Back to the Basics of Teaching and Learning

Back to the Basics of Teaching and Learning

"Thinking the World Together"
Second Edition

David W. Jardine
University of Calgary, Canada

Patricia Clifford
Galileo Educational Network Association, Canada

Sharon Friesen
Galileo Educational Network Association and
University of Calgary, Canada

Routledge
Taylor & Francis Group

NEW YORK AND LONDON

First published 2002
by Lawrence Erlbaum Associates

This edition published 2008
by Routledge
270 Madison Ave, New York, NY 10016

Simultaneously published in the UK
by Routledge
2 Park Square, Milton Park, Abingdon, Oxon OX14 4RN

Routledge is an imprint of the Taylor & Francis Group, an informa business

© 2002 LEA; 2008 Taylor & Francis

Typeset in Minion by
Swales & Willis Ltd, Exeter, Devon
Printed and bound in the United states of America on acid-free paper by
Sheridan Books, Inc.

Library of Congress Cataloging in Publication Data
Jardine, David William, 1950–
Back to the basics of teaching and learning : thinking the world together / David W. Jardine, Patricia Clifford, Sharon Friesen. – 2nd ed.
p.cm.
ISBN 978–0–8058–6320–8 (pbk: alk. paper) – ISBN 978–1–4106–1774–3 (e-book)
1. Education–Philosophy.   2. Teaching.   3. Learning.
I. Clifford, Patricia (Patricia Anne)   II. Friesen, Sharon.   III. Title.
LB14.7.J365 2008
371.1001 – dc22
2008002339

ISBN10: 0–8058–6320–6 (pbk)
ISBN10: 1–4106–1774–2 (ebk)

ISBN13: 978–0–8058–6320–8 (pbk)
ISBN13: 978–1–4106–1774–3 (ebk)

Contents

Foreword

WILLIAM E. DOLL, LOUISIANA STATE UNIVERSITY

This book is, by any standard, amazing. It plays, in a wonderfully hermeneutic manner, with common themes in an uncommon way. A question—what is basic?—and an instance—a young, second-grade girl doing a math problem—entwine and recurse themselves in double-helix fashion throughout the whole book. As the authors—David Jardine, Patricia Clifford, Sharon Friesen—say, they wish to propose the audacious idea that "if you do rich, good, disciplined, living work with children" (notice these adjectives, please) that bugaboo of bugaboos, tests, "are no problem" (p. 8). In fact, to the degree that we worry about and teach for tests, we deprive the learner of the very chance to learn. Learning comes from being immersed, fully, in a situation, not from counting the number of correct answers on a test.

In the simplicity of traditional, linear, reductive thought, basics are those building blocks via which all knowledge is built. When pressed to analyze these, reductionists break the big blocks into smaller and smaller units until arriving at what we all "see" as self-evident. Any second-grade child must know her math facts, those single-digit quantities (1 through 9; zero really does not "count") that make up all addition, subtraction, multiplication, and division problems. Again, in this simple world of school mathematics, powers, roots, recursions, iterations, fractalled dimensions do not count. Only *we* count, in simple, linear terms.

A story: Jardine, Clifford, and Friesen begin their book with "A Classroom Tale." A young child in the second grade is pondering an addition *or* subtraction question (boths and middles are excluded in this world of second-grade arithmetic worksheets). The problem is:

Joan went to the post office. She mailed five letters and three packages. How many more letters than packages did she mail?

The question of the *relevance* of this question shall be passed over. Playing with the fingers of David Jardine, who seeing a puzzled look on the child's face came over to help her and as an illustration for her problem held up five fingers on his one hand and three on his other hand, and looking at his fingers and bending down two fingers of the five extended, as well as extending two fingers on his other (three-fingered) hand, the child easily and loudly said "Two!" But she was still puzzled. "Did I add or subtract?" she queried. The directions, simple as they were, asked her to describe whether she added *or* subtracted. An answer of both was not acceptable. But it is both the child did—pulling down (subtracting) two fingers on one hand, while pushing up (adding) two fingers on the other hand. But alas, the worksheets (textbooks, curriculum guides), in their desire for simple basics, neglect to bring forward the complex and most interesting and truly mathematical relationship between addition and subtraction. What is more *basic* to mathematics than relationship? If mathematics is not about (logical) relationships, what is it about? Relationships, though, were an excluded option on this worksheet.

What other options are excluded in our reciting the mantra—"Back to Basics"? The authors do not wish to dismiss what is basic; rather they want to examine the concept from a hermeneutical perspective, to provide "a more generous, more rigorous, more difficult and more pleasurable image of what 'the basics' might mean" (p. 3). (Note again, please, the interesting adjectives grouped together.) And indeed the authors have provided a journey that is generous, rigorous, difficult, and pleasurable. As one wanders through the book (this is a book to journey in) one questions not only the basics but many educational slogans and shibboleths. One does indeed re-imagine the whole concept of schooling and the potential power that exists in a classroom filled with the fullness and richness of creative experience. Children are creative, adults are creative, life is filled with creativity—life is itself creative. "Treat the work of the classroom as full of intellectual vigor and possibility" (p. 7), say the authors.

Classroom vigor and possibility come from seeing anew, from seeing hermeneutically. In seeing hermeneutically one looks to read any particular event in terms of its fullness, its wholeness, its richness in undeveloped, even unseen, potential. Relationships are, to borrow a phrase from Alfred North Whitehead, the *really real* of life. It is this reality, in all its marvelous complexity, Jardine, Clifford, and Friesen ask us to accept. And they show us, over and over again, in chapter after chapter how this reality exists in every classroom, in virtually every teaching situation.

However, lest one thinks this book is only about teaching situations, let me mention a deeper thread of thinking that runs through the chapters. The authors, especially Jardine, are well versed in Gadamerian hermeneutics, and his ideas on the fullness of life's experiences and the changing visions differing cultural traditions and generations have permeate their thought. Thus to look at an issue like "the basics" differently, interpretively, affects not only the way we might teach addition–subtraction but will also affect "how we live out" life itself and especially our relationship with our children. Such an effect brings with it a host of ethical issues about how we treat the planet with which we live, how we treat those who are other to us (ourselves the others, other), how we treat our children, and how we treat that which we call knowledge.

This is in many ways an inspiring book—a what-can-be book—but more than that it is a book which asks the reader to deal with "hard questions," ones which probe the meaning of life. To read this book is to be transformed. I invite all readers to partake of that journey.

Preface

DAVID W. JARDINE

> No learned or mastered technique can save us from the task of deliberation and decision.
>
> (Gadamer, 1983, p. 113)

Education is laboring under an image of "the basics" that is no longer viable. This image involves ideas of breaking things down, fragmentation, isolation, and the consequent dispensing, manipulation, and control of the smallest, simplest, most meaningless bits and pieces of the living inheritances that are entrusted to teachers and learners in schools. The exhausting and exhausted arguments that swirl around this image of "the basics" are always full of urgency but rarely bring much prospect of relief, pleasure, intellectual challenge or hope to the life of the classroom. What is often ignored in such arguments is that the designation of such things as "basics" is a deeply ethical decision regarding what comes first, what is valued, and what will count in the lives of the students and teachers in the work of schooling. As the burgeoning "information age" swells all around us, this image of basics-as-breakdown can cope with this eventuality only by accelerating the already-manic pace that some schools set, even for the youngest of children.

What would happen to our understanding of teaching and learning if we stepped away from this image of basics-as-breakdown? What would happen if we took seriously the critiques of breakdown that come from contemporary hermeneutics and from ecology and took to heart from these critiques different possibilities for re-imagining "the basics"?

Imagine if we treated *these* things as "the basics" of teaching and learning: relation, ancestry, commitment, participation, interdependence, belonging, desire, conversation, memory, place, topography, tradition, inheritance, experience, identity, difference, renewal, generativity, intergenerationality, discipline, care, strengthening, attention, devotion, transformation, character. Imagine if we treated as *basic* to teaching and learning listening openly and generously to each other, not just to a healthy and sane understanding of others, but also of oneself. If we treated *these* things as "basic" to teaching and learning, students and the living questions they bring from their lives to the life of the classroom become imaginable as basic to the living character of the disciplines entrusted to schools. Moreover, the work that is very often thinly and dully outlined in mandated, grade-level, subject-specific curriculum guides becomes understandable differently. Schools can be treated as dealing, not with the dispensation of finished, dead and deadly dull information that students must simply consume, but rather with troublesome, questionable, unfinished, debatable, living inheritances. This would be coupled with the age-old difficulty of how to enthrall the young with the task of taking up these already ongoing conversations of which their lives are already a part—the "conversation that we ourselves *are*" (Gadamer, 1989, p. 378).

Under this ecological-interpretive image of "the basics," both the young and the old are transformed: the young become essential to the sane and healthy "set[ting] right anew"(Arendt, 1969, p. 192) of the world, and the world becomes a living array of "tried and true" knowledge which is only true to the extent that it is open to being "tried" yet again, here, now, with this child's question, experience, or concern. We are convinced that our children want "in" to the real work of this living inheritance, and that the image of basics-as-breakdown belies this vital desire, ending, often, with boredom, cynicism, and violence.

This book is about an ecological-interpretive image of "the basics." Between us, the three author-editors have 70 years of classroom teaching experience, from two-year-old children to graduate students older than any of us. The reason for mentioning this is specific and difficult. It is not enough to simply propose a different theoretical-philosophical basis for thinking about the basics. It is necessary to interpretive work—"basic," one might say—to show how such a different treatment might work itself out in the lives of teachers and learners. But this doesn't mean simply running through a long list of examples of a theory that is already fully understood and meaningful *without* those examples. It means showing, again and again, how new examples enrich, transform, and correct what one thought was fully understood and meaningful. This means, simply put, that our research is *interpretive* in character. It also means that the classroom events that we are interested in are *themselves* interpretive in character.

This text will be valuable, we believe, to practicing teachers and student-teachers interested in re-imagining what is basic to their work and the work of their students. Through its many classroom examples, it provides a way to question and open up to conversation the often literal-minded tasks teachers and students face. It also provides examples of interpretive inquiry which would be helpful to graduate students and scholars in the areas of curriculum, teaching and learning who are interested in pursuing this form of research and writing.

Regarding the Second Edition: "Thinking the World Together"/Thinking the World Apart

All curriculum requires interpretation. The conservative desire to mandate curriculum as a reified static commodity, to make curricula that are "teacher-proof," to rate teacher performance by student achievement on narrow standardized tests—all of these kinds of measures serve to undercut the one aspect that makes teaching a worthwhile activity, mutually vivifying for both students and teachers: teaching as an engagement with the young over questions of life and death, and the way those questions have been addressed by one's own and other traditions in the past, and ways they can be addressed in the present. This suggestion can be read as relevant whether the curriculum subject is mathematics, physics, literature or philosophy. What matters is an honouring of the work of inducting the young into the broader human life-stream, without which education can only be an act of human alienation. It requires of both teachers and students that they see their work together as a labour of mutual authentication in which the search for truth in any situation must inevitably trump political expediency.

(Smith, 2008)

Much has happened since the first edition of this book. We're looking back over our original dedication of this text and thinking that it just may have turned out to be more meaningful and more troublesome than we thought at the time:

This book is dedicated to the teachers and students who are suffering in the confines of a form of schooling premised on breakdown, and to the teachers and students who have taught the three of us so much about what an enlivening and pleasurably difficult thing teaching and learning can be, once "the basics" are re-imagined.

At this short distance, something more needs to be said. What has come to meet us most strongly since the first edition of *Back to the Basics of Teaching and Learning: Thinking the World Together* is that there is a true, strong, and intellectually and spiritually vital sense in which thinking the world together is itself a form of intimate *experience*, a form of interpretive, deeply sensuous, and experiential *thinking* that helps undo the false and pernicious and spirit-killing suffering of the abstract dispensation of breakdown that has found its way into so many corners of educational experience and so many lives of so many students and teachers. Thinking the world together is a form of *ecological thinking*, where the logic of place or home (Gk. *oikos*—see Gary Snyder's wonderful *Earth House Hold* [1969]) is at issue, and the question of what our place might be and who this "our" refers to needs deep and difficult consideration. I type these words just as news of Benazir Bhutto's assassination fills the airwaves, and just as I was thinking through anew, with a colleague, Rahat Naqvi (see Chapter 18; Naqvi & Prasow, 2007; and Jardine & Naqvi, in press), and with Ahmad Zaidi, how knowledge and thoughtfulness might hold sway in our meetings with others.

It is essential to understand that the suffering caused by a form of schooling simply a "subjective" issue. Equally subjective is a concern for how "democracy" has come to be defined and how it is working itself out in the lifeworld. The objective assessment of the social studies examination trumps such a concern by subjectivizing it and making the one who is concerned an "individual" who simply has an "opinion" with no public possibility of weight or carriage.)

Thus, even though we've decided to cast this second edition of *Back to the Basics of Teaching and Learning* off in a new direction, it is rooted in the same heartbreaking desire: to win back the debate regarding "the basics" from the narrow-minded, psycho-pathologized version of what is basic that is rampant in educational theory and practice. Breakdown and line-assembly, requisite of the scientific management of early-20th-century industrial assembly-line-like production, a movement spawned by Frederick Winslow Taylor (1911) (see Chapters 18 and 21), became inculcated into our imagining of public schooling (see Callahan, 1964; Wrege & Greenwood, 1991). What occurred in those first two decades of the last century was a great coincidence: on the one hand, industry became (understandably) enamored with the assembly line, and the one-piece-at-a-time-in-the-proper-order became the clarion of efficiency and the reduction of waste. Coupled with this is that the worker working such a line became distanced (Marx would say "alienated") from any vibrant connection to what was being assembled, since all that that worker had on hand was "this one piece, do this, never mind the rest." One is not required, in fact not *allowed*, to experience in the task before oneself the way in which that task somehow "fits" into something. Seeing a task this way (as suggested in Chapter 12, experiencing a phenomenon ecologically and hermeneutically, *as* part of a whole, *as* belonging somewhere, *as* somehow "fitting" in a world of relations) simply wastes time. What occurs right at this juncture is something that every school teacher knows intimately: *being interested and invested in what is in front of you is systematically purged from the process as "inefficient."*

Ironically, as Raymond Callahan (1964, p. 20) notes, the efficiency movement of the first decades of the 20th century was touted as profoundly *ecological* in nature (it was promoted thus by President Theodore Roosevelt) because it promoted the elimination of waste. The stopwatch wielded by Taylor was used to measure the movements of workers and to cut out wasted time which he linked to wasted energy, wasted materials and, in the end, wasted money and decreased productivity and profit. It was, of course, this last move that provides us with a vital reminder of some of the bloodlines of contemporary linkages between education and the market economy, between marks, assessment, accountability, increased production, and the commodification of knowledge. It reminds us, as does David Smith's profound work (see especially 2006), of the links between globalization, pedagogy, and the drives and desires of market economics. Smith's work reminds us, too, of how, once teachers and students are abandoned to one-after-the-other fragments and their management, any truths about the living world and how it fits together are difficult to tell and easy to manipulate. In light of management, untruth can become truth if it helps us manage better.

At almost precisely the same time, Edward Thorndike was cultivating an analogous view of the nature of knowledge and its acquisition. Knowledge itself was conceived as a thing built up out of isolated, individual "experiences." Knowledge is thus something to be assembled out of distinct bits and pieces in a process analogous to the industrial production of an object out of its component parts. If one can learn to properly manage (that is, efficiently and with the least waste) the assembly of such an object, one has roiling in the air around the efficiency movement a great epistemological consort for Taylor's stopwatch. Behaviorism (as Thorndike's work was taken up by his successors, B. F. Skinner and others) and the efficiency movement are twinned. As we have attempted to demonstrate in our companion to this text, *Curriculum in Abundance* (Jardine, Friesen, & Clifford, 2006), the core of that twinning is the agonizing reign of regimes of scarcity which compel us to race from bit to isolated bit in hope of some sense of satisfaction of the alienation and homelessness that were wrought by the original breakdown which divested us of our interest in things. Once the world is "thought apart," we lose any sense of how to think the world together unless we have all the parts. We never have a part *in its wholeness*. As mentioned in Chapter 1, adding and subtracting are *separate things*, and my attempt to cultivate that child's ability to think them *together* just muddies the water, slows down the process of assembly, wastes time, and so on. And here is the greatest lie: to overcome our uneasiness with such matters, the only recourse we have seems to be the acceleration of the very process that led to our uneasiness in the first place.

As a consequence of this great confluence, the living disciplines entrusted to teachers and students in schools became *broken apart*, ripe for efficient reassembly according to the rules, not of those original, living disciplines, but according to rules of management and surveillance and the reduction of waste(d time and effort). This is an even older trick that lies at the heart of the work of the natural sciences and that forms an important part of the interpretive critique of the application of natural sciences to the human sciences:

> The object is disassembled, the rules of its functioning are ascertained, and then it is reconstructed according to those rules; so, also, knowledge is analyzed, its rules are determined, and finally it is redeployed as method. The purpose of both remedies is to prevent unanticipated future breakdowns by means of breaking down even further the flawed entity and then synthesizing it artificially.
>
> (Weinsheimer, 1985, p. 6)

In and of itself, of course, there is nothing amiss about this procedure of objective science. But something subtle occurs that is difficult to articulate. In such a breakdown procedure, language (to use one example of a discipline taught in schools) is broken down into an object whose rules of assembly are understood, and the teaching of language is itself broken down into a set of methods which, when deployed properly, will ask of children that they learn to re-assemble, in activities appropriate to their grade level, what has been disassembled and thus "learn [a] language." And, since you cannot possibly engage the rules of re-assembly until you have all the parts, this probably accounts for why we have heard, quite often in fact, that children can't write stories until they first learn and master, in isolation, "all their letters." This couples too easily with a teacher we met who believed that you have to teach the alphabet in alphabetical order, or those who believe that children must learn about primary colors before others, or, as alluded to in Chapter 1, that addition must be taught first, because it arrives (as the next "piece" in the mathematics curriculum guide assembly manual) *before* subtraction. As we have outlined in Chapter 1, what is in fact the *outcome* of an abstract objectivizing process is taken to be what should be taught chronologically first.

Of course, once knowledge is broken down into bits and pieces, and once teaching is conceived of as the efficient and effective delivery and assessment of such fragments, what happens is that the ontology of the efficiency movement gets lodged in our understanding of knowledge itself. As one secondary school "mathematics" teacher said to me last year, what is there to talk about, after all, with the Pythagorean theorem? "Memorize and learn which exam questions to use it on. Period." Once thus ontologically lodged, any suggestion of dislodging such matters—any suggestion of "thinking the world together"—is often met with sometimes heartbreakingly "anti-intellectual" (see Callahan, 1964, p. 8) responses. We are often overwhelmed by the moral indignation that arises whenever any attempt is made to interrupt breakdown and its consorts. Again, Callahan, in his vitally important book *Education and the cult of efficiency* (1964), helped us get a glimpse of this moral air. He cites (p. 52) H. Martyn Hart, the dean of St. John's Cathedral in Denver, who, in the September 1912 issue of the *Ladies' Home Journal*, articulates some of the moral tone that came with the arrival and expectations of the efficiency movement in education:

> The system [of schooling] . . . has indeed become a positive detriment and is producing a type of character which is not fit to meet virtuously the temptations and exigencies of modern life. The crime which stalks almost unblushingly through the land; the want of responsibility which defames our social honor; the appalling frequency of divorce; the utter lack of self-control; the abundant use of illicit means to gain political positions; are all traceable to its one great and crying defect—inefficiency.

It would be simply foolish, of course, to say "They were wrong; now we are right." Such modernist ontologies will themselves no longer do. Rather, what

we are suggesting is something akin to Ivan Illich's idea of "counterproductivity" (Illich & Cayley, 1992, p. 110). Illich doesn't suggest in some abstract, theoretical sense that one way of proceeding is better than another. Rather, he
demonstrates that ways of proceeding wear out, reach limits, and need to be, as
Hannah Arendt put it, "set right anew." This is a *hermeneutic ontology*, which
does not want to fix and settle "what is the case" but wants to propose that "to
be" is "to be susceptible and vulnerable to the future," and therefore "to be" is
to be the long threads of living, vulnerable, contested ancestries and bloodlines
that we have inherited. "To be" means precisely *not* to be understandable once
and for all. Simply put, in education, we are dealing with knowledge understood as threaded through *living* disciplines whose vulnerability to an unan-
ticipatable future is not an error that we must guard against. It is only in and
through such vulnerability that knowledge *lives* in the human inheritance. In
this book, we suggest that teaching our children means entering with them into
this living and learning to live with this life.

We are suggesting—as Illich suggests as a sign of counterproductivity—that
the basics-as-breakdown is starting to create and aggravate the problems for
which it was meant to be the solution. As we suggested in *Curriculum in
Abundance* (Jardine, Friesen, & Clifford, 2006, pp. 6–7):

> There is a certain point where any system operating under the regime of
> scarcity begins to aggravate and, in fact, *create* the troubles for which it
> was meant to be the solution. He demonstrates that in the field of medi-
> cine, for example, we are now experiencing how hospitals are the breed-
> ing grounds of "superbugs." In transportation, he presents a startling
> fact: the faster that air travel becomes, the *more* time we spend traveling
> this way. Moreover, "up to a certain speed and density automobiles may
> expand mobility, but beyond this threshold society becomes their pris-
> oner" (Cayley, in Illich & Cayley, 1992, p. 15) and we spend more and
> more time caught immobile in our cars. The more we accelerate, the
> more we experience "time consuming acceleration" (Illich, 2000, p. 31).
>
> In the field of education in particular, we have witnessed, over and
> over again in our conversations with students, teachers, administrators
> and parents, that the idea of scarcity and lack have produced a counter-
> productive exhaustion, sense of defeat, cynicism, panic, and regret. . . . In
> this milieu, trying to even articulate how that playground conversation
> was potentially a way into great abundance seems hopelessly naive and
> quaint.

If this "cult of efficiency" (Callahan, 1964) is not interrupted and set right, its
only recourse is (as we demonstrate below, especially in Chapters 12, 13, and
21) *acceleration*, increased surveillance, testing all the time, breaking down
matters more and more, and speeding up the expectations of assembly. As we
discuss below in Chapters 2, 3, 12, and 21, time itself starts to shift character.

Time itself starts to be one of the things that are experienced as scarce. As Wendell Berry said so clearly, "for the machine, time is always running out" (1983, p. 76). It is here, again, that we plead in favor of thinking about such matters. Time is not experienced as running out because time somehow "really is" running out. It is thus experienced as a long and complex *consequence* of *treating the matters of education in a certain way*. In the living discipline of poetry, or the ways that triangles arc within circles, time is not running out.

Our feelings are mixed about those teachers we've mentioned who are caught in this breakdown spell, just as our feelings are mixed about the Grade Two teacher who wanted to erase from her student's mathematics worksheet the question, that very question that erupted with *mathematical* interest. These teachers have been *had* by a long train of thought and action, and are therefore as much *victims* of this logic as its perpetrators. But they—all of us in education—are also *culpable*, and intellectually and morally responsible to break this spell, to question this logic on behalf of their students and the disciplines entrusted to them. For educators, the worst consequence of basics as breakdown is that it has led too many of us into believing that we don't need to learn to *think* about what is happening to us and our students. This is breakdown at its worst: the promise to render knowledge and teachers and students and the living disciplines entrusted to them into manageable bits and pieces that can be anonymously assembled, and the deliberate ridicule and belittling of genuine questions, concerns, speculations, imaginings, and creative intellectual ventures as simply glitches in the assembly line's smooth operation—this is the deepest and most educationally reprehensible betrayal. This is where the anti-intellectualism of the profession of teaching must be called to account as inadequate to the matters at hand, and the practice of teacher education needs itself to break the spell of simply preparing new teachers to "survive" in "the real world"—tellingly named by a war metaphor "the trenches."

Thinking the World Together

If we provide enough room for restlessness so that it might function within the space, then the energy ceases to be restless because it can trust itself fundamentally. Meditation is giving a huge, luscious meadow to a restless cow. The cow might be restless for a while in its huge meadow, but at some stage, because there is so much space, the restlessness becomes irrelevant.

(Trungpa, 1988, pp. 48–49)

We were attracted to the citation on meditation by Chogyam Trungpa because it provides a helpful analogy to our thinking on "the basics." What very often happens in schools when students become restless and encounter difficulties with the work they face is that teachers (and sometimes assessors, testers, and remediators) zoom in on that trouble, narrowing attention, making the "meadow," the "field of relations," available to that student less huge, luscious, rich, and spacious. Possibilities are not extended and opened up but rather closed down. Tasks are simplified, shortened, broken into more manageable pieces, because the student's restlessness is conceived, of necessity, as a "management" issue under the logic of breakdown. In the face of restlessness, lesson plans "lessen" (see Chapter 2) as we more narrowly "target" schoolwork to the individual child's "needs" (see Chapter 5, where a "difficult child" is treated by his classmates and teachers in a different way). This sort of pedagogical intervention is commonplace under the auspices of basics-as-breakdown. The more trouble a student has, the smaller and simpler and less interesting the "bit" doled out to them. In the process of such narrowing, the restlessness does not become irrelevant. It becomes paramount. The need, the desire, to "manage" simply intensifies. But, under the auspices of basics-as-breakdown, this restlessness now no longer has places that are patient and forgiving and rich and rigorous enough so that our troubled relations might be able to work themselves *out*.

The interpretive understanding of the basics that we present here issues out of this sense of relatedness and expansiveness. We've often used with the teachers and students and student-teachers we work with images of buoyancy, where an idea "lifts up" and, so to speak, takes on a life of its own (see Chapter 21). This is in the nature of interpretive work, where, as Gadamer (1989, p. 360) puts it, interpretation "breaks open the being of the object." As mentioned in Chapter 1 (see also Chapters 10, 11, and 12) "addition" is not understood *to be* an isolated substance that is what it is independently of everything else (the definition of "substance" from Aristotle through Descartes and beyond). Basics-as-breakdown bears this ontology: any relations between such basic pieces are taught *as if* the pieces made sense *without* the relations and the relations were therefore "revocable and provisional" (Gray, 1998, p. 36). Instead of this, interpretation breaks open this seemingly isolated fragment into its field(s), its place(s), its histories, its imaginal and linguistic and intellectual possibilities. This is understood both synchronically and diachronically: a large field of contemporaneous relationships opens up while at the same time (so to speak) a certain openness to future questions becomes part of what understanding entails, as well as the opening up of the ancestral voices of the past that echo in the work at hand. Addition (to refer again to that introductory example of "Did I add or subtract?") is understood to be *abundant in all its relations* (and only stripped of such abundance in the name of surveillance, control, and manageability). We've spoken, in the first edition, in our later book *Curriculum in Abundance* (2006), and now, here, in this second edition, of a version of "the basics" that involves relation, ancestry, commitment, participation, interdependence, belonging, desire, conversation, memory, place, topography, tradition, inheritance, experience, identity, difference, renewal, generativity, intergenerationality, discipline, care, strengthening, attention, devotion, transformation, character, and the like.

We've added chapters in this edition that take up the ecological aspects of this phenomenon (see especially Chapters 12, 13, 14, 16, and 17), the hermeneutic aspects of it (see especially Chapters 3 and 21), and the curricular aspects of it in the areas of mathematics (Chapters 9, 10, 11, and 12), reading and writing (Chapters 3, 4, 5, 7, and 20), and social studies (Chapters 3 and 18); included also are chapters on child development (Chapters 8, 9, 14, 19, and 20), information and communications technologies, and so on.

We must add that, in pursuing this more ecological and intellectually sound image of the basics gleaned from an understanding of the inheritance of living disciplines of work, we never promised that this would make anyone's life *easier*. Breakdown "is . . . a way of institutionalizing, justifying, and paying highly for a calamitous disintegration and scattering out of the various functions of character: workmanship, care, conscience, responsibility" (Berry, 1986, p. 19), and setting this matter right anew is tough work. But there is something to be said about the pleasures of entering into the suffering and troubles inherent in a living place of work. There is something that most of the students we've encountered find alluring and attractive about being able to do "the real work" (Snyder, 1980) instead of the false and fake "school work" that is perennially cut off from the bloodlines of the world (see Chapter 19).

If we may, we need to be blunt. You don't have to be very intelligent or well read or curious or thoughtful or reflective to hand out worksheets and mark them according to a pre-given key. "Basics-as-breakdown" dumbs down those who fall for it, and it does so *on purpose*, as a condition of its ability to maintain efficient control over schooling. In light of breakdown, the life of the living disciplines will not appear because such an appearance has been disavowed in advance as a condition of efficiency. And we understand full well that, when we speak of living disciplines to those caught in the thrall of breakdown, it is often the case that many simply have no clear referent for what we are talking about. As one Grade Six teacher said years ago, "I don't have time to spend six months making papier mâché igloos. We've got exams coming!"

In the version of "the basics" that we are proposing, something else is asked of us as teachers and, in its own way, this is tremendous news. We are asked, as teachers, to be public intellectuals who think about the world, who think about the knowledge we have inherited and to which we are offering our students living, breathing access. We need to be precisely what we hope our students will be: curious, knowledgeable, adventurous, well read, questioning, creative, and daring in their intellectual ventures. Only thus will the life of the living disciplines appear. This, again, is an ecological point: how we enter into a living field, how we treat it, and how we have prepared ourselves to be open to what arrives will have an effect on what comes to meet us.

Acknowledgments

This book is the product of 15 years' work, and our work has been generously supported by the Social Sciences and Humanities Research Council of Canada, as well as the Izaak Walton Killam Memorial Fellowship Fund. The former provided the three of us with valuable financial support and the latter provided me with an even rarer gift—the gift of time that, in these days of accelerating rush, was welcome indeed. We would also like to acknowledge the careful work of the reviewers of this text, who caught all those embarrassing things that are so hard to find by oneself, and the staff at Routledge, first for agreeing to publish this work and second for taking such good care of both it and us as we proceeded. Special thanks to Naomi Silverman for her unwavering encouragement and support.

We would especially like to thank Dr. William E. Doll for graciously agreeing to write a foreword to our text. He has been a tireless supporter of our work over the years and a good friend.

"Something awakens our interest—that is really what comes first!" (Gadamer, 2001, p. 50). This Preface was first drafted in mid-February, 2002, a few days after Hans-Georg Gadamer's 102nd birthday (he died that March). For several years, the same joke has come up in my yearly graduate course on his text *Truth and Method* (1989): hermeneutics might not be true, but it seems to be good for you. The citation above comes from an interview with Gadamer at age 93. It remains an inspiration for us to hear from this old man that *this* might be first: being compelled by the world and awakened to have living questions of one's own, full of deliberation and decision. We are grateful for Gadamer's example and his work.

The cover of this book is a painting by a Grade One student taught by Sharon and Pat during their tracking of Coyote (see Chapter 5). It is called "Thinking the World Together." We found it an excellent image for the movement from breakdown to interpretation that we have been pursuing in our work: thinking of the rich and generous ways that things belong together, beyond the seemingly accelerating scattershot work of a great deal of schooling.

In these post-9/11 times, our fervor for surveillance and management has increased the heat but not the light around the idea of "the basics." Open inquiry and questioning have come to be understood in some quarters as unpatriotic or, even more, pernicious, a "cultural choice" (see Chapter 18). These certainly are interesting times, and we have come to understand that the arguments we are pursuing regarding the basics are most certainly not simply epistemological matters or issues of objective research. What is afoot, here, is about how to live our lives and what good work is, and how we can contest the rampant and vicious anti-intellectualism that is draining the life out of not only schools but also public life itself. What is afoot here, too, is power and persuasion and "untruth" (Smith, 2006) right in the midst of schooling itself— raising our children up to believe that the lie can be true or, worse yet, that "truth" is only opinion and that nothing holds sway in the work of living our lives together. As the "enfraudening" (Smith, 2006) escalates, the importance of these issues gets put into more and more stark relief. Therefore, our dedication must spread to those doing interpretive work in educational theory and practice. The solidarity and good will and courage of this community of scholars are needed now more than ever. We thank those who have given us the gifts of their time and words and support, and thank that wide array of interpretive scholars who are ready for the suffering that comes with insight and speaking truth to power.

Finally, we re-dedicate this book to the teachers and children who are suffering in the confines of a form of schooling premised on breakdown. And we thank all of those we've worked with who have taught us so much about the love, the intellectual challenge, and the pure pleasure of taking good care of the living disciplines entrusted to students and teachers in schools.

David W. Jardine
Bragg Creek, Alberta
August 3, 2007

Permission Acknowledgments

BC, China. In *Sunflower Splendor*, Lui and Lo, eds., Indiana University Press, 1990, page 9.

Chapter 17
Jardine, D. (1997). "All beings are your ancestors": A Bear sutra on ecology, Buddhism, and pedagogy. *The Trumpeter, 14*(3), 122–123.

Chapter 18
Naqvi, R. and Jardine, D. "Some say the present age is not for meditation": Thoughts on things left unsaid in contemporary invocation of "traditional learning." Reprinted by permission from the *Journal of Educational Thought*, University of Calgary.

Chapter 20
Jardine, D., Clifford, P. and Friesen, S. (2000). Scenes from Calypso's Cave: On globalization and the pedagogical prospects of the gift. A special theme issue of the *Alberta Journal of Educational Research 46*(1), 27–35, on "Globalization and Education," H. Smits, guest editor.

Chapter 21
Jardine, D. (in press). On the while of things. *Journal of the American Association for the Advancement of Curriculum Studies*. Reprinted with permission.

1
Introduction
An Interpretive Reading of "Back to the Basics"

DAVID W. JARDINE, PATRICIA CLIFFORD,
AND SHARON FRIESEN

The issue isn't finding new terms to replace old terms. The old terms are fine. It's a matter of seeing the old terms differently, shifting away from both nominalism and realism to rhetoric and metaphor.

(Hillman, 1991, p. 42)

Our curricula, textbooks, and teaching are all "a mile wide and an inch deep." This preoccupation with breadth rather than depth, with quantity rather than quality . . . [leads to a] splintered character and poor work. How can we develop a new vision of what is basic?

(Schmidt *et al.*, 1997, pp. 3, 11)

To Begin: A Classroom Tale

During a round of practicum supervision several years ago, I (David Jardine) happened into a Grade Two classroom. The children were filling in a photocopied worksheet, purportedly dealing with questions of addition and subtraction. Here is an example of the question layout:

There are four horses in the field. Two of them run away. How many horses are left in the field?

Beside each question was a little black-line cartoon (in this case, of "horses"), a line upon which to put your answer, and, above this line, a plus and a minus sign, one of which you were instructed to circle, to demonstrate the operation you used in solving the question.

One student waved me over. She said, "I don't understand this one at all." The question she had trouble with was this:

Joan went to the post office. She mailed five letters and three packages. How many more letters than packages did she mail?

Eager to help out, I squatted down beside the student's desk and put up five fingers on one of my hands and three on the other.

"OK," I said, moving the appropriate hand slightly forward in each case, "she's got five letters and three packages. She's got more letters . . .".

The student suddenly grabbed the thumb of my "letters" (five digits extended) hand and bent it down. She then bent down my little "pinky" finger as well, leaving three fingers extended. But then, with a puzzled look, she considered my other (three-fingers-extended) hand. Carefully, she pulled my thumb and little "pinky" finger up, now leaving five fingers extended where there were three, and three fingers extended where there were five.

"Two!" she said, a bit too loud for the enforced quiet that worksheets inevitably demand. "Yep, two, you've got it."

The student looked back down at the worksheet's requirements. Suddenly, this: "But, you know, I'm not sure. Did I add or subtract?"

The two of us talked, hushed, about the work she had done with my fingers, moving them up and down, adding, subtracting, taking two away from five and then adding two back on to three. Back and forth. She and I finally agreed that *this question of hers was really good*: "Did I add or subtract?"

"You have to do both," she ventured.

She and I also agreed that the other questions on the worksheet are too easy. "You just have to *do* them" she whispered, as if this were some secret knowledge that perhaps we'd better not let out.

Another Beginning: "Back to Basics"

There is a long-standing allure to the idea of "back to the basics" in educational theory and practice. It drives not only reactionary school reform movements (e.g. Berk 1985; Holt 1996) and critiques or defenses of "liberal" or "progressivist" education (e.g. Lazere 1992; Grumet 1993). The idea of "the basics" also subtly underwrites how curriculum guides are conceived and organized; it defines how disciplinary knowledge is envisaged and delivered; it determines what the work of the classroom is understood to be; it provides images of how children are thought of regarding their participation in and necessity to the work of the classroom; it lays out what teachers are expected to know and to do, and how teaching and the assessment of teachers' and children's work are organized and evaluated. Even more subtle, but far more pervasive, powerful and diffuse is the use of "basics" as an often unexamined, incendiary clarion in public discourse and the public press (Freedman, 1993).

In this book, we don't want to give up on the notion of the basics, despite the fact that it is too easy in these post-modern times to condemn the very idea of "basics" as all too modernist, all too Eurocentric, all too pretentious and grating on the ear. We agree with James Hillman: the old terms are fine. What isn't fine is that educational theory and practice seems stuck when it comes to imagining what this term "basics" might mean in the living work of teachers and learners, except in the taken-for-granted and exhausted ways that the profession has inherited. Many of those in educational theory and practice have lost the ability to hear in this old term the myriad of alternate voices that haunt and inhabit it.

Rather than turning our backs on this troubled inheritance, in this book, we want to understand its meanings, motives and desires, and we want to learn how to spot its (often unintended) appearance in the hallways and classrooms of schools and in the languages used to talk of teaching, learning, curriculum and education.

But we want to do more than this: we want to offer what we believe is a more generous, more rigorous, more difficult and more pleasurable image of what "the basics" might mean. We want to offer an image of "the basics" that is more deeply and intimately in line with how it is that living disciplines actually *live* in the world, how scholarship and thoughtfulness and knowledge are actually cultivated and protected and cared for in the life-world.

We have to be careful here, however. Following the work of contemporary hermeneutics, we are not going to offer this alternate image as somehow naively "really" the basics, and demean the inherited version as "not really the basics." We'd like to suggest that we have all had enough of that exhausting and exhausted fight. All we want to show, as Lewis Hyde suggests, is that "the way we treat a thing [like 'the basics'] can sometimes change its nature" (1983, p. xiii). We want to ask: what might seem most important to us? how might we talk differently? how might we act differently? what new or ancient roles might we envisage for ourselves and our children in the teaching and learning and understanding of the disciplines that have been entrusted to us in schools? what, in fact, might "understanding" mean, given this alternate image of "the basics"? what would classrooms look like?

In the rest of this introduction, we want to sketch out some of the key ideas in the commonplace, traditional, taken-for-granted version of "the basics" and how the version we will be exploring, what might be called an interpretive or hermeneutic version of "the basics," operates on different fundamental assumptions. As will be demonstrated in detail below, even though talk of such fundamental assumptions might sometimes seem abstract and too distant from the tough and troubled realities of the classroom, it is never simply a matter of differences in philosophy. This difference in fundamental assumptions leads, of necessity, *to very different concrete classroom practices in our schools*.

Traditional and Interpretive Images of "the Basics"

Education is being driven by an analytic idea of "basicness" inherited from a limited, literal-minded, and out-dated version of the empirical sciences. This idea can be simply stated even though its consequences are profound: that which is most real or most basic to any discipline we might teach are its smallest, most clearly and distinctly isolatable, testable and assessable bits and pieces. In the tale cited above, the worksheet that the child was doing had clearly isolated, and made testable the child's understanding of the different operations of addition and subtraction. And, even if we find troubles with that particular worksheet and its wording or its reliability as a measure, under the auspices of this analytic idea of "the basics," the aim is to improve it by more clearly, carefully and meticulously marking off, isolating and separating distinguishable knowledge, skills and attitudes. With such improvements, a particular child's mastery of specific knowledge, skills and attitudes can thus be equally clearly, carefully and meticulously tracked, tested and assessed. Children's abilities regarding such masteries (and, via provincial or state testing scores, the accountability of teachers, classrooms and schools) can be then unambiguously rank-ordered, from first to last. Furthermore, as happens in the city of Calgary in Alberta, Canada, such rank-orderings are published in the local newspapers in the name of the public's "right to know" about the performance of their children's schools. And this, in consequence, sets off, every year, energetic, but always eventually exhausting and exhausted debates, often full of more heat than light.

In this book, we contend that such fragmented "basics" are, in fact, *abstractions* that are the *outcomes* of a highly complex, theoretical, analytic process. In an odd turn of events, what is in fact an abstract and arcane product of analysis is believed to be what must be taught chronologically first, to the youngest of children. Under this idea of "the basics," therefore, educators not only deliver *to the youngest of children* the products of a highly specialized theorizing; at the same time, both common sense and the work of developmental theory show that (in particular) young children *are not especially party to this form of analytic thinking*. School children are therefore subjected to the outcomes of a form of abstraction that they themselves cannot especially understand.

An image that is often invoked here is one of "breakdown." In order for something *to be itself* and not be unwittingly mixed up with other things, it is necessary to *break it down* into its component parts. Therefore, *to understand something* means *to break it down* (Jardine & Field, 2006; Weinsheimer, 1987) and to learn how to "control, predict and manipulate" (Habermas, 1972) the now-subsequent relations between such components (such relations having become "revocable and provisional" [Gray 1998, p. 36]). Therefore, in order *to teach something* (to young children especially), it becomes necessary to *break it down*. Moreover, if students in a classroom encounter difficulties in understanding some phenomenon we have broken down, we must *break it down even further*. We must, for example, further sub-divide the sub-skills, further simplify the reading material or the mathematics questions or the science tasks we give children. And, failing this, if it cannot be commandingly broken down, it must simply be erased altogether. As that Grade Two child's teacher suggested when shown what the conversation was about regarding the mathematics worksheet:

"Yes, that question is confusing. I'll take it off the sheet next time."

We need to be clear about this. Whether that Grade Two girl "correctly" circled the "correct" operations on that mathematics worksheet is reasonably easy to unambiguously assess, once mutual agreement is reached regarding which answers will count as correct. Assessing the quality and worthwhileness of the brief conversation and the mathematical and pedagogical potentials it might have held is a different matter. That conversation is full of ambiguity, leading questions, interventions, and exaggerations, possibilities that are not especially easy to control, predict and manipulate. Counting up the number of correct circlings on that worksheet is easier, quicker, more efficient and clearer than exploring ideas of how addition and subtraction are inverse operations and that, mathematically speaking, one is not even *comprehensible* without the other. Talking about the inverse character of operations opens up large, contested, ongoing and interweaving conversations that have defined and troubled the history of mathematics. We can be much more decisive and assured about that worksheet's "mark" than we can about the more elusive question of whether this conversation (if properly followed up) might "mark" this child's memory (see Chapter 3) and learning and confidence. Marking such worksheets is less troublesome than the pedagogical and mathematical quandary of whether this "belonging together"—"you have to do both"—should be raised with the whole class and if so, how a teacher might properly do so. And this is to say nothing of the terrifying question of whether this child intended or understood any of this *at all*.

Moreover, as many student-teachers have courageously admitted, the mathematics worksheet is easy for *teachers* to "correct" by counting the circlings. What isn't so easy is for an individual teacher to face the question of whether he or she actually *understands* this mathematical "belonging together" of adding and subtracting. What about venturing out into the field rife with all the intimate ins and outs of reversible and inverse operations? Can I handle myself in such a field, can I find my way around, and am I adequately experienced in such matters?

In our Grade Two tale, the adult who engaged that girl treated her questions as *mathematically interesting*. It is not helpful, at this point, to ask, for example, "Were these questions actually mathematically intended, or just calls for attention?" What is of interest in an interpretive treatment of "the basics" is this: once this girl began to take up the possibilities that the conversation offered—all the images, for example, of putting together and taking apart 2 and 3 and 5, which started to sketch out for her the beginnings of a rich topography of relations—it became clear that *treating* her questions in this way, with *mathematical* (rather than psychopathological—"What's she up to?") interest, was beginning to change their nature. The playful, however-much-initially-attention-getting game of moving fingers back and forth, up and down, was beginning to show something of a living mathematical relatedness that could begin to be opened up if it was treated a certain way.

But there is an important caveat here. The motives or the results of treating the basics-as-breakdown should not be simply rejected outright as if they indicate something that is simply false or always and everywhere wrong or misleading. It is undeniable that *sometimes* breaking things down is *precisely* what is pedagogically required in the day-to-day work of schooling, or in dealing with specific difficulties of particular children. It is often a valuable and valid *response* to problems and issues that might arise—"Where is the specific trouble this student is having in thinking about that mathematical phenomenon?" However, we contend that under the inherited image of "the basics," breakdown has become no longer a *response* but a *premise*: "breakdown" runs ahead of teachers and learners and turns the living field of mathematics, for example, into something broken down in such a way that, paradoxically, it is now *all* problems. We know, for example, of a Grade Eight student doing pages of problems in a mathematics textbook and looking up the answers in the back of the book, who asked a teacher who drifted by, "Is *this* what mathematicians do?" And we know of a former head of a university Mathematics Department who told us that he could not recognize his own discipline in the work most children do in schools under the name of "mathematics education." Couple this with its correlate: when a child asks a question in the milieu of breakdown, that question means that the child has a problem that needs to be fixed. Imagine if mathematicians treated questions as indicators of nothing more than malfunctioning that needed to be corrected and prevented from happening in the future.

Once things are broken down into isolated, seemingly unrelated fragments, the only work of the classroom seems to be monitoring and management. As one student-teacher frighteningly reported: "In my practicum placement, *every* lesson is a lesson in 'classroom management'." Once the richness, rigours and relatedness (Doll 1993) of the disciplines are broken down into fragments, there is nothing to hold students' or teachers' attention in place and, of course, attention wavers. That Grade Two girl just may have been seeking attention, but one of the reasons for this is that that mathematics worksheet did not deserve or especially need much attention. If teachers continually place such worksheets in front of children (we've witnessed settings where *eight* such sheets were done before morning recess), *of course* there will be "discipline" problems, because any of the ways in which *the work that students and teachers are doing* might have some "discipline" to it that might sustain attention have been eradicated ahead of time, all, again, in the name of this abstract idea of "the basics-as-breakdown."

An interpretive reading of "the basics" inverts this situation: it is only by working *in the midst* of the living discipline, for example, of mathematics and in the face of this living child's beginning venture into that terrain that a sound *pedagogical* judgment can emerge as to whether "breaking things down" might be needed here, now, in the face of these mathematical questions she has posed to us. It is only if you "know your way around" the territory of the "belonging together" of addition and subtraction that you can "hear" that Grade Two girl's query, not as a problem (with her, with the wording of the worksheet, with the instructions given etc.) but as a mathematically interesting question. This is, in fact, how hermeneutics understands the idea of "becoming experienced" at something, having been "around" (*peri-*) and having become someone because of such experience, someone "experienced" in mathematics. Having learned to live with trying to treat children's questions as full of mathematical portend (this was, after all, a mathematics class), one gradually become "experienced" at hearing the nuance and difference that each new situation brings. As Gadamer (1989, pp. 353–8) suggests, becoming experienced, hermeneutically understood, means become more and more sensitive to the fullness and uniqueness of experience itself, ready to experience the difference that *that* Grade Two girl's questions bring to this troublesome, living human inheritance.

But of course, there is a paradox here. This ongoing movement of "becoming experienced" occurs only if you treat the work of the classroom as full of intellectual vigour and possibility, and not as full only of problems that need fixing. Treated interpretively, the question of the belonging together of addition and subtraction is not a *problem*. That Grade Two girl did not have *a problem*. "You have to do both" was not the correction of an error that puts an end to questioning.

Therefore, it is not simply that the way you treat a thing can sometimes change its nature. There are implications in this interpretive treatment of "the basics" for how teachers and student-teachers might become experienced in treating that child's query as mathematically interesting and not simply as a problem that needs repair. And, just to throw in another twist: that Grade Two girl *herself* was, in some small way, being taught how she might treat *her own* questions, not as problems that need repair, but as mathematically opening and interesting.

In this book we fill out this interpretive treatment of "the basics" with images from the philosophy of ecology (e.g. the work of Wendell Berry [1983, 1986, 1987, 1989, 1990], Snyder, [1977, 1980, 1990, 1995]). This discipline has provided the authors with a rich language of relations, ancestry, interdependence, ideas of place and living, sustainable communities and the "continuity of attention and devotion" (1987, p. 33) these matters require and deserve. Ecological discourse has helped us express and articulate things we have experienced as teachers: the idea of sticking with a subject, a topic, a place (like the belonging-together of addition and subtraction) and not fragmenting, trivializing or cheapening it for the sake of our own efficiency; the task deepening our understanding of the topics we are teaching and not taking the easy way out;

the long lesson of learning to live with what we've learned about this place and these relations, learning that others have lived here before, deciding, then, what we shall do with this odd inheritance by linking it up with all its relations and histories and hidden kin.

This book is full of tough questions: what does it mean to conduct oneself well in the living, difficult "territory" of mathematics or science or poetry or the depths of a novel? What does it mean to lead our children carefully and generously into such territories? How can teachers, with some grace and sense of proportion, help students understand that their work can be a real part of the life of these places, and can make a real difference? What does it mean to become "experienced" in such matters? What are the dangers here? What is the good news? What, too, does all of this have to say about the nature and place of "educational research" in such matters?

Between the three of us, we have 75 years of teaching experience, and we have seen such rich, pleasurable, difficult interpretive work occur in real, ordinary school classrooms, with real, ordinary children and teachers. We have also seen that *even state-mandated testing scores go up* when such rich, pleasurable, difficult interpretive work is done. So this alternate, interpretive version of "the basics" is not proposed as an alternative to such tests. We are proposing something a wee bit more audacious: if you do rich, good, disciplined, living work with children, the (basics-as-breakdown) tests are no problem. If you "teach to the tests," the very idea of "good work" might seem like a great idea but a waste of precious time (Jardine 2000; see Chapters 2, and 21). Or, worse yet, we either become cowards and say simply "who is to say what good work is?" or we come to identify "good work" with the efficiencies of basics-as-breakdown test-passing.

Obviously, that Grade Two girl's questions did not have tags on them that say "this one good." Those involved in educational theory and practice have all had enough of *that* sort of moralizing pretence and all of weakening, argumentative "who is to say" exhaustion that ensues. However, as teachers, we *are* faced with a choice as to what we ought to do. We can say that that Grade Two girl was just looking for attention, or that the worksheet has a wording problem. However, if we are prepared to take this risk ourselves, that Grade Two girl's questions *can* be treated generously, as really good mathematical questions that open up a pedagogical territory worth of teachers' and students' attention and devotion.

What Follows

We began this introduction with a classroom tale because of a central interpretive tenet: in attempting to understand the life of the classroom, it is never enough to simply put forth general principles, frameworks or ideas. Ideas, hopes, presumptions, principles, frameworks, methods, and prejudices about teaching, learning, children, and curriculum must face what Hans-Georg

Gadamer (1989, p. 38; see also Jardine 2006) called "the fecundity of the individual case." The individual case of that Grade Two girl's questions is not merely an instance or example of something fully understood beforehand. Rather, her questions, treated interpretively, have the potential to "co-determine, supplement, and correct" (p. 39) what we have heretofore understood, thus adding themselves to the ongoing experiences of mathematics we might then pursue. Individual cases are thus treated, not as individual and individualized narratives in interpretive work (this would simply further entrench a new locale of "breakdown"). Seemingly isolated and individual cases are treated as sites where the discipline of mathematics that schools have inherited is in the process of being "set right anew" (Arendt 1969, p. 192).

We have been using the example of mathematics in this introduction for a specific purpose. Mathematics, as only one of the many disciplines with which schools have been entrusted seems most amenable to the image of "basics-as-breakdown." Moreover, the inverse its true. Mathematics seems *least* amenable to ideas of ancestry, topography, place, relation, generativity, conversation and so on. Mathematics is "the hardest nut to crack" and has therefore become, for the authors, one of the most interesting challenges to face in an interpretive treatment of the basics.

2

A Curious Plan
Managing on the Twelfth

PATRICIA CLIFFORD AND SHARON FRIESEN

The Mock Turtle went on:
"We had the best of educations in fact, we went to school every day."

"And how many hours a day did you do lessons?" said Alice, in a hurry to change the subject.

"Ten hours the first day," said the Mock Turtle, "nine the next, and so on."

"What a curious plan!" exclaimed Alice.

"That's the reason they're called lessons," the Gryphon remarked; "because they lessen from day to day."

This was quite a new idea to Alice, and she thought it over a little before she made her next remark. "Then the eleventh day must have been a holiday?"

"Of course it was," said the Mock Turtle.

"And how did you manage on the twelfth?"

(Carroll, 1865/1966, pp. 95–96)

Introduction: Planning a Lived Curriculum

Every September, teachers and students gather together in our classroom to learn. Each of us, teacher and child alike, walks through the door bringing experiences and understandings that are ours alone. Yet, each person is also embarking on a journey that he or she will come to share with others. This journey is made anew every year with every class.

Travelers prepare more or less carefully for the adventures they hope to have, but the itineraries, maps, and plans do not in themselves create the voyage. The journey is an experience, lived as just the thing it turns out to be: moment-by-moment, day-by-day, month-by-month. As teachers, we prepare for each year's journey in big ways and in small ways. We make decisions, design plans, and outline key strategies to help us set directions for the coming year. In this article, we hope to share some of our decisions, plans, and strategies, therein describing the factors we consider as we prepare for an authentically engaging journey with each new class of children.

Some travelers keep diaries, which we, too, have done, recording actual situations that took place in our classroom from September 1991 to June 1992. In terms of its multi-aged, open-area configuration, our class was like others in the primary division of our school. The number of children varied throughout the year, as families moved in and out of the community. At any time, the two of us team-taught between fifty-five and fifty-eight children in grades one and two. In many ways, our classroom would be familiar to anyone used to teaching in middle-class neighbourhoods. In other ways, however, there are important differences. First of all, the children in our class vary more widely in their abilities, backgrounds, emotional and physical needs than one might expect. In this class, ten students were second-language learners. One child was in a wheelchair. Several had behavioural problems severe enough to warrant the interventions of social workers, psychologists, and psychiatrists since before the children entered grade one. Some had been identified as gifted, others as learning disabled.

Since the mid-1970s, the school in which we taught had maintained a tradition of multi-aged, open-area classrooms as part of its demonstration function for the local university. Because innovative structures and teaching practices are expected and encouraged, we were supported in our request both to teach together and to conduct action research. From the earliest days of our work as a team, everyone knew what we were setting out to do. Never content simply to replicate existing best practices, our school wanted to find out what would happen if we did what teachers at our school, University Elementary School, have always done: question, challenge, and change fundamental assumptions about the education of young children.

Using excerpts from the diaries we kept from 1991–1992, we hope in this chapter to illustrate some of the struggles and successes we encountered. We feel the examples we will give suggest a quality of children's thought and work that some may find astounding, given the fact that our students are only six and seven years old. We believe, however, that this is an example of the kind of work and thinking in which *all* children could engage and that all teachers could endeavour to bring forth. We would like to pose serious questions about how teachers can prepare themselves to create situations in which the voices of children genuinely inform the construction of each year's curriculum. For some teachers, administrators, and staff developers, these questions may be uncomfortable to hear because they call into question much of what is currently recognized as sound professional practice. We maintain that many of such current practices stand squarely in the way of the kinds of educational reform our profession needs most urgently to begin.

When schools open each year, one of the first things many teachers do is begin making long-range and unit plans that outline what they hope to accomplish by Christmas or, perhaps, for the whole year. If you are a school administrator reading this chapter, we want to give you some things to think about as you request such plans. If you are a classroom teacher, we would like to give you things to consider before you actually sit down to plan. If you are a teacher of teachers, we would like to give you pause as you prepare student teachers for their work with children. We would like, in short, to add our voices to the conversations aimed at ensuring that lessons do *not* lessen from day to day, from year to year, for children who have no choice but to come to school. We are committed to developing a classroom where teachers and children are passionate, robust learners. This commitment requires something more than new programs or new methods. It calls for what we can only characterize as a fundamentally different idea of what is considered "basic" to education, and a different disposition that permits teachers to live more generously with the children in their care.

We are searching for a school curriculum that acknowledges the importance of the lived experience of children and teachers; that understands growth as more than an interior, private, individual matter of unfolding development; that situates teaching and learning within the context of an educative community; and that asks hard questions about the fuzzy, feel-good legacy of much of what teachers now do in the name of "progressive" practice. Creating such a curriculum is a life's work. Perhaps it is significant, however, that neither of us came to early childhood education as our first career. One of us worked for five years as a systems analyst, and the other taught senior high school for fifteen years. For different reasons, and on different paths, we had both developed similar concerns about public education long before we met each other. We were worried about the boredom, dropout rates, and general lackluster performance of many students. In that we were not alone; we were part of a growing public concern that young people in North America were not learning as much as they might. Two things were different for us, however. First, we resisted the return to traditional images and practices that seem almost inevitably to accompany criticism of schools. And second, each of us knew (again, long before we met) that attempts to reform schools by concentrating mainly on the attitudes and achievements of secondary students, or on the attitudes and achievements of those being hired to teach in schools, was unlikely to succeed. Each of us had already decided that the most promising place to create genuinely new practices was with the very young.

We endeavoured initially to find out something about what a classroom would look like if we called into question some of our profession's most ordinary assumptions about teaching and learning. When we first wrote this chapter in 1992, we had studied, taught, and written together for four years. In that time, we learned a great deal, and we fight constantly with the temptation to try to say everything at once. In this chapter, we hope to make a small start by posing three important questions:

How can curriculum remain open to children's unique experiences and contacts with the world they know outside the school?

Why is imaginative experience the best starting place for planning?

What happens when teachers break down the barriers between school knowledge and real knowledge?

David's Story: On Keeping Things Connected

I would ask you to remember only this one thing," said Badger. "The stories people tell have a way of taking care of them. If stories come to you, care for them. And learn to give them away where they are needed. Sometimes a person needs a story more than food to stay alive; that is why we put these stories in each other's memory. This is how people care for themselves."

(Lopez, 1990, p. 48)

We met David and his parents on the first day of school. They had just returned to Canada after spending seven years in Africa, where they had lived and worked among the Masai. Although he was of European descent, David had been born in Africa. He went to a village kindergarten, and played and tended cattle with the Masai children. No one in our class, including us, knew much about Africa. Though we had listened carefully to what David's parents told us at the beginning of the school year, we remembered embarrassingly little of it because we had been trying to learn about our fifty-four other children at the same time. So, as we watched David take his first tentative steps in school, we often forgot that the life David had been living until the end of August was radically different from the one he now had to negotiate in our large, complicated, noisy Canadian classroom.

Throughout September and into October, David spoke very little. He would answer direct questions briefly, but never offered to share much of himself. Once, in response to an assignment to tell a personal story, he told a small group of children how he and his family had gone camping—and had woken up to find lions crouching under their truck. The other children acted the story out, growling and shrieking with frightened delight. But aside from this story, we knew little about David. As time went on, David made a friend in class, hooking up with Jason out of mutual need. David was lonely, and he wanted to establish himself in a new country. Jason needed a companion to coerce, command, and bully. This friendship worried David's parents. David had spent all of his life nurtured within a trusting, gentle community, and he approached his friendship with Jason with the same quality of trust. David got into trouble almost daily because of Jason, and David's parents found themselves having to talk to him about the inappropriateness of some people's intentions. They were heartsick, both about what was happening to David and about the ugly lessons about "the real world" that their gentle, naive son was beginning to absorb.

One day in early October, David arrived at school with a huge book about the Masai and asked if he could show his book to the other children. This was the first time David had ever offered to share part of his life experiences with the whole class, to teach us all what he knew best—life among the Masai. David stood in front of the class with his book. He flipped to a few pictures and spoke softly—so softly that only the children near the front could hear him. We tried to offer a few details about the Masai, but we knew so little. In spite of these difficulties and limitations, the children were entranced. They had so many questions to ask David, so much they wanted to know. This was the second time we had seen the children respond with enthusiasm to David's life in Africa. This time we recognized the power of the invitation that he had offered us. Here was the perfect chance to bring David into the full life of the classroom.

That afternoon, David's mother came to volunteer in the classroom. We asked her if she would speak to us about the Masai. She agreed, took her place in a small chair at the front of the group, and opened David's book. As she spoke, David stood quietly at her shoulder, gently stroking her long hair. He seemed to relax into the memories of that safe, familiar place, trusting the intimacy of his mother's voice and body to secure the connection between here and there.

As our eyes met above the heads of the children, we knew we had been waiting for this all along, without knowing it: waiting for David's life in Africa to come alive for us. Up to now, David had blended in too readily with all the other children. We had had no images to help us understand that this new country, this new classroom, held few connections with the world he had known in Africa.

Our efforts to see all children as contributing members of our classroom community is a kind of standing invitation, but we never know who will take it up, or how they will do it. It appeared that David had decided that *now* was his time, and he made the first essential move. David and his mother shared their life among the Masai with us, and in that sharing helped forge new links between David, his classmates, and us. The class was filled with curiosity, and questions overflowed the hour we spent together. Because of the intensity of the children's interest in David's experiences in Africa and the potential to find, in their pleasure, a new place for David in the classroom, we felt committed to act beyond the delights of that afternoon. We accepted eagerly when David's mother asked if we were interested in using a children's book about the Masai that they had at home.

The next day David brought us *Bringing the Rain to Kapiti Plain* (Aardema 1981). As we read the story to the class, David sat at the back mouthing every word to himself. Once again we saw David relaxed, smiling, basking in the genuine delight of hearing that well-loved story again, this time in the world of his classroom in Calgary. This book was just the beginning of the stories about Africa, for we found others: *The Orphan Boy, Rhinos for Lunch, Elephants for Supper,* and *A Promise to the Sun.* David brought in other things to share with us, such as elaborate beaded collars and knives used to bleed cattle.

Months later, when the children drew maps of their known worlds, David's map showed his house in Africa, the cheetah park, the camping place where the lions crouched under the truck, a Masai warrior. We sensed then how much of his heart was still there and were honoured that he felt safe enough among us to share himself in this way, for as David now tells us, he is "a very private person." We are also keenly aware that we would have known nothing about these places had David not come into our lives. Recently, when we were reading about Mongolian nomads living on animal blood and milk, many children remembered what David had taught them about the Masai. They speculated about why the animals didn't die when they were bled, and looked to David for confirmation that such a thing was, indeed, possible.

We continually ask ourselves: How much of the life that is lived completely outside school is welcomed into the classroom as knowledge and experience that can enrich all those who inhabit a particular classroom? How much of each child gets to come to school? When a child says, "This is me, and I am ready for you to know it," we must try to honour this offering, not shut it out, control it, or hurry to get on with the curriculum. An invitation is more than words. Offered sincerely, invitations create obligations to welcome and to provide. Having extended an invitation to David, we felt compelled to act. David's knowledge and experiences needed to become part of the curriculum, part of the life of the group.

Bringing David into the class in this way opened up new possibilities for him, but it did something just as important for the whole class. All of the children lived the experience of a standing invitation. By observing how we attended to David and to others who also offered *their* stories, the children came to understand the importance of what each of them might bring to the journey our class had embarked on together.

Our curriculum work demands mindful, deliberate improvisation at such moments. It goes far beyond "Show and Share," which can be a perniciously educational practice: "You show me yours and I'll show you mine." Children's sharing is often limited to a slot in the daily agenda. While such activity is designed to bring home into the school, the activity of sharing can, unfortunately, become an end in itself, requiring no further commitment from the teacher than to provide the opportunity for each child to bring in a favourite object or news event. That is not at all what we mean when we speak of invitations. We mean, rather, that each child's voice can be heard, and that their speaking can make a difference to our curriculum decision making. Improvising on children's responses to our standing invitation demands a commitment to recognizing human relationships as a fundamental source of knowledge. At the beginning of the year we could not plan for these moments, but we were prepared for them because we knew that they would inevitably arise. We knew that the children would give us what we needed to know, as long as we remained open to the possibilities.

Determined to foster continuity between personal and school knowledge, we work in a constant state of watchfulness. Children's authentic offerings are often made tentatively. Unlike David's, they can be subtle and easy to miss, but they are nevertheless vital components of a lived curriculum. We know that when curriculum includes only the plans teachers make to deliver instruction, the child who emerges is usually what we might call a "school child," one who is either compliant with or defiant of the exercise of institutional power. It is our belief that when curriculum is divorced from real life, children often lose connections with their own memories and histories. They lose touch with who they are. They may exist in our eyes more as students than as emerging selves, and we wonder if they continue to learn in any passionate sense of that word.

Learning: From the Known to the Unknown

Children develop most fully as passionate learners when they—like all of us— are allowed to claim fully their own experience of the world. We are not, however, talking about the type of experience made relevant to children through its commercial appeal or immediate access: Ninja Turtles and Barbies, video games, superheros, or cartoons. Nor are we talking about the immersion in local experience that some call "the belly button curriculum": me and my house, me and my family, me and my neighbourhood. Much of early childhood education is grounded in a view of learning as predictable development through ages and stages, from familiar to strange, from concrete to abstract, from (supposedly) simple to complex.

In one sense, we accept these assumptions. After all, David *did* want to share his daily experiences in Africa with his classmates in Canada, and we watched David blossom as he accepted the invitation to connect his life in Africa with life in Canada. In another sense, however, what happened to David is best understood as a starting point for even richer engagement. What intrigued the children was not the sharing of "me and my family." They did not want to talk about *their* daily lives in Calgary in response to David's stories. They wanted, rather, to talk about knives and arrows, about drinking blood and milk, about women who shaved their heads, and about children who tended cattle all day long, far from the gaze of watchful adults. What was familiar and well known to David called out to the imagination in each of us. Enriched by David's knowledge, we began to experience new worlds together, creating within our classrooms the kinds of imaginative experiences that Egan (1986, 1992) describes: those imaginative experiences that engage, intrigue, interest, puzzle, and enchant; those imaginative experiences that call forth sustained and key conversations about freedom, loyalty, responsibility, strength, and human relationships. When we speak of imaginative engagement, we mean the kind of engagement that invites children most fully, most generously, into the club of knowers; not at some unspecified time in the future when they are grown up and able to use their knowledge, but today and each and every day they spend with us.

Egan (1992) invited us to consider that "even the briefest look at children's thinking from this perspective opens profound conflicts with some of the ideas that dominate educational thinking and practice today" (p. 653). When we learn to look at children with new eyes, we can see clearly that, by the time they come to school at age five, they have already learned about some of the most complex, abstract, and powerful ideas they will ever encounter. Simply by virtue of their humanity, they have experienced joy and fear, love and hate, trust and betrayal, power and oppression, expectation and satisfaction—all, as Egan notes, before they have even learned how to ride a bicycle (1986, pp. 28–29).

Our study of a familiar fairy tale shows how this view of imaginative experience can challenge dominant educational thinking. Early in 1991, the children in our class listened to *Rumpelstiltskin*, an ordinary experience in a primary classroom. In choosing that story, we were depending on the children's knowledge in important ways. We did *not* assume that they had had direct experience with princes and princesses, much less with malevolent dwarves and alchemic transformations. Indeed, if learning is understood to proceed from concrete to abstract, from familiar to strange, from daily experience to the world of wonders, then *Rumpelstiltskin* should make little sense to children. But they loved the story, debating fiercely about issues such as whether parents, like the miller, have the right to put their children in danger; whether people have the right to ask for help without pledging something in return; whether adults should be allowed to give their children away, and the grief that may follow if they participate in such bad bargains. For children to understand this story, they needed to know about deception, the politics of rescue, false pride, boasting, and the indomitable human spirit.

As Egan (1992) notes, "to teach concrete content untied to powerful abstractions is to starve the imagination" (p. 653). David's story is important to us as teachers because of what it tells us about hearing each child's voice and bringing each child into the life of the classroom. However, it is also important to us because of what it says about children's interest in places far away and times long ago. The great stories of history and literature are as fascinating to the children in our class as David's accounts of Africa. Stories about Leonardo da Vinci, Columbus, Ghengis Khan, Radomes and Aida, Pythagoras, and King Arthur and his court prompted the same kind of lively debate and discussion of big questions about the human condition we saw in their response to *Rumpelstiltskin*. Retellings of *Romeo and Juliet, Beowulf* and parts of Chaucer were as enchanting as readings of *The Lady of Shalott, The Highwayman*, and *The Rime of the Ancient Mariner*. All of these stories have engaged the imagination of generations of adults because of the engagement they demand. We have discovered that these stories touch young children with as much power. They connect both them and us as their teachers with the past, ground us all firmly in the present moment of listening to their rich language and images. They cause us, even compel us, to contemplate together what life holds in store.

Thus, for us, a second important planning issue centers on the "big questions" we offer to and accept from the children we teach. Without those big questions, tied to great literature that engages the imagination, the spirit, the feelings, and the intellect, curriculum is likely to be thin and unsubstantial, fully satisfying to neither teacher nor child. Arising from questions about the human condition that engage each of us because we share the planet together, the curriculum we have created with our children permits them access to intellectual and aesthetic traditions that are thousands of years old. Children often ask some of the same questions the ancients asked, and discover anew, for themselves, the power of learning both to create and to solve important, engaging questions.

We have many, many typed pages of notes we took while the children were discussing stories and films about Columbus, Leonardo da Vinci, Ghengis Khan, the Arthurian saga, outer space, Greek myths, and Chinese legends. These subjects may not be considered the usual fare offered to six- and seven-year-olds. Indeed, we had no idea in September, when we were writing our plans, the various directions our studies would take. How could we have imagined, for example, that Jason would bring us back again and again to the idea that human knowledge is really a model of how we think things work? He asked us over and over how people know when their models are wrong. And over and over, we thought about that question as a way of understanding what adults have come to call "history," "mathematics," "science," "literature," "ethics," and "education." How do any of us find out if our models are wrong?

How could we have anticipated the amazement of Diana, a child in grade one who could not yet read, when she learned that the ancient Greeks had known the earth was spherical, but that people had subsequently *lost* that knowledge for centuries. They had lost precious knowledge about space, Diana's passion. She was offended by what she considered to be the carelessness of her ancestors, and endlessly intrigued by how that knowledge had been retrieved. Had there been one person, she wondered, who had just stood up and said, "Look, you guys, this is how it is"? Or had there been many people at the same time who figured it out together?

Could we ever have guessed that Edward would lean over to Sharon during a reading of *The Rime of the Ancient Mariner* and whisper, "It feels like the ghost of the ancient mariner is in this room right now. Do you think he's here? Do you?" Until Christmas, Edward had hardly spoken to us. He was so withdrawn from others that he often buried his face in the hood of his kangaroo shirt and rocked back and forth during lessons and class meetings. He seldom wrote, preferring to sit by himself and draw minutely detailed mazes of miniature battle scenes, seemingly obsessed with blood dripping from gaping wounds and vicious swords. On a blustery January day, Coleridge's words had reached across time and space to touch a little boy who wanted, for the very first time, to talk to his teachers about the world inside his head. The next day, he picked up the conversation again. "Do you know," he told us, "that an imagination is a terrible thing? The pictures in my mind really, really scare me." For Edward, the thing that had frightened him most—his ability to conjure detailed, vivid images—became the vehicle through which he was able, for the first time that we could see, to connect with others in the classroom.

Would we ever have expected that, after several weeks of reading, discussion, and project work about human discoveries, dreams, hard work, courage, tenacity, and integrity, the children would have pulled together the following questions about knowledge and work, questions to which they—and we—returned again and again in the months that followed:

Where do you go looking for knowledge?

How do you learn the secrets of the world?

The more you learn, the more you get to know what you have to do. Why?

Why do things come alive when you put yourself into your work?

What do you need to give so you can get knowledge?

The children drove us deeper and further than we could possibly have gone on our own, demanding more stories, more history, more problems, more answers. The children stretched our knowledge and our capacity to hear, in their demands, the next best step to take. We haunted stores and libraries, searching for books to bring back to them and for books to help *us* learn more physics, mathematics, mythology, history, literature. When, for example, we read the children *I, Columbus*—excerpts from the log Columbus reputedly kept on his journey to learn what he called the secrets of the world—they asked many questions. Was Columbus the only person who believed that the earth was a sphere? What must it have been like to be Columbus, certain of your own knowledge but wrong in the eyes of many of your peers? Where did Columbus get his maps from, anyway? How did he navigate once he had passed the boundaries of the known world? Where was the Sargasso Sea, and was that where the Ancient Mariner had been becalmed? Why do people say Columbus discovered America when there were people living here already?

As teachers, we saw opportunities in these questions to bring in more and more material about maps and map-making, astronomy, geography, and history. One child brought in an article from the Manchester *Guardian* about Renaissance maps. We found stories such as Yolen's *Encounter*, which raised important issues about the effect of European contact on aboriginal peoples, and we introduced the children to the fact that the First Nations of Canada struggle to this very day with the consequences of voyages of so-called discovery that ended up on shores we now think of as our own.

During each story, lesson, and discussion, we would sit side by side at an easel at the front of the group. One of us would facilitate the children's conversation, and the other would scribe as quickly as possible, catching wherever we could the actual words of the children, and paraphrasing when the talk moved too quickly. Earlier in the year we had tried to tape-record these conversations, but the microphones let us down. First, the conversation was too complex for a machine to capture properly. Second, capturing key elements of the discussion required a teacher's judgment. Which comments and questions did we want to formulate for the whole group? Which were the threads that seemed, even in the moment, to hold real promise of future exploration? Where were the moments that allowed us to make powerful connections between the mandated program of studies and the children's own questions?

At the end of days on which the children had been engaged in such discussions, we would sit at the easel re-reading and organizing what they had said and asked. We would highlight for ourselves what the next step ought to be. What had the children said that we could most profitably mine? Sometimes we knew exactly what resources we could use. We would go to our class library, the school collection, or to the public library for books and films we already knew about and bring them in for future classes. At other times, we would just go looking. If a question seemed sufficiently promising or intriguing, we would look for material we were certain must exist.

Curriculum planning that takes the voices of children seriously represents a kind of openness. Teachers need to remain open to children's experience in the world and construct curricula that are deeply responsive to and resonant with what each child knows, who each child is. Teachers also need to understand that it is only the big, authentically engaging questions that create openings wide and deep enough to admit all adventurers who wish to enter. Three things are important in this regard. First, when children raise the kinds of questions that capture their attention in our studies of literature, history, and mathematics, it becomes possible for each of them to find compelling ways into the discussion and work that follows. Individuals cannot tell in advance when moments of connection will occur—for themselves or for others. Our experience has shown us time and again that questions about fairness, justice, knowledge, learning, courage, and oppression, sparked by stories of substance and worth, seem to free children to engage with complex aspects of the world and of their own experience.

Second, questions are ones that intrigue adults as much as they enchant children. The conversations, the debates, and all of the work that flow out of these questions are deeply engaging for us, as teachers. The children experience our own genuine sense of excitement and commitment to the world of the mind and the spirit as they struggle with us to relive, in the present moment, dilemmas that were equally real to our ancestors. Moreover, when the children see their own questions returned to them as the basis for subsequent work and study, they come to know curriculum as a living, connected experience. Curriculum is not delivered to them through fragmented activities made up by others; it is created with them, inspired by the work of the community of which each of them is a valued member.

Third, the worlds made available to children through stories and philosophizing of this sort form strong links with the complicated, everyday world in which they live. When the dean of the local law school, the mother of one of our students, came into the classroom during our study of *Rumpelstiltskin* and saw a child's comment written on chart paper, she hastened to copy it down: "When parents give their child away for gold, they will regret it later on, when they've had time to think about it." She was about to make a presentation about surrogacy contracts to the legal community, and she was delighted that young children, inspired by this classic tale, had articulated so clearly the dilemma that many legal scholars were now exploring. Thus, teachers must remain open to the power of real literature, real science, real mathematics, and real art to touch all of us profoundly—not only the children.

Real Knowledge and School Knowledge: Examples from Mathematics

Coming to know the world as mathematicians or scientists—like becoming a reader and writer—involves authentic engagement in mathematical and scientific experiences, not the busy work that often comes to count in school as mathematics and science or reading and writing. Many school textbooks and workbooks are organized to encourage mindless recitation. Most mathematics curricula are organized to support the notion that accuracy in computation equals excellence in understanding. Even Alberta's new mathematics curriculum, which states that problem solving is at the heart of mathematics, relegates problems to a separate unit. Many curriculum designers seem to think that problem-solving means doing word problems. It is also clear that many teachers think that they are teaching mathematics when they are merely covering the textbook or the workbook. Unfortunately, the result often is a student who is schooled in "school mathematics"—a form of mathematics that bears little resemblance to the "real mathematics" that mathematicians, physicists, and engineers experience, or to the mathematics that sparks the imagination and ignites a passion for understanding the world mathematically and scientifically.

We want children to experience mathematics as a powerful language of the imagination that allows them to explore big mathematical ideas like balance, space, time, patterns, and relationships. We have come to see that they enjoy thinking about these matters, exploring, debating, solving problems, and learning together. We have found, too, having taught in many different school settings, that too many school children learn only "school mathematics," a dull, lifeless, scary, and irrelevant round of pluses and minuses that usurps the real, much more engaging, thing.

How might it look in a classroom if teachers set about to make math real? The Alberta science and math curricula both state that children in the primary grades must know certain things about time: they must know how to read both analog and digital clocks, know the days of the week, the months of the year, and something about the seasons and the phases of the moon. When we sat down to talk about how to teach this part of the curriculum, we saw that among our options were activities that would encourage children to think that time resided in a clock or a calendar. Such activities would have satisfied the curriculum objectives, but we wanted more. We wanted children to learn that time is a mysterious and puzzling phenomenon.

We felt that if we restricted an understanding of time to the narrow view of "telling time" contained within most curriculum guides, we would transmit a useful skill, but not much more. Instead, we thought that if we paid attention to what physicists ask about time, we might give children access to what is undeniably one of the secrets of the world.

Here is what Bruce Gregory (1990), the Associate Director of the Harvard-Smithsonian Center for Astrophysics, tells us about the human understanding of time:

> Galileo's accomplishment was made possible by his decision to talk about the world in terms of motion through space and time. These concepts seem so obvious to us that it is difficult to remember that they *are* concepts. Time is normally measured in terms of motion, from the swing of the pendulum of a grandfather's clock to the oscillations of a quartz crystal in a modern watch. Apart from such periodic behaviour, how could we even talk about the uniformity of time? In the words of the contemporary American physicist John Wheeler, "Time is defined so that motion looks simple." Wheeler also said, "Time? The concept did not descend from heaven, but from the mouth of man, an early thinker, his name long lost." Einstein demonstrated the power of talking about space and time as though they were a unity, and in the process he showed that both space and time are human inventions—ways of talking about the world.

(p. 70)

To let children in on some of the secrets of this way of talking about the world, we need to let them in on two other big secrets. First of all, they must come to understand that human knowledge is humanly constructed. As a culture, a society, a community—and as a classroom—we make decisions about what will and will not count as knowledge, and those decisions make some understandings of the world possible, as much as they render other perspectives impossible.

If we really want our children to face the challenges of the twenty-first century with confidence and skill, we need to teach them not only that they can acquire current knowledge, but also that they have voices that can shape what their society comes to accept as knowledge. This philosophy of teaching is exemplified in the following illustrations drawn from a series of lessons and activities about time.

We began one morning by asking the children to talk to us and each other about what they knew about time. Seated on the floor in front of the easel, they began to talk. As they offered examples of how time works, we recorded the following comments:

It's something you have to use.

You need to wear a watch to know what time it is.

You need it—you can be late if you don't know the time.

You can run out of time when you are playing or when people bother you.

Sometimes grown-ups say, "You have two minutes to do something!" They really mean get it done quickly.

You need to know time to know how fast you run in a race. You win when you have the least time.

You can waste time.

It is important to tell time.

People get worried if they think they are running out of time.

A day and a night equal twenty-four hours.

Time can be fast and slow.

Time lets you know when you should be doing things.

Time goes fast when you're playing. It goes slowly when you're not having fun.

Everyone in the world needs to know what time is the right time. You need to synchronize time with world events, like the Olympics on TV.

Adults are expected to tell time. Children don't have to.

If your house is flooded, it takes a long time to get it out.

When we're doing projects, people always ask, "How much time until lunch?"

You can tell time by counting by fives.

People need to be home on time.

Clearly, this long list shows that the children had many experiences with time. For example, they knew about clocks and strategies about how to read clocks, they knew time was related to astronomical and geographical phenomena, and they knew time experientially. One of the children asked, "How can you tell time without a watch?" This question was to lead to intriguing explorations into the history of time and time-keeping devices and opened the possibility to explore time and its astronomical relationships. When one child recalled that a member of Columbus's crew was charged with the responsibility of turning the hourglass over when it emptied and keeping track of how often this occurred, another remarked that at one time people used sundials. This idea of the sundial caught the children's imagination, and they wanted to know exactly how a sundial told time. Fortunately, the sun cooperated with us and we went outside to begin some preliminary investigations.

In order to understand what happened next, it is important to know something about how our day is structured. We reserve a two-hour block of time between morning recess and lunch for the integrated study of literature, social studies, science, and mathematics. This time might be devoted on one day to conversations such as the one described above, and on another it might be used for a lesson and supporting activities. Sometimes we read stories and explore the children's responses; sometimes the children conduct investigations and experiments; sometimes we all listen to a guest speaker who can shed light on a question that has emerged on previous days. Often, the children paint or perform plays.

The flexibility of this long block of time permits us to follow up promising questions and comments like the ones about sundials. On this particular day, we had enough time left before lunch to go outside to explore the daytime astronomy of the sun's light and motion. Before leaving the classroom, we asked the children to observe where their shadows were and to try to make them fall in a different direction. Once outside, they turned and twisted themselves about in the sun, succeeding only in making their shadows change shape, not direction. A group of five children called us over to where they were standing. They proudly announced that they had found a way to tell time using the sun and their bodies. The children had positioned themselves in a circle and explained that one of them was at twelve, one at three, one at six, and one at nine, with the fifth child in the centre. They had formed a clock and the direction of the shadow that was cast by the centre person indicated the time.

Inside again, the children made further observations and asked more questions:

If you stood in the same place for a whole day you would see your shadow change places because the earth changes position.

Clouds can block the sun's rays so sundials won't work on rainy days.

Can you tell time with one "hand"?

Why is my shadow longer than I am in the evening but shorter than me at noon?

People can't make time go faster because they're not the boss of the world. Even if you change the hands of the clock, you aren't changing time, itself.

How do we know what the real time is?

How did people start to tell time?

By now, two hours had passed. What had seemed like a simple beginning had flowered into exciting possibilities for future investigations. From the children's work and conversation, we saw themes on which we could now begin to improvise.

On another day, we asked the children to name all the ways they knew to record time. We learned that they knew about months, hours, and minutes; that 60 minutes equalled an hour; that 120 minutes made up two hours; and that 30 minutes was half an hour. Time, some said, could be measured in years, seconds, days, weeks, decades (which we told them meant 10 years), and centuries (which they knew meant 100 years). There were birth years, seasons, milliseconds, generations, and lifetimes (which we all decided together usually lasted from about 70 to about 90 years).

The next question was easy for us to ask: "Which of these measures of time is the longest?"

We even expected an easy answer: centuries. But we didn't account for children like Michael, whose hand shot up at once.

"I know, I know," he said, "it's seasons!"

"Why, Michael? Tell us what you are thinking about."

"Well, you see, seasons keep going on and on. You can have summer and fall and winter and spring. Then you keep having them all over again, and they make a pattern. See?"

And all of a sudden, we did see: not only that we had both locked into a narrow focus when we thought centuries was the best (even the only) answer, but also that Michael understood something important about the concept of relativity: that is, that "right" answers had everything to do with the framework you adopted. We looked at other measurements on the list. We asked if some of *those* could be candidates for "longest" as well. Joseph responded that generations were even better than seasons because generations went on and on with parents and children, and then their children and their children and *their* children. It all ended up in Heaven, he added, where time went on forever and ever. This idea of generations set another conversation in motion. To how many generations could each of us belong in a lifetime? Could they ever be in the same generation as their parents? As the children they would come to have? Would they *want* to be?

And so it went—from topic to topic, question to question, insight to insight. By the end of yet another discussion, we reached a conclusion to which everyone agreed: When you talk about days, seasons, or whatever in a general way, many units of measurement could be considered "longest" because they repeat themselves in a patterned way. As Michael's and Joseph's comments indicate, duration can also be understood as cycles—a fundamentally different framework from a linear one. Moreover, the children spoke of freezing time. They gave the example of designating a time—say, Friday, June 5, 1992, 11:48 am.— which is the precise time we had this part of the conversation. That moment will never repeat itself, they reminded us. The instant it passes, it becomes part of history. You can never, ever go back and do *that* time again the way you can repeat summers, year after year.

As the discussion continued, thoughtful and excited murmurs passed through the group like a wave.

"You mean, if we just waste that time we can't ever get it back?"

"Like, if we just were fooling around right now, we wouldn't get to come back to 11:48 because it was gone forever?"

"No, not gone forever, because tomorrow there will be another 11:48. But *this 11:48 can't come back.*"

We pushed them by asking: "How precisely do you have to indicate a time before you know that that particular moment would never repeat itself?" Clearly, every day had 11:48s in it (and Maria reminded us that there was an 11:48 for the morning and one for the night time because there were always two 12:00s in every day). Fridays would repeat themselves, and so would Junes. But the Friday that occurred on the fifth day of June in 1992—not 1993 or some other year—was the one that would not come back. The 11:48 that belonged to only that Friday was the moment that was now part of our collective history.

This discussion was in June; we had worked hard since September to create an intellectual community. We were witnessing the work and dispositions that we had nurtured throughout the year bearing fruit. The next time the children gathered to talk about time, their observations bore the mark not only of their individual experiences of time outside the classroom, but also of the hours we had spent in exploration together. We decided to ask them what we thought was a harder question: "What is time?" This is what the children told us:

Time is something that keeps on going.

It helps you keep track of the events in a day and also of the day.

It's not in a clock—it's everywhere.

It's something we use.

It's invisible—like air.

It's part of our lives.

We can't hear it, we can't see it, but we can use it and waste it.

We live time, we make it.

You can't speed it up or slow it down.

Planets use time to travel around the sun.

It's a different time in every country. When we have morning other countries have night.

If everything stopped, we would float quickly off to the sun—like a very fast aeroplane ride.

The clocks we use can be wrong—but time itself can't be wrong.

The sun uses time—it takes Mercury less time than any other planet to go around the sun. Pluto takes much more time to orbit the sun.

If we didn't have any time we would be dead. We wouldn't have any time to be born or to live.

Time was in the past and it is still part of the world.

They were also left with questions:

How do we know if our clock is wrong?

When was math invented?

Was there time before there was a universe? Did time exist before the Big Bang?

Where would stars and planets "go" if time stopped?

How did time get started?

As we went over the list, we noticed that much of what they discussed referred to the solar system. We recalled that, for a number of weeks, a group of children had worked together to create an elaborate, scaled model of the sun and the planets with all sixty of their respective moons. All of us had been involved in lively discussions about outer space, gravity, density, and light. The children brought forward into this current conversation on time some of the questions and issues they had visited before. We hadn't planned to integrate or summarize their experiences, but then Scott looked pensively at the ceiling and said, "Time is the whole universe. If there was not time everywhere, there would be no time. The only way time could stop is if the universe stopped." He formulated for all of us an understanding made possible by the history we shared together.

We were excited and honoured to have been part of this conversation. These children were pursuing knowledge, making conjectures, reasoning with each other. They were asking the kinds of questions that Einstein, Feynman, Sagan, and Hawkings ask. They were coming to understand that mathematics is a way of speaking. It is a language that permits those using it to experience the world in particular ways. It is a tool that allows the exploration of other, larger ideas. The ability to think mathematically is not simply the ability to produce number facts. It is not even the ability to solve word problems. If we want to nurture children who are passionate about science and mathematics, we have to start right (in both senses of the word) from the beginning:

> Because the discourse of the math class reflects messages about what it means to know math, what makes something true or reasonable, and what doing math entails, it is central to both what students learn about math as well as how they learn it. Therefore the discourse of the math class should be founded on math ways of knowing and ways of communicating.
>
> (*Professional Standards*, 1991, p. 54)

Did the children ever learn to tell time? Absolutely. It took only one hour for fifty of them and an additional 30 minutes for the other five to learn *that* kind of math language, too. Many of the grade one's and all of the grade two's could tell time to the quarter hour, and a substantial number mastered the grade-three objective: they could tell time to the minute. As for problem solving, a group of children created, and then set about solving, their own problems. Nathan, for example, wanted to know how many seconds were in an hour. A group of five children who had already completed the required exercises on telling time and who were interested in solving Nathan's problem gathered around him. While the rest of the class worked in small groups with clocks and question sheets, Nathan and his friends figured out what they thought they would need to know in order to solve the problem and then set about doing the computation. This was no mean feat, considering that none of them knew how to multiply. But they *did* know that mathematics is about patterns and relationships, so they were able to draw upon what they knew about addition, set organization, and place value to solve this real and interesting problem.

There is more to our story of time. The children's questions about the beginnings of clocks led the class to ancient Egypt and Stonehenge, to early calendars and struggles to align solar and lunar years, to the mythological sources naming months and weekdays.

Unfortunately, like the sands in an hour-glass, we ran out of time. But we were left with a wonderful and exciting starting place for the following September. We were going to teach these same children again the next year.

Conclusion

These are not easy times for public education. Beset on all sides by calls to do better work on behalf of children, it is difficult not to feel defensive or defeated when others far from the daily life of a classroom call for school reform. For a long time, teachers have been charged with implementing theories developed by others. Those who have been teaching for a long time have seen many theories come and go, and have worked hard to keep up with what was expected of teachers because of such changes. Increasing numbers of teachers have, however, begun to sense that the educational conversation is changing in important ways. Often excluded in the past, the voices of teachers and children are being welcomed as ones that can inform both theory and practice in unique ways. For it is teachers who spend their daily lives in the presence of children; teachers who are better placed than anyone to see what can happen when they begin to think differently about their work with children.

In our daily work, our reflection, and our writing, the two of us have taken seriously the challenge of thinking about education differently. We began our work together knowing *that* we wanted to challenge basic assumptions about primary practice. As our research proceeded, we began also to be able to talk about *how* we thought changes in teaching practice might come about. First, we came to see, in the relationships that we established with each child in our care, the importance of offering invitations to connect the life each child lived fully and completely outside the school with the life we were offering inside its doors. For us, David's story was perhaps the most dramatic and obvious of fifty-four other stories we could have told. As we sat together at the end of the school year thinking about the children and the journey on which each had embarked with us, we understood for ourselves that the successes—and the failures—of our attempts to connect with each child marked the successes—and the failures— of our ability to work with each in pedagogically fruitful ways.

We do not think that observation will come as any great surprise to good teachers. Nor will it come as a surprise to anyone when we say that living out the implications of this understanding is an awesome responsibility. What *did* come as more of a surprise to us was to see, in our relationships with the children, the power of imagination to build connections that were not only personally gratifying, but also educationally profound. Imaginative engagement in questions and issues that were big enough to enchant each person in class, child and adult alike, created the space within which each child could move with strength and freedom. Each found his or her own ways into the conversations and the work throughout the year, and each voice contributed uniquely to how the school year turned out for all concerned.

Perhaps what is most unexpected about what we found as we began to explore the world with children in the ways we have described here is the extent to which they learned more than we had ever imagined possible. We heard some of them recite parts of Tennyson by heart on the playground, loving *The Lady of Shalott* (1986) as much as David had loved *Bringing the Rain to Kapiti Plain*. We did physics experiments with some, and investigated ancient number systems with others. Together, we and the children built models of the solar system, medieval castles, and the Great Wall of China. We thrilled in their re-tellings of ancient Chinese legends and plots of Italian operas. With each and every study, the children kept pushing: tell us more. Given access to real science, real mathematics, real literature, and art of substance and merit, they seemed insatiable.

We began this article with a quotation from *Alice in Wonderland*. Like many teachers, we are fond of Alice. Indeed, there are days when we find ourselves, like her, wandering around asking foolish questions about matters that seem quite settled to others. The Mock Turtle and the Gryphon listen patiently to Alice's bewildered inability to understand what schools are for, and we wonder what—if anything—they made of her question, "And how did you manage on the twelfth?" We wonder if they clucked their beaks, rolled their eyes, and wished she would just go away.

Having begun to create for ourselves a completely different framework from the one presented by the Turtle and the Gryphon, however, we are no longer left to resolve the beastly paradox that so bedevilled Alice. Lessons need *not* lessen from day to day, month to month, year to year. Children and teachers *can* find new and powerful ways to come to know each other through real work that engages their minds, hearts, and spirits.

We can all, in fact, manage quite nicely on the twelfth.

3
Cleaving with Affection
On Grain Elevators and the Cultivation of Memory

DAVID W. JARDINE, MICHELLE BASTOCK,
JENNIFER GEORGE, AND JUDY MARTIN[1]

I

It is necessary that a man should dwell with solicitude on,
and cleave with affection to, the things which he wishes to
remember.

(Thomas Aquinas, paraphrasing the *Ad Herennium*,
cited in Yates, 1974, p. 75)

II

I (J.G.) have the fortunate opportunity to work with half of my students
again for a second year. Now the older and wiser ones, my new Grade Two
students will be the leaders of the new inquiry. In the beginning I was dead
set against continuing with the grain elevators because I could not conceive
of a way to bring my new Grade One students up to speed. I was resigned
to the fact that "the Elevator Kids" would have to be a noon hour club and
that elevators would not be a part of my classroom work this year—so
why were there so many grain elevator posters still in my room? Could it
be that, like the Grade Two children, I was not ready to let the project go
either?

Early in September I received a phone call from artist Karen Brownlee, who
illustrated a grain elevator book for the Centennial titled *Alberta Remembers*
(Tingley & Brownlee, 2005). She wanted "the Elevator Kids" to come and speak
at her book launch.

III

In honor of Alberta's Centennial, the majestic beauty of the grain elevator is celebrated by artist Karen Brownlee and author Ken Tingley in 128
vibrant paintings with descriptive text. Based on the artist's Rural Prairie
Communities series, Alberta Remembers pays homage to this rapidly
disappearing icon that played such a central role in the development of
the Prairie West. Includes forewords by Jane Ross, Curator, Western

Canadian History, Royal Alberta Museum and Daniel T. Gallagher, Curator Emeritus, Canadian Museum of Civilization.

(Book Description entry for *Alberta Remembers* [Brownlee & Tingley, 2005] on www.amazon.ca)

IV

When I told the class the next morning, one of the Grade Two boys, Charlie, said: "Thank goodness. I was wondering when we would get busy again!"

Now what? How could I possibly prepare half of my class for a book launch while not involving the younger half of my group? But that's exactly what I did—after all, I was not going to do grain elevators again, remember!

The book launch went off without a hitch and then the trouble started. Mysterious notes passed during math, science, and occasionally "phys. ed." turned out to be innocent drawings of grain elevators. The drawings also re-emerged on the backs of spelling tests and on the covers of scribblers. But it was when I caught some Grade Two children sketching grain elevators during our trip to Tepee Village (instead of sketching tepees) that I knew I had missed something.

Back in class we shared our copy of the *Alberta Remembers* book together at the carpet. I watched closely as the Grade Two students, "the Elevator Kids," sat high on their knees, eyes wide and excitement boiling, as they spoke about every page. I also watched the vast majority of the Grade One children sitting quietly back, looking around the room, wondering what all the fuss was about.

Then it happened. As I turned the page with a broken-down elevator full of holes and I read the caption "She used to mark the prairie and now you can see the prairie through her," I saw the eyes of one Grade Two boy well up with tears.

"That's sad," he said.

"That's not sad! What's so sad about that?" snapped a Grade One boy.

What happened next left me at a loss for words with an absolute feeling of obligation.

"That's because you don't know them!" shouted the Grade Two boy, his tears ready to burst. It was at that moment, and with a lot of reassurance from my Galileo mentor, Judy Martin, that I knew I had to find a way to help them know. I decided that I would ask the Grade Two children to teach the Grade One children all that they know about grain elevators.

As I pondered presenting them with this task I was reminded of the question most people ask me when they hear about "the Elevator Kids": "Tell me about the project. How did it start?" I still get this question and it gets harder and harder to answer all the time.

V

I've (D.J.) recently been reading Mary Carruthers's work on the medieval arts of memory (Carruthers & Ziolkowski, 2002; Carruthers, 2003, 2005) as well as

Francis Yates's wonderful work *The Art of Memory* (1974) and Brian Stock's (1983) work on 11th and 12th century images of written language. This study began on the advice of Michelle Bastock, a recent PhD graduate of the University of Calgary (and a representative of the Galileo Educational Network Association [founded by Sharon Friesen and Patricia Clifford—see www.galileo.org] who worked with Jennifer George for two years in her classroom as a teacher-mentor), whose wonderful dissertation on the relation between word and image opened up for me this new area of exploration and intrigue (see Bastock, 2005; see also Chapters 4 and 21 below).

I was especially interested in these matters for many reasons. In my own work, rarely do I hear teachers and students talking about memory except perhaps under the guise of rote memorization of spelling lists and the like. However, and in direct contradiction to this, some classrooms I've witnessed (intriguingly, very often the youngest of grades) are taking on the task of remembering in a different way. J.G.'s reflection above on the urgency with which a Grade Two child attested to the work he had done and remembered from the previous year, and that child's profound invocation of the connection between knowledge, memory, and care—all this links, somehow, to Aquinas's words cited above, that dwelling with solicitude on and cleaving with affection to the things which we wish to remember is somehow an apt description of what can happen in the classroom, with the youngest of children. Knowing the world/knowing oneself and caring for the world/oneself are linked (see Foucault, 2005).

The cultivation of memory is a way of working in the classroom, a way of caring for the living worlds of knowledge we are inheriting and caring, too, for teachers and students alike in their working their ways through those worlds and the nature and worth of those inheritances. Memory, here, is no anonymous storage but an intimate, formative task.

Therefore, those old books on the medieval art of memory can be read as commentaries on the nature and vagaries of classroom practice. They provide clusters of images and ideas that allow us to think about classroom practice out from under the burden of fragmentation and its consort of memorization and rote repetition (see our Preface and Chapter 18).

Under the image of basics-as-fragmentation, only the most meager forms of memorization are possible.

The memorable, on the contrary, requires something else.

VI

In J.G.'s Grade One/Two class, the question that was posed was "What stories do we have to tell?" This question gave rise to clusters of investigations for teachers and students alike:

• What story is it that each of us might have to tell?

- Where might such stories abide?
- Where is the memory of these stories "held" and *how* is this memory held and by whom?
- To what are we beholden in remembering and retelling such stories?
- "What stories are we *compelled* to tell?"

This sense of compulsion—desiring, needing, longing, demanding to speak, to write, to remember, to think, to know, to hear what others have to say, to learn, to contribute, to judge, to ponder, to speculate, to absorb—is something that teachers recognize in very young children. Moreover, it is precisely that which is often deliberately bred out of children very early in their schooling (the fixing of the wiles of the deliberately willful child, the "little monster," shall we say [see Chapter 5; see also Jardine, 1998a; Jardine & Field, 2006; Jardine & Novodvorski, 2006]).

This sense of "being compelled" is not simply a psychological urge. As Jean Piaget has demonstrated (see Jardine, 2005), young children are profoundly concrete, imaginal, playful, bodily, and substantive in their ways of knowing. "Being compelled" isn't adequately understood as merely an "inner drive." It means *being driven*. To cleave to the phenomenological adage regarding the intentionality of consciousness, it means being driven *by something* ("Consciousness is always consciousness *of something*" [Husserl, 1970, p. 13]), not simply having a drive. Hermeneutics and its phenomenological ancestry are not about subjective willing as a starting point for thoughtful work.

Rather, as Hans-Georg Gadamer (2001, p. 50) attests, "*something* awakens our interest—that is really what comes first!"

One of the first experiences that J.G.'s class undertook in exploring this question of compelling stories was asking themselves what the oldest object in their house might be. Such a venture has many wonderful and compelling characteristics. First of all, the question is directed towards something that is concrete and fleshy and substantial, something with Earthly, bodily texture and tactility. Children found old World War army-issue blankets or worn porridge bowls, or letters written in an old hand, or photographs or maps, and so on. It is also necessarily an intergenerational exercise that involves things that are handed down, handed over, inherited, saved, kept, protected, things that carry memory beyond the sheer materiality of their arrival. These artifacts are not at all anonymous or faceless or silent things. They are full of faces, stories, travels, pleasures, sorrows, voices. They are full of witness and suffering, of promise and betrayal. They are imbued with relatedness, and even when they witness fragmentation and loss they help us connect to it and find our way. Such things don't just lie there. They face us and ask something of us. We are witnessed by them.

They are memorial, somehow. Memory is somehow *already housed* in such things, "incarnated," if you will (see Gadamer, 1989, pp. 418ff.; see Chapters 14 and 15 for the ecological ramifications of this idea). But, clearly and obviously, such inherited objects are only thus incarnated if you have cultivated in yourself the ability to *experience* their incarnate character (again, experience is always the experience of something, and something being experienced as incarnate of memory is a way of experiencing something that is not just an objective property of some indifferent object, but a form of cultivation [of oneself and thus, of necessity, of the thing itself (-as-experienced)]. For more on this only-seemingly contradictory idea, see Chapter 21). Otherwise, of course, "you don't know them" and they can be ignored like any object of indifference. It is not enough for that Grade Two boy to simply point to the objects that the class had explored the previous year in Jennifer's class as if their memorability were simply given and present for all to see. Work of a certain sort is needed in order to be able to experience that memorability. Cultivation of experience and memory is required in order to learn to cleave with affection to those cultivated objects about which memory has been cultivated. (Again, this reads like a paradox or a tautology, but it isn't.)

Properly treated and cared for, these objects become, as Gadamer put it, much closer to being "inheritances" than simply objects of indifference. They are not so much objects that we "have" as they are objects that, so to speak, have and hold (some part of, some tale or secret about) us:

> [It] no longer has the character of an object that stands over and against us. We are no longer able to approach this like an object of knowledge, grasping, measuring and controlling. Rather than meeting us in our world, it is much more a world into which we ourselves are drawn. [It] possesses its own worldliness and, thus, the center of its own Being so long as it is not placed into the object-world of producing and marketing. The Being of this thing cannot be accessed by objectively measuring and estimating; rather, the totality of a lived context has entered into and is present in the thing. And we belong to it as well. Our orientation to it is always something like our orientation to an inheritance that this thing belongs to, be it from a stranger's life or from our own.
>
> (Gadamer, 1994, pp. 191–192)

We are attached to these things "beyond our wanting and doing" (Gadamer, 1989, p. xxviii) (they can affect and define us even if we have never cultivated an awareness of them—this is why a mere phenomenology of conscious experience is necessarily inadequate here), and that attachment grows as we learn about them. They define us in some small way in our very attempt to unearth their origins and travels.

We are *known* by them (see Abram, 1996; Palmer, 1993).

Cleaving with affection to them, therefore, is, in part, learning to experience how these artifacts are already imbued with affect and learning how to let ourselves be affected by them. Again, this is the paradox of learning to experience how these things open up worlds that go beyond our experience and house and shape that experience (it is here, again, that the phenomenological adage of the intentionality of experience reaches its hermeneutic breaking-point).

Next, these artifact ventures are an exercise that is about the life and family of each particular child, but the attention to that particular life and family is, again, mediated through a concrete, image-filled, world-provoking, object ("the totality of a lived context has entered into and is present in the thing"). These ventures therefore are profoundly intimate and particular to each child while at the same time avoiding the abstract psychologism (Husserl, 1972) of a lot of "me and my family" classroom activities. This is accomplished, simply, by having a topic (Gk. *topos*, "place") in which and around which children and teachers gather. These experiences provided ways of encouraging children to think about themselves and their families in ways that are organized around an artifact that calls up memory and ancestry and that, shall we say, "houses" each of our lives in a community of relations (in this way, this work is similar to the work done by Jennifer Batycky, also in a Grade One classroom [see Jardine & Batycky, 2006, pp. 213–226]. Ecologically oriented examples are found in Chapters 12–14 and 16–17; see also Jardine, 2006b).

This says something profound about what the "community" of the classroom might mean. It is not a collection of individuals tethered to each other psychologically. Rather, those tethers are mediated through the common worldly work that is done that allows us to experience each other "in place" rather than through the psychologistic utopianism of "individuality" and "uniqueness." We (children and teachers alike) found ourselves in a public space with others. More strongly put, we each found ourselves, right in the midst of the intimacies of our family's artifact, to be *public* subjects. Right in the midst of the intimacy of our family artifact, languages are involved, histories, geographies, images, bloodlines mixed into the world(s). As we cultivate our affection and memory for these artifacts, our affection becomes worldly because the artifact draws us out of our selves into a world that shapes our lives and is not just shaped by it (here is the beginning of a critique of constructivism [see Jardine, 2005, 2006d]).

Another compelling feature of this work was that, inevitably, there is a story (sometimes multiple stories, sometimes, as we all know living in families, *contradictory* stories full of silences and effacements) to be told that goes along with the object in question. It was someone's, handed over, purposefully or by default or accident, to particular intended or unintended hands. We are reminded here of Bronwen Wallace's (1987, pp. 47–48) wonderful insight about anthropological artifacts, that "the shards of pottery, carefully labelled and carried up through layered villages flesh out more hands than the two that made them."

Next, these objects inevitably have come from *somewhere*, not just someone, so they involve territories, countries, travelling, journeys, leaving home (sometimes to get to something better, sometimes to get away from something worse, sometimes both). Maps are implied, histories of immigration and travel and the like are hidden in these objects. Hidden, too, are lost tales of settlement, indigenousness, families, love, conflict, colonialism, and displacement. Of course, this starts to sketch out a life's work, but the tethers are there in Grade One, strong and healthy. We suggest that these children will remember something of this experience because this experience, in its multifariousness and richness and in the ways it was treated, stands in a "horizon of . . . still undecided future possibilities" (Gadamer, 1989, p. 112) which have the potential to appear in this world of ours, rife as it is with tales of settlement, indigenousness, families, love, conflict, colonialism, and displacement. These children may, in the future, be able to experience and remember something when they see, contemporary with this writing, refugees from northern Israel and southern Lebanon fleeing war with only what they are able to carry.

An aside: as teachers, we deliberately chose, as often as possible, to pursue experiences with children that have the potential to "come around again" and thus, possibly, *last* and perhaps *come to something*. (Memory and futurity seem linked?) As teachers, we also realize that this possibility is out of our hands. This is an ecological point. Wendell Berry (1986) talks about how the farmer's planting of trees along the farm's lane is a sign of the decision to *stay put* and not simply give up on a place. As I've (D.J.) passed abandoned farms in southern Alberta, those lines of trees, especially against the background of so much prairie, are full of remembrances if I allow myself to see and do the work requisite of such remembering.

Something of this phenomenon has occurred inevitably in the many classrooms where we've seen similar ventures pursued. Some children come from families that left everything behind because of sometimes very difficult circumstances (broken families, refugees from war-torn countries, families whose material goods have been ruined or lost). Of course, this requires great delicacy to handle, and each case will demand something of teachers and students alike. But even the absence of such objects has great and powerful stories to tell us all.

VII

This gracious, difficult work (work, not of rote memorization, but of, somehow, cultivating the experience of something memorable) plays with an etymological twist hidden in Hans-Georg Gadamer's *Truth and Method* (1989, pp. 240–262)—the German-rooted relatedness of experience (*Erfahrung*) and ancestors/ancestry (*Vorfahrung*). Experience, here, is imagined as a journey (*Fahrung*)—an undergoing, a "suffering" (pp. 256–257)—linked to those who have journeyed before us (*Vor-*). There is even a link between *Erfahrung* and the Latin-rooted English term "experience" in that both invoke the idea of danger—*Gefahr* (German, "danger") and the root shared by "experience" and "peril" (see the Latin root *periculum*). Such wild etymologies are not meant to be a scientific-linguistic outline, but are playfully intended as *reminders*, that even our language, in its most ordinary usage, hides reminiscences of things past ("every word breaks forth as if from a center and is related to a whole, through which alone it is a word. Every word causes the whole of the language to which it belongs to resonate" [Gadamer, 1989, p. 458]. Words, too, are like inheritances; they bring memory with them. The work of the classroom is coaxing them to break forth). One need think, in English, of the phrase "That was quite an experience" to realize that not just anything qualifies to be called "an experience" in this sense.

The difference, it seems, is, at least in part, memory. But this is not memory understood as simply the compiling of information for later recall. What is at work here is a deeply embodied, fleshy, intimate sense of memory and knowledge and their cultivation. Teachers and students alike are each *becoming someone* because of what they have learned and remembered.

And this most pedagogical of tasks—becoming someone—is linked somehow to places that are traversed, territories that are journeyed through. We're tempted to push this one step further and suggest that these places or territories, properly understood and "taken up," are the *topics* that curriculum guides entrust to teachers and students in schools. More on this later.

VIII

Not only is fragmentation a disease, but the diseases of the disconnected parts are similar or analogous to one another. Thus, they memorialize their lost unity, their relation persisting in their disconnection. Any severance produces two wounds that are, among other things, the record of how the severed parts once fitted together.

(Berry, 1986, pp. 110–111)

We will simply point out here something that shadows the work we are doing—the loss of memory, the erasure or effacement or violation of memory, the deliberate or accidental replacement of the memory of one with that of another. All these threads and more are of great importance, perhaps especially so in the present context because the case can too easily be made that such violations are, in many classrooms, precisely the work of schooling itself. We think, in a very simple case, of the teeming lives that children bring to the early years of schooling (see Chapter 2) and how such lives are so easily ignored or rendered by the flattening expectations of schooling. This may be the not exactly "hidden" curriculum, but something quite deliberate and systematic and publicly pronounced and pursued. The efficiencies promised by Frederick Winslow Taylor required replacing memorability and its cultivation with memorizability, since only the latter fits with the clarion of efficiency that rages through education around 1911 (see Boyle, 2003; Gatto, 2006; see also our Preface and Chapters 18 and 21).

Perhaps this is a way to think through anew what the fragmentation that underwrites much of contemporary education means—the erasure of memory and the corralling of education into that which is memorizable (i.e., that which can be methodologically controlled and monitored and assessed). This erasure links, too, to images of individuality and publicness, wherein we "den[y] any authority to the past. It nullifies precedent, it snaps the threads of memory and scatters local knowledge. By privileging individual choice over the common good, it makes relationships revocable and provisional" (Gray, 1998, pp. 35–36). Thus memory loss is, to paraphrase Wendell Berry's (1986) text, memorialized in fragmented curriculum bits and pieces wherein memory has been erased, as well as being memorialized in an exaggerated sense of individuality wherein the worldliness of each child has been replaced by an abstract (rather than concrete and worldly) sense of precocious "uniqueness" (see Jardine, Clifford, & Friesen, 1999; Jardine & Field, 2006).

IX

The children in J.G.'s classroom were asked to talk to those they live with about these objects and their histories and stories, and to bring them to school and share what they had found. Children sometimes interviewed family members, took digital photographs, made sketches, and the like. Over the course of two years (J.G. began with a mixed class of Grade One and Grade Two children. In the second year, the Grade Ones remained with her as a Grade Two class, and a whole new group of Grade One children joined the class), these objects and their stories became part of the fabric of memory of the class as a whole.

Memory and its cultivation thus took on what, at first blush, might seem like a paradoxical character. Each child's work was intimately connected with them as an irreplaceable individual whose memory was being cultivated, and yet, at the same time, that cultivating and cultivated work added itself to the memory and work of the class as a whole.

Because of the worldly character of the artifacts themselves, children's "differences" made the communal order of memory richer, more diverse, more "multifarious" (Gadamer, 1989, p. 284):

> The community is an order of memories preserved consciously in instructions, songs and stories, and both consciously and unconsciously in ways. A healthy culture holds preserving knowledge in place for a long time. That is, the essential wisdom accumulates in the community much as fertility builds in the soil.
>
> (Berry, 1983, p. 73)

Thus arrived tales of everything from grandfather's blankets from World War II to ornate rugs from the Middle East, tapes of grandmothers reminiscing, and images of people escaping with little more than their lives. We have literally dozens of these sorts of stories archived away on-line and available to readers at their leisure.[2] The trouble with citing finished examples here is that something inevitably gets "lost in translation." What gets lost is all the slow work that occurred when this story first emerged, all the ways in which it was lovingly treated, day by day, by teachers and students alike. What gets lost is how certain things were remembered or forgotten, exaggerated or diminished. The finished product too easily leaves out how all the revisions and re-reading and re-writing, all the efforts, moment to moment, to compose memory, shape it, form it, express it, word it. What happens in showing the "finished products" is that we too easily lose the fact that such matters must be whiled over in order to be what they are (see Chapter 21). It is always troublesome to witness how all of this living, emergent, cultivated detail is inevitably occluded in the *outcomes* of this work. Examples can count as examples only if they can function as *reminders of something*. But they need, in our case, to be reminders of more than the general *idea* of memory as a warrantable classroom practice. *Actually* cultivating memory—all those miraculously small moments and moves and gestures and returns—is not necessarily experienceable as "present in the thing" (each child's completed story has hidden in it the conditions of its appearance). It is the formative movement of the cultivation of memory that is at issue here and what it means for a teacher to cleave with affection to such cultivation in her and in her students.

X

This leads to another pedagogical clue regarding memory that I (D.J.) had found years ago regarding education and learning and the young, a clue which, in part, provides a new spin to the interpretive critique of Cartesianism that is commonplace in contemporary curriculum theorizing: "Education cannot tread the path of critical research. Youth demands images for its imagination and for forming its memory. Thus [Giambattista] Vico [b. 1668] supplements the *critica* of Cartesianism with the old *topica*" (Gadamer, 1989, p. 21). Some-how, regarding the path that education must tread if the demands of youth (someone new to a place, someone who hasn't especially "been around," someone "inexperienced") are to be met, images, the process of cultivating memory, and topics somehow fit together. The clear and distinct methodolo-gism of Descartes (*critica*—we can hear here echoes of Frederick Winslow Taylor's efficiency movement) needs productive, substantive, imaginal, story-laden, allegorical, bloody, bodily, Earthly, supplementation. Without such sup-plementation, method can come to act with no sense of place and proportion, impulsively, in ways that are profoundly "inexperienced." We end up with Grade One classrooms where children would not be allowed to write about their grandfather's blanket because, as we've all heard, "they don't know their letters yet," as if the methodological abstraction of letter formation were more basic, and chronologically prior to the human desire to tell a tale and have its memory last. We speculate, therefore, that teachers who remain spell-bound by the fragmentation that underwrites schooling can become experts in the methodologies of skill development while remaining profoundly inexperienced in the world of language.

In this passage about Vico, I recognized something that I had experienced elsewhere. When a graduate student asks me about how to do hermeneutics, my first impulse is always to ask, "What is your topic?" Following Vico, Gadamer is suggesting that anyone new to something ("youth," so to speak—Vico's *pedagogical* point is not necessarily or solely a *chronological* one) cannot begin the task of coming to understand through being told what *method* to use (*critica*, from Rene Descartes' [b. 1596] *Discourse on Method* [1640]), just as I, as an advisor to graduate students, can't become experienced in how to proceed unless I have some sense of where we are working (see the young boy's comment at the beginning of Chapter 9). A method has no face, no body, no memories, no stories, no blood, no images, no ancestors, no ghosts, no inhabitants, no habits, no habitats, no relations, no spirits, no monsters, no familiars. All these fall to Cartesian doubt because they are not clear and distinct and methodologically controllable. They are, rather, attractive and intimate and not fully determined (they have a future, whereas the purpose of *critica* is to methodologically outrun the future by determining ahead of time how it can possibly appear).

Method doesn't help us get our bearings and learn our way around, because, so to speak, there is no "place" to it, no topic, no sentinel or artifact. We don't become *experienced* through the application of a method because a method, properly taken up, must be taken up as if I could be *anyone*. Nothing accrues to the one wielding such a method, and nothing about the one wielding such a method must affect that method's enactment.

On the contrary, the formation of memory, Vico suggests, requires supplementing questions of "how to proceed" with more substantive, affectionate questions regarding one's *topica*, one's "topic" and the images and forms and figures—the bodies, one might say—that haunt that place. Thus, answer to the question "*Where* am I?" holds part of the answer to the question of how to proceed. Differently put, how could I know how to properly proceed if I don't know where I am? (see Chapter 9). I cannot warrantably devise a method and then simply subsequently aim it at some topic. Topics, hermeneutically conceived, productively supplement, correct, transform, or "set right anew" (Arendt, 1969, pp. 192–193) our desire to proceed without heed to where we are. Topics hold our ways through them in place (but if and only if we allow ourselves to learn *from* the place and *in* place how to pay attention properly *to* the place). The place tells us something of what *it* needs from *us* if we are to "understand." *This* is what it means to "learn" about this place—to realize, to deeply experience how it is that this topic *asks something of me* beyond what I might ask of it. It means, in part and in short, to become able to learn from the place, from the topic. Hidden here are vaguely ecological images of places, topographies, territories and a sense of bodily bearings. Hidden here, too, are images of education as involving someone coming to "inhabit" a topic and learn our way around *from the topic itself.* "We can entrust ourselves to what we are investigating to guide us safely in the quest" (Gadamer, 1989, p. 378). This is an adage that is hermeneutic, pedagogical, and ecological.

Pedagogy thus requires the cultivation of topographical imagination, and, as with ecological consciousness, this involves places, relations, ancestors, faces, ways, stories, songs, generationality, intergenerationality, and the vigorous presence of life beyond the merely human. Only in such cultivation can pedagogy avoid the excesses wrought by setting individual students loose into a territory as if each one is "the 'god' of your own story" (Melnick, 1997, p. 372; see Jardine, Friesen, & Clifford, 2006, pp. 137–148), as if somehow we are each able to constructivistically make up the topic in a narcissistic pool of self-satisfied and self-confirming reflection (see Bowers, 2006; Jardine, 2006; Johnson, Fawcett, & Jardine, 2006). Stripped of substantive memory (stripped of topographical Earthliness and surroundings that house, shape, resist, and transform our actions), *critica* can let us act as if we've got no relations and all we need to proceed is procedural "know-how."

An ecological disaster in the making (see Chapter 14).

Gadamer's work does not take us in this particularly ecopedagogical direction. However, in its dispelling of the natural-scientific link between method and truth, it does house a recovery of a deep linkage between the cultivation of memory, the cultivation of a sense of place ("*topica*/topics, from Gk. *ta topika*, lit. 'matters concerning *topoi*,' from *topoi* 'commonplaces,' neut. pl. of *topikos* 'commonplace, of a place,' from *topos* 'place' " [*OED*]) through the cultivation of a topographical imagination, and the cultivation of character (*Bildung*—an idea inherited from von Humboldt [2000/1793–1794]; see Pinar, 2006). Put less haughtily, there is a link between what I remember, how I imagine and remember and know and experience my whereabouts, and who I have become (see Chapter 13). Becoming experienced in the ways of a place (learning my way around [Gadamer, 1989, p. 260]), as ecology profoundly reminds us, means becoming *someone.* As Gadamer (1989, p. 16) insists, "it is time to rescue the phenomenon of memory from being regarded merely as a psychological faculty and to see it as an essential element of the finite historical being of man." That is, through the dialectic of remembering and forgetting, I become myself and no one else even though *what is being remembered* tethers this remembering self into a worldliness and publicness. Memory, in this sense induced by Vico, is always *mine.* I, in this sense invoked by Vico, am not an abstract and empty Cartesian "I am" (an anonymous epistemological subjectivity that wields an equally anonymous methodology) but am, rather, a person, *this* person, distinguishable through the life I've led through the world and what has accrued to me through my experiences in the world. Even in those vile cases where a person's memory has been defiled or distorted or replaced with that of another—even (and unfortunately and despicably) in these awful cases, remembering serves this formative function (see, for example, Morris & Weaver, 2002). And, of course, to the same degree, even when defiled, defiled memory is not simply psychological. Even a defiled memory remembers *something* and lives in a world thus remembered and experienced.

XI

Regarding these inherited objects that the children were encouraged to explore, it is here that the part of the work of teaching becomes clear. Jennifer brought in a story about her own artifact, a hope chest owned by her grandmother. This initial version is deliberately quite meager:

> *My Grandma's Hope Chest*
> This is my Grandma's hope chest. I got it when she died.
> It sits at the end of my bed. I put things in it.

The pedagogical motive here, with regard to memory and its cultivation, is double.

First, it is clear that a teacher interested in pursuing such work cannot stand outside of it and merely "instruct" children in it. To help children learn how to cleave with affection, teachers must themselves cleave with affection to those things that *they* wish to remember and must take on the task of showing such affection in the classroom. To teach a "topic," a teacher must *go to the place* and see what becomes of them when they do, what is asked of them by the place in order to become experienced in it. And this must be done in the witness of the children they are teaching (see Chapter 13, where the issue of simply living in the presence of someone who knows what they are doing is discussed).

The second aspect of the motive for Jennifer bringing in her own artifact is that, as teachers, we need to find ways to draw children into this sort of work in order for the cultivation of memory to take hold of their imaginations and hearts. We need to charm kids, help them see how they are part of what is at work—part of memory and its passage, part of asking and saying and writing and recording the passing of things. The story Jennifer initially brought in to the class was deliberately brief and not especially initially rich or informative. This was done on purpose. This is the loving and affectionate "trick" that we pull, hoping it will do the trick (see Chapters 5 and 20 for more on the link between hermeneutics, tricksters, and pedagogy)—"snake-charming" is the term that Sharon Friesen and Pat Clifford have often used for this initial gesture, drawing children into the living *topica*, the living place of human work, with all its possibilities and foibles.

Jennifer took notes on the overhead as they discussed her "hope chest" story and what more they might want to know. Again, here, the living character of the cultivation of memory intervenes—it is impossible to write enough or eloquently enough or often enough to demonstrate *how* this can be done genuinely, how to "get inside of such questions" in the classroom and feel their living import in this sort of work of the world. We have often speculated that, if we just had a videotape, or a tape recording, or more notes, or, well, whatever, we might outrun this trouble of showing what the cultivation of memory might look like, second to second, in its emergence here, with this class and that child's offhand comment which was taken up just like that and then this, etc. However, we realize, again, that we are speaking, not about some objective properties of classroom events, but about *how classroom events are treated*. As with ecology, how you treat a place will have an effect on what the place might show of itself. There is thus a connection between memory, experience and, as we will explore in more detail below, *composition* (both in the sense of a work produced through gathering and in the sense of the cultivated "composure" of the person doing the exploring; see Chapter 21).

Jennifer incorporated the students' suggestions into a second piece of writing. Again, we halt: the children's comments themselves were listened to and *remembered*. Suggestions were incorporated, exaggerated, edited, all with an eye, not to simply reproducing what the students had said, but memorially composing it. This is part of the medieval art of memory, that memory is formative and *compositional*. It requires judgment and forgetting, parsing and connecting, forming and shaping. It is a creative, inventive process of making something of what has occurred. Remembering and its consequences are being formed and performed, minute by minute, and the what is being remembered is slowly appearing, forming, composing itself:

> *My Grandma's Hope Chest*
> Hello, my name is Jennifer. This is my Grandma Agnes's hope chest. I got it when she died. It had some of her special things in it. Things like her wedding dress and mittens that she was knitting for me. Now I keep my own special things in the hope chest. I will pass it on to someone special some day.

Jennifer did the same thing again, using the new feedback for a "final draft." Again we intervene: what is, of necessity, missing here is, for example, how one usually reticent girl may have asked on the second morning a delicate question of J.G.'s Nana's death, and how her subsequent editing suggestion had shaped the conversation that ensued, and how, on this third morning, that girl remembered and asked if J.G. had a new piece of writing. Or how another usually talkative child has remained pointedly silent and whose voice would burst out a week from now. These intimacies of classroom life are always necessarily hidden, because even a description of them, however fulsome, cannot reproduce for a reader how they are then treated and remembered, day to day. This limitation merely emphasizes, for us, how profound is the cultivation of memory in the fabric of classroom life. So much of what occurs in classrooms where "the basics" are no longer defined by fragmentation has to do with things not having to be constantly "dropped" but rather remembered and carried, often in surprising ways, into future compositional work (as with the example cited in Chapter 1, you don't have to "drop" addition to get on with learning subtraction. Perhaps that worksheet she was given can be a clue as to the erasure of memory in a lot of classroom material. Some material [purposefully?] disallows remembering):

My Grandma's Hope Chest
When my Grandma Agnes was a girl she had a hope chest. It sat at the end of her bed. She kept lots of things that were important to her inside of it. She kept her wedding dress that she wore when she married my Grandpa in her hope chest. When my Grandma died she passed the hope chest on to me. Inside it I found some half knitted mittens that she was making for me the month that she died. I also found a Canadian Pacific Railway envelope. Inside the envelope I found some souvenirs. They were souvenirs from a train trip that my Nana and I went on when I was five years old. The train trip must have meant a lot to my Nana. Someday I will pass my Grandma's hope chest on to someone special. They will become the new keepers of the story.

XII

In medieval European times, it was commonplace for students to engage in specific practices aimed at the cultivation of memory (see Carruthers, 2003, 2005). It would be wrong to assume that the sole reason for this was because of the lack of available books, such that students had to retain knowledge in memory. In fact, the reverse is almost true: books were understood to be not merely repositories for knowledge, but simply (yet, of course, not so simply) *reminders*. This is age old, linking back to Plato's *Phaedrus*:

You are father of written letters. But the fact is that this invention of yours [writing] will produce forgetfulness in the souls of those who learn it. They will not need to exercise their memories, being able to rely on what is written, calling things to mind no longer from within themselves by their own powers, but under the stimulus of external marks that are alien to themselves. So it's not a recipe for memory, but for reminding that you have discovered.

(Plato, trans. 1956, p. 275)

But, in the 11th and 12th centuries, this began to change in the burgeoning European imagination: "Men [*sic*—but perhaps an apt one given the historical circumstances] began to think of facts not as recorded by texts but as embodied in texts" (Stock, 1983, p. 62). Once books became understood as repositories, a great shift, foretold by Plato, began to occur. "As fact and text moved closer together, 'searchability' shifted 'from memory to page layout' " (Stock, 1983,

p. 62). No longer was it necessary to cultivate in oneself a memory of, say, Aristotle or biblical texts or Gadamer's *Truth and Method*. One could leave such matters "housed" in texts (or, now, "on-line") and simply search them out or refer to them when the occasion might warrant. Even the *layout* of texts shifted at this juncture. Reference works, which were heretofore organized topically (around memorable clusters of things that had memorial affinities, relations of kind, imaginal family resemblances [Wittgenstein, 1968, p. 32]), began to be organized *alphabetically*, leading to what Illich & Sanders (1988) referred to as the alphabetization of the modern mind. Even references (like the reference to Stock, 1983, p. 62 above, or Illich & Sanders, 1988) were transformed. In this book, as is standard current practice, references are inserted *after* a cited passage in order to document where the text was found and to allow readers to find their way to the text which is the repository of the citation. Prior to the 12th century in Europe, references were given *before* the cited text. This was not a matter of "authorizing" the citation to follow (although this is probably part of the motive), but of allowing readers to call to memory the images and topographies of the work about to be cited and its author, so that the reader might be ready to "hear" its reminders. References given prior to citations gave readers a chance *to prepare themselves* (Carruthers, 2005, p. 100) properly and adequately for the words that followed.

The shift away from memory (which I carry with me and which defines who I am) to an understanding of texts in which knowledge is "stored" outside of and detached from and irrespective of memory entailed that, as I made my way in the world, the sojourn was no longer necessarily taken in the company of what I remember, in the company of those ancients the memory of whose voices might fill me up with experience and wisdom. Only on the basis of books becoming understood as repositories is it possible to conceive of "myself" as some sort of autonomous individuality somehow independent of ancestral bloodlines and hauntings, independent of the great human inheritances that I bear in my blood and breath and bones. What is hinted at here is a long history of "experience" being considered "innocent" and access to the world being naively conceived as democratically equal to all (which, we've seen in the past 50 years, eventually becomes "everyone has their own opinion," and the opinion of someone who has studied and cultivated a memory of some topic is itself "just another opinion"). See Ivan Illich's (1993) commentary on Hugh of St. Victor's *Didascalicon* for lovely wanderings on these ways, and how our image of ourselves as an interior subjectivity arose parallel to new images of the nature of texts. Illich (1993) further argues (supported by Carruthers [2003, 2005] and Stock [1983]) that, to use Gadamer's terms, only on this basis do I come to imagine myself as a subjectivity who has experiences which are possessed as "interior" (*Erlebenisse*) states, and no longer especially experienced sojournally (*Erfahrung*). Against such a background, a person experienced in some topic becomes understood only as an expert who oppresses others. (I [D.J.] was once in a Grade Three classroom where children were finishing up some writing, and I looked at one boy's work and found in it great musical cascades of description. I told the boy that his work reminded me of Dylan Thomas and that he might want to check this out. Later, the classroom teacher privately reprimanded me: "In this classroom, we don't impose our opinions on others. The only thing you are allowed to say to one of my students is 'Tell me about your writing?' After all, its *his*, not *yours*." Introducing this child to one of his ancestors was not experienced as an opening of his work into the world of writing, but as the imposition of one will over another. Endemic, here, again, is a sense of the world of writing being broken down in the face of authorial property rights—another thread of the breakdown of a knowledge commons into rules of enclosure [see Neeson, 1996].)

As we know from Descartes' meditations, methodical doubt has severed our relations to the world and its ancestries (*Vorfahrung*). Experience (*Erfahrung*) became experience (*Erlebenisse*), worldly venture became possession and interiority, and mathematics, as a methodology, became necessary to any transcendence of such subjectivity. Knowledge is no longer rooted memorially and is no longer linked to character and its cultivation. It is rooted, now, only methodologically. Only once these pre-Cartesian moves are made regarding memory, texts, experience, and subjectivity/interiority does it become possible for the *critica*-methodologisms of Cartesianism to take such easy and firm hold on the newly emerging sciences of his day and ever since (especially, as we all know, in the halls of schools and their renderings of the world into manageable test results). Once experience becomes imaginable as a subjective interiority, Cartesian methodology's promise to speak boldly and commandingly and masterfully about "the world" becomes a tempting promise.

However, as so many critiques of Cartesianism have demonstrated, this objective world is no longer the memorial and topographical and imaginal and Earthly world understood by the invocation of "the old *topica*." This objective world is a world that has been rendered by methodology into that which can be controlled, predicted, and manipulated at the wont of human agency. "Places" are no longer first. Human agency is first and knowledge becomes, in the work of Immanuel Kant, a *demand made upon things* and no longer a memorial and intergenerational heeding (see Jardine, 2005).

Unlike the sorts of anonymous rote memory touted in many schools (paradoxically, looked at from the 12th century, often the rote memorization of "facts" considered to be housed in "texts"), memory in the more bodily, topographical sense and its careful cultivation, hinted at by Vico and visible in the medieval arts of memory, are thereby connected deeply to how I carry myself in the world, how I call myself up in the face of what comes to meet me.

XIII

Clearly, in this simple case of Nana Agnes and her granddaughter's writing, the teacher was "teaching writing," but we glimpse something about the tethers between writing, memory, and community that are basic to its character. "Writing" is not taken up as a "skill" whose practice can properly occur independently of some memorable/memorial cluster of images that concretely *desire* written expression. Otherwise, as Plato warned, writing begins to weaken memory, memory work becomes occluded, and we end up, in schools, simply memorizing what is in the textbook (and textbooks end up not containing anything memorable but only memorizable).

On the contrary, what we are seeing here in early elementary school is that writing and its skilled practice remain linked to the traversing of the topic/topography at hand and to the specific work that the children were engaged in, such that their writing is not simply a "dump site" for what is already known but a site wherein knowledge is practiced and articulated and "composed." As such, reading is also an activity, not simply of retrieving what is stored, but of being reminded of what has been compositionally known and what has been ventured or experienced. Writing and re-writing and reading and re-reading are themselves compositional memory exercises. (In my own [D.J.] case, I have often experienced how those books on the medieval art of memory need to be read in a very particular way that I have had to learn and practice—as speaking to something I remember of my own work and life. Otherwise, they can be quite boring and attention easily drifts. They need to be treated in a certain way if they are to "speak" and "be heard" [and, of course, this is not a singular matter. These texts "speak" to many issues and can therefore be "read" in many ways, because these texts lay out a topic that is rich and variegated in its remembrances].)

This is vital to emphasize. There is no use pretending that the difficult work of learning to read and write and communicate with others simply disappeared with this activity of artifactual reminiscence. Rather, what happened was that the difficult work of learning to write was placed into the embrace of something that the children deeply experienced as not only *worth* writing about but urgently *needing* to be written and written well. Family memory thus became the "site" for the practice of the very curricular mandates that Grade One and Grade Two teachers are required to fulfill (including writing, reading, editing, learning to use appropriate computer technologies for the photographs and writing that was done, threads of the social studies curriculum regarding Alberta and Canada and immigration and the like, art and artifacts, mathematics and calendar years and chronologies, to name a very brief few). This family artifact work was therefore not a "special project" or some sort of "extra" that was done after or over and above the meeting of curriculum mandates. It was, rather, one of the sites of that meeting, a site that proved to be especially amenable to the cultivation of a wide array of curricular topics.

Even more than this, the difficulty with learning to write and write well (to return to this particular curricular phenomenon that is commonplace in Grades One and Two) was experienced by these children to be a *human* problem and not just a problem that they have. The children in this classroom came to learn that the difficulty of writing is in the character of writing and in the character of wanting to write well about memorial family matters, and not just a personal flaw or pathological issue. Writing is difficult to become experienced in, and gaining such experience takes work and takes a lifetime. The wide array of children's difficulties in this regard does not become erased or effaced but each trouble becomes part of the world of writing itself to which young children's work and efforts belong. Even one boy's terrible trouble with forming letters becomes a place of regard and commiseration and work. It belongs with the work being done; the topic *needs* his attention and practice to these matters. And, of course, what each individual child needed help with, needed practice on, needed examples of, needed to read more about, needed to be more patient with, needed to try again and again, and so on—each of these was each child's own need, but each child's own need was worked on and worked out in concert and "in place" ("on topic") with others. The young—the authors included when it comes to a new topic—need images for their imaginations and for the formation of their memories, and thus "how to write" needs the guidance and imaginal richness of the *topic*.

XIV

> Thinking is not a disembodied "skill"; there is no thought without matters to think with [an interesting insight to parallel with Edmund Husserl's regarding phenomenology, that there is no thought without it being thinking about something]. People can only think with the contents of their memories, their experiences. And human memories are stored as images in patterns of places (or "locations" or "topics").
>
> (Carruthers, 2003, p. 89)

The ancient arts of memory involved cultivating in oneself multiple, interweaving, ordered, cared-for storehouses, "architectures," if you will, that are full of names and faces and images and ideas and tales and voices and experiences. The precise schemes varied, everywhere from what was called a "memory theatre" (an image used by Giulio Camillo [see Yates, 1974, pp. 129ff.]) to

> the feathers on the six wings of a seraphic angel, a five-story, five-room section of a house, a columnar diagram, the stones in the wall of a turreted urban tower, the rungs of a ladder, the rows of seats in an amphitheatre. Gardens were also popular, with orderly beds of medicinal plants and fruit trees separated by grass and surrounded by a wall.
>
> (Carruthers & Ziolkowski, 2002, pp. 5–6)

Many of the medieval efforts to portray this process of cultivating memory utilize architectural images—rooms, recesses, niches. Students were often trained to picture a great empty house with a memorable array of empty rooms as the "places" where images could be carefully and thoughtfully stored. This architectural urge is understandable, since the rootedness here is one of creating and composing, but also of building, of formation and "forming" or becoming oneself (*die Bildung* [see Gadamer, 1989; von Humboldt, 2000; Pinar 2006]). Students were then shown how to deliberately place significant clusters of images in each room, mindful all the while of the order and sequence of the rooms and their images. Each imaginal item to be remembered had to be digested, meditated upon, ruminated over, worried, cared for, situated, studied, and then *placed* in *places* the traversing of which became imaginable. Images that were vivid and memorable (even grotesque and exaggerated) were especially encouraged, since the impressions that these made on memory were understood to leave a lasting impression (see Yates, 1974, p. 9). Such vivid images (recall Vico and, of course, Piaget's work on imagination and embodied knowing) were best able to be recalled when, asked to remember, one would move, so to speak, from place to place, room to room, and "see" the images in each *topos* and "read" them for what they remind one of.

This idea of territorially traversing one's memory and knowledge is directly in parallel to how "medieval public memory, in pilgrimage and in liturgy, was conducted processionally, as a way among sites" (Carruthers, 2003, p. 116). This might just give those in education a new way to re-imagine what "field trips" are about. It is vital to a cultivation of a new sense of "the basics" to remind ourselves of the ancientness of *going to a place* in search of knowledge, and all the images of journeys and returns that our human inheritance has to offer us.

Memory, therefore, is *topographically composed* and, in composing memory, one is, so to speak, composing oneself, gaining composure in the face of the world—becoming educated, one might say, in the "ways" of places and their inhabitants. This is often linked to a metaphorical extension of the Latin word *silva*:

Within his memorial "forest," [*silva*] a trained student, like a knowledgeable huntsman, can unerringly find the place (*loci*) where the rabbits and deer lie. Quintillian observes: "Just as all kinds of produce are not provided by every country, and as you will not succeed in finding a particular bird or beast if you are ignorant of the localities where it has its usual haunts or birthplace, as even the various kinds of fish flourish in different surroundings, . . . so not every kind of argument comes from just any place and for the same reason is not to be sought out in scattered and random places." As the huntsman finds game and the fisherman fish, so the student finds his stored material—by knowing its habits.
(Carruthers, 2005, p. 62)

The ecological images here are astounding. One can also think about how such matters involve understanding the ways of the soil and the seasons of the sun. For more on this ecological-pedagogical idea, see Chapter 16, where an ancient Chinese poem sketches out how, to every thing, there is a seasonality.

XV

> In no other area of experience, whether it be the cognitive field, the practical field, or the affective field, is there such total adherence of the subject's act of self-designation to the object-oriented intention of experience. In this regard, the use in French and in other languages of the reflexive pronoun "*soi*" (self) does not seem to be accidental. In remembering something (*se souvenant de quelque chose*), one remembers oneself (*on se souvient de soi*).
>
> (Ricoeur, 2004, p. 96)

Education—the memorial formation of character—is not a simple matter of "giving students a prodigious memory for all they might be asked to repeat in an examination" (Carruthers, 2003, p. 9). Something more is at work, an experience that is familiar but difficult to articulate. I'm reminded, here, of an old Zen adage:

> A Ch'an master once wrote that the wise enshrine the miraculous bones of the ancients within themselves; that is, they do not regard teachings of ways to enlightenment as an external body of knowledge or information to be processed as an acquisition or believed or revered as inflexible dogma, but rather apply it as far as possible to themselves and their situations, vivifying the way of enlightenment with their own bodies and lives, not just in their thoughts.
>
> (Cleary & Cleary, 1992, p. xviii)

The work of enshrining is, as St. Bede suggested, a meditative, memorial activity, "a process of meditative composition or collocative reminiscence—'gathering,' *colligere*" (Carruthers, 2003, p. 33). What is gathered in memory must be worried over, worked, revisited, re-read, mumbled, "murmured" (Carruthers, 2005, p. 164) and, in so doing, I become someone, so that, when an invitation to write a paper like this one comes up, matters can be called up from the recesses of memory, not as "raw data" but as inhabitants of *places*. In speaking of Quintilian, Carruthers (2005, pp. 297–298) insists that "composition is not an act of writing, it is rumination, cogitation, dictation, a listening, a dialogue, a 'gathering' (*collectio*) of voices from their several places in memory." It is a matter, then, of becoming someone thus composed, someone who can act with composure in a territory. "*Memoria* is most usefully thought of as a compositional art. The arts of memory are among the arts of thinking, especially involved with fostering the qualities we now revere as 'imagination' and 'creativity' " (Carruthers, 2003, p. 9). Carruthers (p. 11) notes, too, that *invenio*, the Latin root of the English term "inventiveness," is also the root of the term "inventory." Inventiveness and creativity are impossible if we have nothing to think *with* and thus the cultivation of memory (the composition in oneself of a memorial "inventory"), unlike the training of rote memorization, becomes a source of creativity (invention). Unlike God, we cannot think and create *ex nihilo*. To think and create, we must "follow the trail" (Carruthers, 2005, pp. 62–63) and its *vestigia* (p. 20), its tracks or footprints. This is what constitutes an *investigation*. The wider and richer one's ventures, the more one has to work with in experiencing the world. One becomes "experienced" and, as Paul Ricoeur suggested above, to remember the object is to remember oneself.

This ties, inevitably, to a very different view of what knowledge is and what happens to oneself in the process of coming to know. Carruthers (2005, p. 199), in citing Augustine, talks in near body-liquid terms:

> "Cogitation makes us expand, expansion stretches us out, and stretching makes us roomier." For Augustine, the pieces brought together in *cogitatio* make a sum greater than its parts. Knowledge extends understanding not by adding on more and more pieces, but because as we compose [a composition, recall, which is intimately linked to memory and its cultivation] our design becomes more capacious, it dilates.

The gatherings of voices in memory, then, and our cultivation of them and our care and devotion to this process of self-formation actually *expand* "myself" to include, now, this weird voice of Augustine talking about becoming "roomier" as a result of learning and its meditative-memorial practices. I become different in learning about this heretofore unheard-of connection between this dissolution of the self-containedness of the Cartesian-*critica* "I am" and the great body-function of *dilation*.

XVI

To paraphrase Bronwen Wallace's words (p. 36), the articulation of personal artifacts fleshes out more hands than those that handed these things along, and more hands than those that received them. Memory lives and is housed and articulated beyond the confines of subjectivity, even though each of us faces the intimate, inward task of its cultivation. So already with the family artifact there is a world, both surrounding the artifact itself and surrounding the types of work needed to cultivate an understanding and memory of it. Education becomes a public practice on topics that are themselves public.

So what about the grain elevators? This family artifact experience with children cultivated a memory hollow in which subsequent experience is then cradled and nurtured. In the cultivation of memory and the composing of oneself that is required, we can then experience what comes to meet us by having along with us the ancestors we "remember" from having learned how to remember. Our "selves" have become "roomier" or, to use the hermeneutic adage, the world has become open to interpretation. And here is the great, seemingly paradoxical situation: "keeping ourselves open" and "keeping the world open" (Eliade, 1968, p. 139) are the same thing. As we become experienced, having cleaved with affection and made ourselves "roomier," the world's roominess can be experienced. Just as with objects treated with the objective methods of the objective sciences, so too with memorial objects treated with affection. "The way we treat a thing can sometimes change its nature" (Hyde, 1983, p. xiii). (This is why the arguments regarding "the basics" are not simply a matter of, so to speak, "pointing to the object" and attesting to its interdependence and interpretability. Understanding the interpretive nature of "the basics" requires understanding *myself* differently, as compositionally engaged in and obligated to the living inheritance of the world.)

Remembering the thing is remembering oneself. Writing about it is writing oneself. Taking or drawing a picture of it is portraying oneself.

Something happened, and the exact details never function properly as a cause for what happened. Jennifer regularly saw a grain elevator outside of town on her way to work, and then, one day, it was gone. And she has family ties to Gleichen, straight east of Calgary, Alberta, and it was on the grain line and had its own elevator, and on the first trip David took to his new job in Calgary in 1986 the first recognizable thing you met entering Calgary from the south was the Midnapore Elevator (which has since disappeared). And the authors and the children in the classroom are living in Alberta, not elsewhere, and these things scatter the landscape in long trips to meet friends in Lethbridge, 250 kilometers south through Claresholm and Monarch and Coaldale, so on and on. Topographical, substantive, image-filled, ancestral happenstances that have been remembered, stored, and that cue off reminders when that one grain elevator happened to disappear one day to one of the authors. This is little more than the slow work of living a life and allowing oneself to notice, and becoming experienced in noticing. And we're often surprised to find what has been stored away.

These grain elevators are disappearing and, from their family archive work, these kids know something already about how things house memory and how their disappearance dovetails with forgetting, and how Aquinas is almost right: you must cleave with affection to and dwell with solicitude on that which you wish to remember, but, as a result, you can come to experience how things (like all the topics named so meagerly in curriculum guides) can hold memory— hold part of the answer to who we are and just who this "we" might be—and are not just objects of indifference. So Aquinas's words get inverted: as a grain elevator disappears, we learn, through the cultivation of memory and character, to be affected.

Detailed talks with Michelle and Judy ensued about these structures being centerpieces for many towns, and, of course, on the prairies they function, too, as guides, as directional markers, as gathering spots for decades of lives and work and gossip, as somehow "sentinels." Even though we can cultivate in ourselves the ability to *experience* (*Erfahrung*—"experience" as suffering or undergoing) the disappearance of these grain elevators, it takes time and work and conversation to come to understand what has happened, what is being suggested in the experience of being addressed by such matters.

Sentinels. This is an odd turn of phrase, but, as Vico suggests, the young (anyone new to something, we teachers in those early speculative meetings several years ago over several weeks, and now still ongoing) need images for their imaginations and for the formation of their memories. Sentinels, looped into the other great and looming topography that we collectively knew was approaching. "Alberta history" and "Maritimes history" and "the North" were coming up in Grade One and Grade Two social studies and needed to be "covered." How we *treat* these curriculum mandates can sometimes change their nature. Histories. Memory. Memorials.

Holders of public memory. Links to travels and territories. Sentinels. Grain elevators, lighthouses, inukshuks. Yes!

Teacher planning, here, works substantively and imaginatively. It is, as with medieval work, the imaginative opening up of a *topos*, a place, a topography in which to house images that themselves house memory. Since the young need images for their imaginations and for the formation of their memories (this includes myself as a teacher who might be "new" to a topic), planning itself must needs be imaginative, speculative, memorial, and topographical. Teacher planning, first and foremost, must "entrust [itself] to what [is being] investigat[ed] to guide [it] safely in the quest" (Gadamer, 1989, p. 378).

XVII

J.G.'s students were quickly taken with their teacher's grain elevator tales, with the old yearbook she brought in from Gleichen, Alberta, and what quickly spread was calls to the local Alberta Grain Elevator Society, letters to the Alberta premier, visits to local elevators, detailed, worried-over illustrations of how they work and their landscapes, and a field trip to meet the then minister of whatever in Edmonton, Alberta. What occurred was that the artifact work had worked a niche in memory, and its vestiges allowed children and teachers alike to have an "experienced" response to the grain elevators and their memorial place in the life of Alberta. History itself became incarnated, not in a thin line of dates and names (like the sorry work of that Grade Ten student regarding the social studies topic of "sovereignty"), but in buildings, places, functions, designs, rail-lines, settlements, and the seeming passing of such matters in the disappearance of these sentinels of Alberta life. When the premier of Alberta, in a public meeting of various schools involved in the Galileo

Educational Network, mentioned a particular town, one Grade One child remembered, on the spot, when the elevator was built and when it disappeared.

Or, as Gregory the Great suggested, "we ought to transform what we read into our very selves, so that when our mind is stirred by what it hears, our life may concur by practising what has been heard" (cited in Carruthers, 2005, p. 164). Or, from *Truth and Method* (Gadamer, 1989, p. 340), "[we] belong to the text [we] are reading. The line of meaning that the text manifests . . . always and necessarily breaks off in an open indeterminacy. [We] can, indeed [we] must accept the fact that future generations will understand differently." Or, as Hugh of St. Victor proposed, "reading is ethical in its nature, or 'tropological' (turning the text onto and into one's self)" (Carruthers, 2005, p. 164). "Understanding begins," so goes the hermeneutic adage, "when something addresses us" (Gadamer, 1989, p. 299). To interpret and remember a text is to read and remember it as if it were addressed to me. "Perhaps no advice is as common in Medieval writing [on reading and memory], and yet so foreign, when one thinks about it, to the habits of modern scholarship, as this notion of 'making one's own' what one reads in someone else' work" (Carruthers, 2005, p. 164). Once "made one's own," grain elevators and the memory they incarnate become objects of affection, and it starts to make perfect sense that one cannot experience the sadness of their disappearance if you have not come to know them.

Readers can visit the website where the grain elevator work, as well as the family artifact work, is located.

XVIII

One last reflection for now. Clearly, the matter at stake in the cultivation of memory in the medieval period was salvation and an experience of God. This constitutes, so to speak, the *telos* of dilation:

> "New" knowledge, what has not been thought, results from this process, for dilation leads ultimately, even through the deepest "cavi" of memory to God. Augustine characteristically speaks of this as a "going through" [*Erfahrung*?]. How shall I reach God? he asks. "I shall pass through [*transibo*] even this power of mine which is called memory; I shall pass through I to reach Thee, sweet Light." God is indeed beyond memory, but the only way there is through and by means of it, "*ascendens per animum meum ad te.*"
>
> (Carruthers, 2005, p. 199)

This, of course, goes too far, even for me (D.J.) as an ex-Anglican altar boy. But there is another place in which Carruthers (2005, p. 67) cites a beautiful passage from E. K. Rand's Aquinas Lecture of 1945 that helps illustrate the effects of this cultivation of memory in a way that is more palatable and more experientially available in the most ordinary of classroom events:

St. Thomas has learned from many men of wisdom, but on the present occasion they are summoned to court [to discuss, in this particular instance, the nature of temperance with a waiting audience], summoned from their chambers in his mind. I am not going to name them all, but they are hovering outside the courtroom in crowds, ancient Greeks and ancient Romans, members of all the philosophical schools, some of their poets ... and Christian poets like Ambrose, doctors of the Roman church and of the Greek, Popes all down the line, saints and heretics—at least the mighty Origen—writers of the early Middle Ages from England, France and Spain, writers of the Renaissance of the twelfth century, writers of his own day, the Hebrew Rabbi Moses, or Maimonides, the Arabs with Averroes at their head, mystics, monastics, and meta-physicians, writers of law books and decretals, Church councils and liturgy, yes, Holy Scripture, Old Testament and New and the glosses thereon.

When St. Thomas, with his great memory and experience, shows up and bears witness to a particular phenomenon, a Great Council of Beings shows up surrounding him, just as, when the wanderer who is experienced in the ways of a forest shows up, that place's ways can be experienced because the wanderer is surrounded by his or her "being experienced" in the ways of that place. The cicada's burr *reminds* (see Chapter 13) only those who are experienced in such matters. "Only in the multifariousness of such voices" (Gadamer, 1989, p. 284) do Aquinas's experience and knowledge exist. He is both inventively and inventorially wrought.

And this, too, is what we witnessed when a Grade Two boy was able to hear his younger classmate's lack of affection for grain elevators. That Grade Two boy summoned up what he knew and remembered and spoke, emotionally and articulately, to the question at hand surrounded by a great council of memorial experience. And the Grade Two class initiated the work of introducing their younger classmates to these disappearing sentinels, taking out of the teacher's hands the need to decide how to proceed.

We know full well that this Great Council that shows up surrounding Aqui-nas (or any one of us) is not Absolute, that it is surrounded (I would suggest, *necessarily* surrounded) by a dark and irremediable penumbra of absences. We don't learn everything. None of us is everyone. None of us is cut out for living just any life, and none of us will live forever. We are not perspectiveless and timeless beings whose knowledge floats and whose life is a matter of indiffer-ence. I am defined by what I can thus remember, what necessarily exclusive and incomplete host of voices haunts my inner life and work and therefore haunts the world(s) that open in front of me. This composed and cultivated memory constitutes my openness to what comes to meet me from the world.

No amount of effort allows any of us to avoid this process of suffering through the remembering and forgetting of the world and becoming someone in the process.

As memory increases, so does this suffering. I become more susceptible to the world's affect as I become more experienced.

This is basic.

Notes

1. Because of the multiple authorship of this chapter and how it is composed, all authors will be referred to in the third person. In those cases where a specific author is speaking or referred to, the author's initials will be provided.
2. See http://www.galileo.org/schools/district-cbe/princeofwales/stories/index.htm

4

Children's Literacy, the *Biblia Pauperum*, and the Wiles of Images

MICHELLE BASTOCK AND DAVID W. JARDINE

We have been exploring how forgotten aspects of ancient theological debates regarding words and images might silently and subtly inform more immediate pedagogical conversations about children's picture books.

The recent rise in the quality and quantity of beautifully illustrated children's books has been extraordinary. Teachers and parents can attest to this proliferation and to the great joys to be had in reading such books with children. Many teachers have told us that they have fallen in love again with "kids' books" because the tales and images have become vivacious again—troublesome, lively, rich, and engaging *for them* as well as for their students.

In the face of such a "pandemonium of images" (Jardine, 1992, p. 90), we are faced once again with age-old hopes and fears regarding the informative yet wily nature of the image, and what it means, in an increasingly image-laden world, to be literate. We found an especially fascinating example from the 14th century CE, the *Biblia Pauperum* (see Manning, 2001, and Figures 4.1 and 4.2), wherein selected tales from the Bible were "told" with illustrations instead of words, so that those who could not read the Word (the poor, the illiterate, the child) could still partake in their meaning, still feel drawn to the great saving narratives.

The use of images as a living, alluring text has not been at all theologically uncontentious, however. At the Second Council of Nicea (787 CE), great debates were had over the status of images:

> At Nicea a subtle differentiation was made between *adoration* of images (idolatry) and the *veneration* of images. The eight sessions of statements emphasised the distinction between the image as such with full divine power and the image as signifying or pointing to that power. It concluded that the divine was *not* inherent in the image; images were not repositories of power. Rather, they were useful for didactic purposes. They were not presences or presentations, but representation, illustration and allegories to remind the faithful of abstract theological figuration transcendent to the image.
>
> (Hillman, 1983, p. 71)

The terms and fears and power of this debate can be seen in the most commonplace of events in the classroom—reading a lusciously illustrated book to young children. Teachers understand how easily the illustrations in such books can, as we say in a commonplace way, "capture" children's attention and lead to fervent conversations and speculations. Phenomenologically speaking—that is, from the perspective of lived experience—images have a sense of power and allure to them, a sense of *agency*. Many of us can recall leafing through books over and over again, knowing them by their series of pictures long before we could decode any words, long before there was any need to do so. When faced with a powerful image, we undergo the experience of being *affected*, of something been *done to us*, rather than the experience of our *doing something*. Like a good question that strikes us and demands something of us, the experience of an image is "more a passion than an action. A[n image] *presses itself upon us*" (Gadamer, 1989, p. 366). This is why hermeneutics characterizes the initial moment of understanding as one of being *addressed* (Gadamer, 1989, p. 299) by something that "*happens to us* over and above our wanting and doing" (p. xxviii). Understanding involves moving into a territory (*topica*; see Chapter 3) full of images, and somehow being "moved" by *its* movement (the root of the word *passion*. See Chapter 20 for more on this character of "movement" as another "basic" of teaching and learning), being changed by *its* lessons, *its* teaching of *us*.

It is little wonder, then, that these matters were of great theological concern. In the presence of images, fixed doctrine that might be rote-memorized and rote-repeated (see Chapters 3, 18 and 21) "give[s] way to movement" (Caputo, 1987, p. 2), motility, passage (*Erfahrung*). Under such sway, even words start to become deliteralized, suggestive and ambiguous and multivalent, rather than simply definitional or declarative. The text before us, in such cases, requires us to *do* something. It poses questions to us and draws us into *its* questions. Such an imaginal sense of textuality is at the heart of hermeneutics—texts need interpreting, not just rote-repeating.

This, of course, won't do, either in light of a fundamentalist understanding of textuality or in light of the efficiency movement's rendering of interpretation into a form of *waste* (see our Preface). "Dogmatic thinking must rely upon an unambiguous text. This is one of the reasons why the Roman Catholic Church could develop a set of dogma" (Dan, 1986, p. 129) (and this in spite of the fact that that Church trails behind it a long and complex and multifarious ancestral and imaginal trail of names and faces and places). And in a great parallel that remains profoundly hidden, schools, too, can only operate if the "text" which students must master and the terms of that mastery itself are themselves unambiguous. Only thus is state-wide "testing" warrantable and accountable and feasible. We find, here, a great bloodline of the desire to identify "the basics" with "the unambiguous" and therefore find origins of the literal-mindedness that underscores schooling. In our too-cautious haste to separate schooling from religious matters, such matters remain not only hidden. They remain *at work* in the seemingly secular day-to-dayness of schooling and remain equally beyond articulation. We are *had* by such matters without having on hand a legitimate sense of any recourse to *understanding* such matters.

The early Church believed that "paintings [and stained-glass windows and Church statues and the like] were an aid to worship [because] the mediæval congregations were largely illiterate" (Bull, n.d.) and that "pictures were the Bible of the poor [*Biblia Pauperum*], the uneducated" (Corbett, 1907/2003). However, in *c.*600 CE, Bishop Serenus of Marseilles was concerned that his parishioners were engaged in superstitious worship of the holy images in his church. To prevent this, the bishop destroyed all the images in his church (Carruthers, 2005, p. 221). Pope Gregory the Great intervened:

> It is one thing to worship a picture; it is another by means of pictures to learn thoroughly [*addiscere*] the story that should be venerated. For what writing makes present to those reading, the same picturing makes present [*praestat*] to the uneducated, to those perceiving visually, because in it the ignorant see what they ought to follow, in it they read who do not know letters. Wherefore, and especially for the common people, picturing is the equivalent of reading.
>
> (cited in Carruthers, 2005, p. 222)

This is not unlike a contemporary pedagogical argument for the illustrations in children's literature. Images are not dangerous and idolatrous and worrisome provided that they are understood and accepted only as a *means* for understanding what is written in the words of the text. Images, in elementary school classrooms, are introduced as *vehicles*, "carriers" of meaning. To re-cite James Hillman's words (p. 60), they are not *presences* that have something to say to us, something to show. They are simply re-presentations, pointers to something else, (albeit convenient and effective) stand-ins, in Christian-literacy terms, for "the Word."

Here, of course, is where the fight starts and where the fear lies regarding the wily character of images. At the Second Council of Nicea (787 CE) and in line with the troubles that Bishop Serenus had witnessed, it was argued that images could easily charm, mislead, and sway. They are, by their very nature, open to interpretation, full of ambiguity, multiplicity, diversity, charge, and a potentially dangerous vivacity. As any elementary school teacher knows, when we sit with a gorgeous picture book with young children, we *invite* a pandemonium of responses, a multiplicity of possibilities, and it is very difficult (and, we suggest, for good teachers, not especially desirable) to close down the "multifariousness of voices" (Gadamer, 1989, p. 285). In light of an interpretive understanding of "the basics," teachers purposefully "ignore the orthodox who labour so patiently trying to eliminate the apocryphal variants from the one true text" (Thompson, 1981, p. 11).

Such a way of proceeding would have been considered, at the Second Council of Nicea, precisely a violation of the Singularity of Voice that is at the core of Christian dogma. The Word is singular. The One does not become The Many in the proliferation of images. Therefore:

> A distinction was drawn between the *adoration* of images and the free formulation of them on the one hand, and the *veneration* of images and the authorized control over them on the other. Church Councils split hairs, but the roots of these hairs are in our heads, and the split goes deep indeed. At Nicea a distinction was made between the image as such, its

power, its full archetypal reality, and what the image represents, points to, means. Thus, images became allegories. When images became allegories the iconoclasts have won. The image itself has become subtly depotentiated. Yes, images are allowed, but only if they are officially approved images illustrative of theological doctrine. One's spontaneous imagery is spurious, demonic, devilish, pagan, heathen. Yes, the image is allowed, but only to be venerated for what it represents: the abstract ideas, configurations, transcendencies behind the image. Images become ways of perceiving doctrine. They become representations, no longer presentations, no longer presences of power.

(Hillman, 1983, p. 56)

Underlying the power of the image to teach (the illiterate, the young) is an abiding fear of the image, a fear that it might lead to a breaking up of the unity and coherence of the Word, a fear that, so to speak, all hell might break loose (parallel this to the abiding fear that methodologically based research has of interpretive methodologies that begin with *topica* and not *critica* [see Chapter 3]. Hermeneutics is often treated like an "undisciplined child" [see Jardine & Misgeld, 1989]—just as the image is considered, for example in Piagetian theory, as more "childish" than the methods of logic and mathematics [see Jardine, 2005]). After all, children can be tested as to whether they can properly decode words below the pictures and we, as teachers, can easily agree upon an officially approved version of what such decoding can be. However, if they start meditating and speculating about an image, trouble potentially brews, as Figure 4.2 from the *Biblia Pauperum* clearly attests.

Insofar as truth is identified with the Word, images become suspect, a little wild, arousing too many wiles (see Chapter 5 for a consideration of the imaginal figure of Coyote and his wiles). They begin to appear multiple instead of singular, ambiguous and interpretable instead of clear and distinct and, in education, perhaps at best "enjoyable" and "fun" and "engaging," but also, in the end, unmanageable and difficult to assess. Our relation to them becomes profoundly ambivalent. Roiling conversations with young children over the images they encounter in a picture book are, in consequence, too easily forgone in favour of managing and assessing their skills at decoding the words below the pictures (that "underwrite" the pictures, just as stock market quotations similarly "underwrite" television news [our own *Biblia Pauperum*, perhaps? By analogy, television news tells us that underwriting the myriad world of images we see before us is the One True Text that those images point to: the Market. See Smith, 2008]).

In early elementary school, images are patiently allowed to help with decoding the words of a text, but children must mature (see Jardine, 2005) and eventually forgo such dependence (see Bastock, 2005). Reliance on images is at best childish and, at worst (as the great theological histories of the image show us),

animalistic, bodily, devilish, willful, deceptive, seductive, and untrue (Jardine, 2005). What occurs, therefore, is that, bereft of images and their imaginal topographies, "the imaginative process withers, only reinforcing the ego's literalism" (Hillman, 1983, p. 65).

Thus, at Nicea, we come to understand how Figure 4.2 cannot be allowed to be open to interpretation. It calls out, theologically, to be "depotentiated" (Hillman, 1983, p. 71). After all, just imagine what could be imagined regarding this image of Eve and her tempter. With children's picture books, then, the images are allowed as mere temporary stand-ins, mere pointers to the words, mere representations, not dangerous and potent presences that might carry us away. They are "crutches" to "support" those less able (another theological inheritance is this interweave of the child, the unable, the illiterate, the poor, the innocent). The wiliness of the image has thus been neutered. The pictures in children's books are not powerful presences that might charm us and draw us and whisper to us. They are simply pointers to abstract psycholinguistic figurations involving the development and management of children's literacy decoding skills.

Of course, teachers know that this is not what *happens* when we read beautifully illustrated books with children (Bastock, 2005), nor does it at all account for North American culture's drooling, spell-bound, almost morbid fascination with images and their voracious consumption. What is at work here is no mere psychological or psycholinguistic research finding about "children's literacy." Something far more ancient howls here. The ancients knew that we should be careful in such matters, but they've fallen silent. Contemporary education acts and speaks with little or no memory of such great and troubled ancestries. And, of course, we have not yet even *alluded to* Judaic or Islamic bloodlines, let alone the great makyo-nightmares of Buddhism (Aitken, 1982, p. 46) or the great Vedic gods of Hinduism. Without "a special effort of memory" (Gadamer, 1989, p. 482) in this regard, teachers and students alike are left unable to richly and generously articulate what they experience first-hand in reading beautifully illustrated books to young children.

A Parting Thought

There is a dialectic to the word, which accords to every word an inner dimension of multiplication: every word breaks forth as if from a centre and is related to a whole, through which alone it is a word. Every word causes the whole of the language to which it belongs to resonate and the whole world-view that underlies it to appear. Thus, every word, as the event of a moment, carries with it the unsaid, to which it is related by responding and summoning. The occasionality of human speech is not a casual imperfection of its expressive power; it is, rather, the logical expression of the living virtuality of speech that brings a totality of meaning into play, without being able to express it totally. All human speaking is finite in such a way that there is laid up within it an infinity of meaning to be explicated and laid out.

(Gadamer, 1989, p. 458)

What is at work in this contestation over images and words is a struggle between the ability to corral and command meaning, and the experience of transcendence that comes from encountering something "over and above our wanting and doing" (Gadamer, 1989, p. xxviii). Central to our alternate image of "the basics" is a shifting image of the agency of knowledge and, therefore, a shift in the image of the work of schools. Coming to know and experience the world and its ways is not an ego-issuance but a true encounter in which I experience my own limits by experiencing something from beyond the limits of my own experience. This is the great phenomenological paradox that images help us encounter. It is also a great paradox that words can induce when allowed to be moments of "breaking forth." James Hillman, we suggest, is correct: "Literalism is the enemy. Literalism is sickness" (Hillman, 1983, p. 3). And, if we don't take literalism too literally, we can understand how this encounter of that which meets me from beyond myself is precisely at the core of pedagogy itself:

"Education is suffering from narration-sickness," says Paulo Freire. It speaks out of a story which was once full of enthusiasm, but now shows itself incapable of a surprise ending. The nausea of narration-sickness comes from having heard enough, of hearing many variations on a theme but no new theme. A narrative which is sick may claim to speak for all, yet has no *aporia*, no possibility of meeting a stranger because the text is complete already. Such narratives may be passed as excellent by those who certify clarity and for whom ambiguity is a disease to be excoriated. But the literalism of such narratives (speeches, lectures, stories) inevitably produces a pedagogy which, while it passes as being "for the good of children," does not recognise the violence against children inherent in its own claim. Because without an acknowledgement and positive appreciation of the full polysemic possibility which can explode forth from within any occasion when adult and child genuinely meet together: a possibility which resides precisely in the difference of every child, every person, a difference about which one can presume nothing despite the massive research literature (e.g., about children) available to us, and despite the fact that our children come from us, are our flesh and blood. Without an appreciation of the radical mystery which confronts us in the face of every other person, our theorizing must inexorably become stuck, for then we are no longer available for that which comes to meet us from beyond ourselves, having determined in advance the conditions under which any new thing will be acceptable, and thereby foreclosing on the possibility of our own transformation. This radical difference of every child, every other person, renders our pedagogical narratives ambiguous but at the same time hopeful, because the immanent ambiguity held within them opens a space for genuine speaking, holding out the promise that something new can be said from out of the mists of the oracle of our own flesh.

(Smith, 1999, pp. 135–136)

5

"Whatever Happens to Him Happens to Us"

Reading Coyote Reading the World

PATRICIA CLIFFORD, SHARON FRIESEN,
AND DAVID W. JARDINE

Introduction

COYOTE

by starlight hush of wind the owl's shadow voice,
the campfire embers glowing inner universe
by firelight smoke curls weaving faint the voices,
coyote voices faint the pain and smell of pitch,
fire, I sing you stars,
fire, I breath obsidian
& again the owl's shadow voice leans back
into times past
singing firs fire,

brittle spine bent bowed toward the fire,
voices low to murmur a child whimper,
deer fat sucked upon to gentle dreaming,
the mother her song the night cradles,
child, the owl, too, has young,
tiny hearts and warmth of down,
& old man coughing guttural spit to fire,
young people giggle beneath hide fondlings
soon to sleep,
again coyote voices drown the mind in a loneliness
of deep respect in love of those who camp
just up the hill,
& tiny crystals of tears spatter the dust,
my people,
legs that cannot ever carry me back to you,
soul that holds you
forever.
Peter Blue Cloud, cited in Snyder (1977, p. 56)

Pathologizing Difference

When Robert Coles was a resident psychiatrist, one of his professors kept insisting that he tell stories, not clinical synopses, of the patients with whom he was working. He would say to Coles (1989, p. 28), "At times I feel you're explaining *away* those people—and I know you don't want to do so; I know you are a friend of theirs, and they are friends of yours." Today, we propose to tell the story of one child whom we will call Manuel, a child who came to us three years ago full of problems. Grounded in the "stubborn particularity" (Wallace 1987; see Chapter 12) of one child, we offer his story not to explain him away, but instead to offer ways of reading differently the difficult, "abnormal," troubled children who haunt the margins of educational practice and theorizing.

What we propose is, in some sense, quite radical, for we call into question the pathologizing of difference that underpins so much of the way education understands children, their lives, their experience, and their reading and writing of the world. We question the usual understanding of classrooms as collections of individuals whose separate worlds connect from time to time and who come together simply so that each can mind their own business (Dressman 1993). We want to interrogate the very idea that difference can be merely "known" and thereby, if teachers and researchers are diligent enough, eradicated as a problem of practice, and we want to challenge what is, sometimes, education's neurotic compulsion (Evetts-Secker 1994) to tame and understand the exotic "other". Instead, we believe, the intractable, irreducible differences of individuals can form the ground of true freedom, for in:

> coming together in their pluralities and their differences, . . . [students] may finally articulate how they are choosing themselves and what the projects are by means of which they can identify themselves. We all need to recognize each other in our striving, our becoming, our inventing of the possible. And yes, it is a question of acting in the light of a vision of what might be a vision that enables people to perceive the voids, take heed of the violations, and move (if they can) to repair. Such a vision . . . can be enlarged and enriched by those on the margins, whoever they are.
> (Greene 1993, pp. 219–220)

Manuel came to us in Grade One already wearing almost every one of the flattening, professional pseudonyms available for troubled children. He was "physically challenged", "severely disabled". He possessed, we were told, "a file this thick" documenting his "behavioral difficulties" (this file, it turned out, did not exist). He could not count reliably, could not print between the lines, could not sit still, could not resist touching his classmates or calling out in lessons. Unable, it seemed, even to *recognize* any given task at hand, Manuel certainly had problems devoting time to the classroom agenda. Sometimes he would wander like a lost soul, apparently unconnected to anyone or anything around him. At other times, the mere prospect of a day at school with his friends made him so happy, so excited he would have a coughing fit and his breakfast would slide out on the floor. Manuel was a puzzle. Of that we were certain. In him, we saw the puzzle of difference constructed as either remediable or irremediable deficiency by the institutions that had already labelled him for us. The walls had gone up, and Manuel had already been offered two choices: learn to be more normal, more ordinary, or face exile forever beyond the pale. Meanwhile, he bore the brunt of feigned clarity that comes from this odd, harsh-edged, school board version of educational psychology.

Manuel's parents had felt compelled to leave their homeland to come to Canada because the only classroom that could be made available for such an unusual child was one that already contained nineteen autistic children. That's how it started for Manuel in kindergarten in his own country, half a world away. His parents were afraid, almost literally, for his life when they moved to Canada.

And his welcome, here, was that the very first teachers who took him in kept him for only one day and asked that another placement be found for him because they already felt themselves overwhelmed by the number of problem children in their charge. All three of us recognized, in Manuel's arrival, a scenario we had played out with other children: the principal appeared at our door early one morning.

"Will you take him? No one knows quite what to do with him."

And of course we took him in, for we knew what leaving him outside the door, outside the walls of our classroom might mean. Unable to find a home, exiled from his own life, Manuel might well have become a latter-day Caliban, a monster child labelled and enslaved by the malefic generosity (Greene, 1978; see Jardine 1998a, Jardine & Novodvorski 2006) of school—a child confined to its margins.

The margins of the institution are not places anyone would necessarily self-select. Certainly, there exist boundaries that are full of adventure and the possibility of transgression, transformation, and movement (see Chapter 20). But there are also boundaries that imprison and demand either inclusion or exclusion, either normality or pathology—and those were the boundaries that had already begun to close around Manuel.

Not without care, not without concern for his difference, of course. The impulse behind institutional labelling and classification, however toxic the effects, may well have generous roots in professionals' wanting to help, wanting to do well by the child—wanting to fix his wounds and put an end to everyone's suffering. But fixing is such dangerous enterprise. It seeks to eradicate difference; but it also eliminates openings and possibilities, especially the unhesitant, grotesquely self-certain fixing we have come to expect from many educational psychologists in our respective professions. "Fixing" has a dark, colonial shadow that educators do not always acknowledge—outsiders stream

in to classrooms, find an ambiguous and difficult child like Manuel, and proceed, with clarity and confidence to order us around, all, of course, "for [our]
own good" (Miller 1989).

As *Coyote Columbus* incites, too often "they act like they got no relations"
(King 1992).

Children like Manuel can sometimes show that what is often dismissed as in
need of identification, naming, intervention and eventual transformation by
the institution may become understood in a totally different way. Monster
derives from the Latin *monere*, the word for portent, for warning (Jardine
1998a; Werner 1994). Manuel and marginal children like him can sometimes
offer warnings or demonstrations to the clear and confident centres of normality in the classroom, and the ordinary, taken-for-granted course of things that
classrooms often portray and defend. Such children can bring about the transformation and renewal of the centre, providing that centre can remain vulnerable and open to their arrival—provided, that is, that those at the centre are
able and willing to read their arrival more generously than the institutionalized
discourses of marginality and normality have often allowed. The troubles that
Manuel brings may thus be understood as what James Hillman calls lacunae,
weak places which give opportunity:

> Perception of opportunities requires a sensitivity given through one's
> own wounds. Here, weakness provides the kind of hermetic, secret per-
> ception critical for adaptation to situations. The weak place serves to
> open us to what is in the air. We feel through our pores which way the
> wind blows. We turn with the wind; trimmers. An opportunity requires
> . . . a sense . . . which reveals the daimon of a situation. The daimon of a
> place in antiquity supposedly revealed what the place was good for, its
> special qualities and dangers. The daimon was thought to be a *familiaris*
> of the place. To know a situation, one needs to sense what lurks in it.
>
> (1979, p. 161)

Coyote Stories and the Work of the Imagination

At one point in the year we taught Manuel, we began reading stories about the
native trickster figure, Coyote, a creature from the boundaries and margins,
whose wild energy and tricky ways were enchanting. We read picture books
together; listened to told stories; drew pictures; studied the art of native illus-
trators and of artists like George Littlechild. Because we, as teachers and as
researchers, had become fascinated with what we were now calling "borders
work," the interrogation of taken-for-granted protocols under which we live,
we offered the children the heady opportunity to inhabit some of the spaces
that a character like Coyote offers. While nominally attached to curriculum
requirements that we study native people in Alberta, the Coyote stories took us
far away from the rampant literalism of the prescribed program of studies. And

we could never avoid the coincidence: Coyote himself, in such stories, always reaching out beyond prescription and teaching thereby.

The possibility of creating a world that is different from the world as taken-for-granted-as-normal is the work of the imagination (Bogdan 1992; Coles 1989; Hillman 1983). The possibility that things might be otherwise than they seem can be apprehended only in the imagination, and the strategies for resistance and for unnaming (Le Guin 1987), reshaping, and renaming the world come only from imagination as well. It is no wonder, then, that these teachers and students loved Coyote so much, for Coyote, both fool and savant, was given the power to create anything he could imagine. Calling to each person from the boundaries of their world of normal experiences, Coyote howls holes in the taken-for-granted, the assumed, the unuttered, and the unutterable. But he does not simply howl such holes: he incites those who meet him "in" through such openings, such opportunities for understanding, with his silly grin and his all-too-human foibles and the energy and foolish wisdom he exudes.

That is, he teaches. And he teaches by teaching us the limits of the world. And he teaches such limits through their violation, through "keeping the world open" (Eliade 1968, p. 139) so that the lessons of balance and respect can be learned once again, here, by this child that:

> child, the owl, too has young,
> tiny hearts and warmth of down.

Like almost every child in the class, Sinead decided to write Coyote stories. We never asked the children to do this; never required or even suggested that they take up Coyote for themselves. They just did it anyway, so fully had this ratty creature captured their hearts. Through one of Sinead's stories (and, we suggest, also through the feral agency of Coyote herself), Manuel the monster child is welcomed in from the margins and given a home. A close reading of Sinead's story will show something of how one of the children in Manuel's class did the generous, generative work that was so difficult for many adults in Manuel's life to accomplish.

COYOTE AT THE CHRISTMAS CONCERT by Sinead O'Brien
Sinead, Robert, and Manuel were helping Ms. Patrick and Ms. Charleston decorate the gym for their Christmas concert. Sinead asked Manuel, "Is your dad coming to the concert tonight?"

"Yes. Bah humbug," said Manuel, fake-laughing and throwing his head back.

"Oh really," thought Sinead to herself.

"Come help me lift this," yelled Robert.

"I'll be there in a second," replied Cheryl, who had just come back from gym.

. . . . .

"We come as clouds, the . . ." the class recited together, practising for the evening's performance.

"WE COME AS CLOUD," yelled Manuel, walking into the classroom. Sinead rolled her eyes.

"Guess what? We're going to read The Christmas Carol," said Joanie as she came over to Cheryl and Robert.

"YES!" yelled Robert.

"YES!" yelled Manuel, jumping up and down.

"I already knew that," said Cheryl.

Just then, Mrs. Smith came on the speaker. "Boys and girls, may I have your attention."

"No you can't," thought Sinead.

"Students in the gym, may I have your attention."

"I'm not in the gym, so I don't HAVE to pay attention," thought Sinead again.

"Remember to have your best manners on tonight and great voices. We want our parents to be impressed, don't we? Of course we do."

"Not me," thought Sinead to herself.

"Good afternoon."

RRRRRRRRRRIIIIIIIIIINNNNNNNNNNNGGGGGGGGGG.   The bell rang.

"Try to wear something nice tonight," said Mrs. Cliffrie.

. . . . .

"Ayeeeya aeeeeya," sang the choir, beginning a native song.

Coyote, coming in the door, heard the wonderful singing. After his hard day with Grandfather Rock, he sure did feel like singing—especially when they got to the part with the "Harpoooooooooooooooooooooooon him?" That tricky Coyote, he started singing along with the choir. OOOOOOOOOOOOOOO. OOOOOOO. OOOOOOOOOOOO OOOOOOOOOOOOOOOOOOO. OOOOOOOOO.

"What fun," thought Coyote to himself.

But not very many parents in the audience thought that listening to OOOOOOOOOOOOOOOOOOOOOOOOOOOOOOOOOO was the most pleasant way to spend the Christmas concert.

"Who's making that racket?" someone whispered to Zoe's dad.

"I don't know," said Don under his breath, "but it certainly isn't Zoe or Jeremy."

Robert's mum turned to look. "Oh no, Don. I can't believe it. That's not a child at all. It's a big dog or something."

"Oh don't be ridiculous, Pam. There can't be a dog in here. It must be someone's child." and he turned around to see whether it was anybody he knew.

"Oh NO! It's a coyote. A coyote! COYOTE AT THE CHRISTMAS CONCERT!" And he fainted dead away.

Suddenly, from the other side of the gym, a sound started to build. It was Coyote number two, Manuel the Magnificent. He wanted to sing, and he did. And guess what? Everyone else started singing and even Sinead was happy and they had the best Christmas concert ever—at least for that year.

Imaginary Figures and the Real World

The voyage out of the (known) self and back into the (unknown) self sometimes takes the wanderer far away to a motley place where everything safe and sound seems to waver while the essence of language is placed in doubt and profoundly destabilized. Travelling can thus turn out to be a process whereby the self loses its fixed boundaries—a disturbing yet potentially empowering practice of difference.

(Minh-Ha 1994, p. 23)

Sinead's reading of Coyote stories is a reading that touches the very world we live in, that makes the world "waver and tremble" (Caputo 1987, p. 7) and, as a result, makes the world become more multi-vocal, complex, ambiguous, and alluring than it was before. Such readings do not simply add stockpiles of "images" or "concepts" to the one doing the reading. They reveal layers of the living world, add meaning to the creases on the faces I see. They are readings that, in other places, we have called "edgy readings" (Clifford, Friesen & Jardine 1995), the sense of which is eloquently captured by bell hooks (cited in Greene 1993, p. 220):

Living as we did—on the edge—we developed a particular way of seeing reality. We looked from the outside in and from the inside out. We focussed our attention on the centre as well as on the margin. We understood both. This mode of seeing reminded us of the existence of a whole universe, a main body made up of both margin and center.

And, of course, it is especially Coyote (not unlike Hermes) who tracks the passages and openings in between inside and outside, between centre and margin. One could add, between young and old, between new and established, between teacher and learner, since Coyote is a figure who most often appears in the elders stories to and for and about the young and their ways in the world.

As we considered the text of Sinead's story, it became clear that Coyote was not just a "concept" or an image or a literary figure housed inside this and other writings and readings we had done. Reading Coyote stories did not mean simply decoding the literal meaning of what she heard or read, nor did it mean instrumentally using Coyote simply as a "metaphor" for what was somehow "in fact" an otherwise literal, "real" world of "children with Attention Deficit

Disorder [A.D.D.]" (again reinforcing the boundary between "the normal" and "the special"). Rather, the living figure of Coyote became part of her living world, re-figuring that world, adding to it and transforming its multiple relations. Reading *texts* about Coyote pulling tricks, getting into trouble, and teaching lessons thereby, and reading the *world* of the upcoming Christmas concert became strangely akin. The boundary between text and world gave way. Coyote became part of the text(ure) of the real world, not simply a figure within various written texts within that world.

In Sinead's story, Coyote is not just the wild animal with which we are all familiar. Neither is he just a figure in a wide open range of stories presented to children. Through Sinead's reading and writing, Coyote has somehow escaped the orbit of such literalism. He may be understood, through Sinead's own work, to be a living, breathing figure that haunts the living, breathing world—and not just "Sinead's world", as might go the individualistic, psychologistic formulation. As Native tales show, Coyote does not live inside people's heads. His tracks are real tracks, if only one knows how to "read" the world for them. He is, to re-iterate Hillman, "the daimon of . . . [the] place, . . . [revealing] what the place is good for, its special qualities and dangers":

> While laughing at Coyote with their friends and family, native children learn how to behave and how not to behave. This is why Coyote is a sacred fool. This clown gives us a way to know and accept ourselves. His foolish mistakes and his heroic imagination teach about balance and respect. This is the balance in ourselves and in our interrelationships with all life-forms.
>
> (Anges Vanderburg, Flathead Indian Elder)

In Sinead's story, it is not only Coyote who becomes de-literalized. Manuel, the classroom, the Christmas concert, parents and their concerns and embarrassments, school administration, interruptions, teachers—all of these become *readable* beyond their mundane, taken-for-granted, literal, surface features. They take on a spacious, generous, imaginative character. The "real" world of the Christmas concert is no longer a mere actuality. It opens up into the ephemeral temporality of "in-between"; into a world constituted by *possibilities of interpretation*, a world that could, therefore, be read other-wise than the protocols of everyday life might allow. Manuel, therefore, is not "really" a child with A.D.D. who can incidentally be read-as-Coyote; neither is he literally Coyote (as if we can overcome the strangulations of educational psychological discourse by simply appropriating another, more exotic discourse with the same literal-mindedness). *Both* Coyote and A.D.D. become possible ways to read a real child who exists in the cracks and edges between these (and many other) readings.

Reading in this edge sense opens up to a world of meaning, attachment, and consequence; a world that, if deeply understood, generously counterposes the world as taken-for-granted, putting that world, the "normal" world, into per-spective. It makes horizons of action, belief, and hope visible as not simply "the way things are", but as readings that *could have been read otherwise*. Instead of a world in which margin and centre are at odds, margin and centre might only make sense only in relation to each other. Coyote stories show how those living together in a classroom might get along well, with some sense of balance and respect, not *in spite of* figures like Coyote but *because of them*.

Teachers and the disciplines they teach, in an odd way, owe their lives to such figures. Such figures herald places of movement, of difference, of openness and transformation, or regeneration and the "original difficulty" (Caputo 1987, p. 1) entailed in having "life itself" (Smith 1999, 139) erupt right in the midst of multiple shared and contested worlds.

Reading in this way thus de-literalizes the professionalized understanding of real-world, upper-case events like Attention Deficit Disorder, Hyperactivity, Learning Disabilities, Developmental Delays, all of which had been attributed to Manuel. It opens up the possibility that these "disabilities" can be under-stood otherwise. Horizons of meaning are not fixed; educational categories and typifications that freeze children into codes and into terse objectifications, just might thaw and release under Coyote's address; boundaries might flutter and shift, holes and spaces open. And through those holes would pour children like Manuel, now with proper names and obligations (Caputo 1993), with bodies and hearts and minds that we might know other-wise.

Recognizing Ourselves in the Mess of the World

Interpretive readings set Coyote loose. Coyote, the trickster who loosens and violates boundaries, works in Sinead's story to blend and blur two "realms": the "real" world of the concert at which there was a "real" disruption and "fictional" tales of Coyote as a disruptive character. Through Coyote stories, Sinead makes the world in which she and Manuel live *readable* again beyond its surface actualities. The "real" world becomes an imaginative space readable in its possibilities, containing both the discourse of A.D.D. and the goofiness of Coyote. The "real world," interpretively understood, thus becomes a place in which we must decide what reading might be best here, now, in these cir-cumstances. Reading becomes a deeply ethical and pedagogical act. What way of proceeding would best evoke balance and respect in the circumstances faced by teachers and children in a classroom where "native life" is a man-dated curriculum responsibility? Because of Coyote, Sinead makes visible, just for a moment, all the parental concerns and pretence, all the rhetoric of school announcements and protocols, all the howls of children full of excite-ment. We can now "recognize ourselves in the mess of the world" (Hillman 1983, p. 49). Coyote stories are about us, about this real world and these real children.

Which is not necessarily to say that this news is good news for everyone. The pedagogical context in which such edgy readings are accomplished is crucial, for:

> this fluidity of boundaries between self and the world, ordinary existence and imaginative experience, consciousness and repression of consciousness, identity and loss of identity—makes the reading experience fraught with the potential for the kind of destabilizing that student readers may neither expect nor welcome, depending on where they might be in terms of feeling, power, and location, especially in a classroom.
>
> (Bogdan 1992, p. 192)

Sinead's reading of the Christmas concert could have exploded like a bomb in the middle of a classroom where protocols were never read, never challenged, never really understood or understandable as living decisions made in response to a living world. Sinead, herself, might have become problematic: the wilful girl-child who lacks respect for her elders and betters. Or her story could simply have disappeared, mis-read, beneath the weight of the everyday crush of events in a busy school. "That's nice, Sinead. Thank you for sharing your story with us", someone might have said as they plunked her into Author's Chair (Calkins 1986) and unleashed a barrage of profound illiteracies:

"How long did it take you to write?"

"Where did you get your ideas from?"

"I like the part with the howling. What part did *you* like the best?"

Sinead's story allows for the possibility of reading the howling of the Christmas concert as a lesson badly in need of learning. Reading and retelling Coyote stories helped Sinead, and can help anyone charged with Manuel's education, to "read" the stories of children like Manuel in ways that are more generous, more open, more forgiving than the flattening, psychologizing discourse of education generally allows. And she demanded from her teachers a response to her writing that was deeper and more difficult than the well-intended niceties of "tell me about your writing." As her teachers, we were *addressed*, we were directly *claimed* by her work. Through it, we were helped to "read" like children like Manuel not as deficient and in need of fixing, but, like Coyote, as bumping into the limits of the world, opening them again, making them newly visible, audible, readable, understandable.

But there is a deeper, more urgent claim at work here: by way of Coyote's lessons, Manuel, this real, difficult child, this wild thing whom others would not, could not allow in the world of their classroom, *became one of us*, that one, Coyote-like. As remembered in Sinead's story, Manuel becomes understandable in the sense of livable, bearable, here, with us. He became a child who once bore a tale of suspicion and isolation, and who now bears as well the possibility of a more generous tale of tolerance and necessity and relation and community. He came to have a place in the classroom uniquely his own, one without which the classroom would have been a very different environment, lacking the sharp-edged reminder of the protocols of the world we so comfortably assume. And other children in the classroom often protected Manuel when outsiders arrived with their clinical gazes and tightly gripped clipboards. They helped him "do normal" until the troubles passed. In this way, just as surely as Manuel became one of us through Coyote, this "us" *became different because of him.*

De-romanticizing Coyote

Of course, we cannot romanticize here. Coyote would be difficult to be around as often as he would be wonderful to be around. He is a playful trickster and a greedy, arrogant, self-centered fool who never, ever learns and who often falls out of trees at exactly the wrong time and ends up dying, rotting, and smelling up the place.

Reading Coyote stories as a reading of the world of the classroom does not simply dispel the negative characteristics of Manuel. He was not always and everywhere a joy and wonderful to be around. Sometimes his openings of boundaries and his violations of protocols are tolerable and revealing. Sometimes they are most decidedly not. The issue becomes not only pedagogical. It is an ecological and ethical one as well: how much disruption can a living community of relations *sustain*? What course of action is best in the circumstances we individually and collectively suffer? And how does Sinead's story help us address this question in better ways than we might otherwise have done? Her story does not necessarily help us tell which openings are tolerable and sustainable and which are not. It does remind us that there is a *difference*, and there can be a lesson of balance and respect to be learned through Coyote's ways.

The question about disruption can never be answered in advance or alone. What Coyote does, however, is teach us about the issues of balance and respect from which an answer might come, here, today, this time around, in this place and at this time with these children, about this bit of wisdom of the world. Coyote puts the difficult child (and the difficult work of pedagogy) back into perspective, back into "place", back with all his relations. The opening up of boundaries is thus both good news and bad news and sometimes both at once. And the point may be that we have to learn to take the good with the bad and tolerate disruption in the classroom if it can help us read our world more generously and help us treat children on the margins more generously as well: more like one of us, with more humour and forgiveness and protection. Again, the lesson of balance and respect. Coyote loose again.

Through interpretive readings, we can perhaps resist pathologizing the figures who disrupt our complacency. Through interpretive readings we might come, in however grudging a way, to honour those who live on the margins as essential to the life and vigour at the centre. We owe such figures a debt of gratitude for the lessons they might teach us. Such figures might teach us about the character of pedagogy as boundary work. The portals they open for us provide opportunities, images, and the will we need "to name the impossible space we inhabit" (Bogdan 1992, p. 218). Understanding, seeing from below and from the edges, we learn to converse with "the world as coding trickster" (Haraway quoted in Bogdan 1992, p. 218).

Embodied, irretrievably grounded in partial perspectives and located in "the tangibly real that makes claims on people's lives in the infinite playing out of the creative imagination" (p. 219). But we should not leave with unwarranted optimism, for Sinead's story also leaves us with a disturbing picture of what might become of Manuel. Our classroom opened a space for Manuel that was large enough to house his special ways in the world and Manuel himself helped make that opening possible and transformed us and the classroom and the work we pursued in the process. We refused either to cut him loose or to abandon him to psychological isolation and caricature. We refused to pin him down, for:

> the symbol which Trickster embodies is not a static one. It contains within itself the promise of differentiation, the promise of god and man. For this reason every generation occupies itself with interpreting Trickster anew. No generation understands him full, but no generation can do without him. And so he became and remained everything to every man—god, animal, human being, hero, buffoon, he who was before good and evil, denier, affirmer, destroyer, and creator. If we laugh at him, he grins at us. Whatever happens to him happens to us.
>
> (Radin, cited in Bright 1993, p. 183)

We might well ponder how best to deal with those who know beyond a shadow of a doubt that Coyote is but a fiction and that Manuel, undoubtedly, is just a child with A.D.D.

Coyote reminds: whatever happens to him happens to us.

6

The Transgressive Energy of Mythic Wives and Wilful Children

Old Stories for New Times

PATRICIA CLIFFORD AND SHARON FRIESEN

The Wilful Child

Once upon a time there was a child who was wilful, and would not do what her mother wished. For this reason God had no pleasure in her, and let her become ill, and no doctor could do her any good, and in a short time she lay on her deathbed. When she had been lowered into her grave, and the earth was spread over her, all at once her arm came out again, and stretched upwards, and when they had put it in and spread fresh earth over it, it was all to no purpose, for the arm always came out again. Then the mother herself was obliged to go to the grave, and strike the arm down with a rod, and when she had done that, it was drawn in, and then at last the child had rest beneath the ground.

(Grimm Brothers 1972, p. 534)

This is an old and terrible fairy story, that, if interpreted literally, should never be told (Evetts-Secker 1994). As a cautionary tale warning to children about the perils of disobedience, it is a brutal and terrifying narrative that is best left hidden within the pages of ancient books. Read symbolically in other ways, however, the tale invites us, as teachers, to think about much that is wrong with schools today—and to consider the potential within each of us to offer, through wilful transgressions, genuine hope for change.

Speaking as women, we are immediately on shaky ground when we mention transgression. Our mythic foremothers Lilith, Eve and Pandora tried transgression already. Read as cautionary tales, *their* stories have come to us through the ages as warnings: don't presume equality; don't pursue knowledge; don't disobey the master or displease God. Women who do not do as they are told, we have been instructed, are the source of all evil in the universe. And their stories, told from generation to generation, re-inflict the primal punishment of the initial sin upon each one of us, generation after generation. What we propose today is a new reading of those ancient tales of wilful women. Read literally, their cautionary purpose is oppressive, and read only literally, they deserve the same fate earned by so many forgotten, grisly Victorian stories. Opened to new readings of possibility woven within their folds, however, such stories (while still uncomfortable to contemplate) become disturbing in a completely different way. The energy of their single acts of rebellion transformed utterly the worlds in which these women lived, making those worlds, and not just the women's acts, readable in new and exciting ways.

Eccentric Children and Teachers

Let us situate that awful story about the wilful child in North American classrooms. Sent to school as very young children, both boys and girls learn very early that the Procrustean standards of "normalcy", "being good", and "doing school" create a very narrow band of acceptable thought, speech and action. Children are forced to learn very quickly how to discipline their bodies, how to color between the lines, how to print neatly, how to please their teachers by doing "their work" in a neat, orderly and timely fashion. Those who will not, or cannot comply with what schools and teachers demand are rapidly and effectively marginalized under the claim that early intervention is in the best interest of the child. They are scrutinized for symptoms of learning disabilities, behavioural disorders, developmental delays, experience deficits. The institution of the school, geared up and waiting for the first signs of abnormality, like not being able to read by Christmas of Grade 1, not talking properly in the first month of kindergarten, or not forming letters correctly right from the start, begins its work of culling the abnormal into "learning resource rooms" and burying their difference under a dead weight of pathology.

Children learn early on in school that they have to "be good" in order to survive. School robs far too many of them of the ability to feel, touch, and embrace the world with energy, imagination and ferocious appetite. Instead, school reduces children's experience to a round of activities, exercises, and programs that exist nowhere except in school. Being good in school means being quiet, obedient, orderly, passive. It means staying "on task" no matter how dull, meaningless or demeaning the task may be. Despite the rhetoric of education that claims an interest in the development of creativity, critical thinking and independent judgment, the daily experience of far too many children is that the genuine exercise of these faculties generally lands them in hot water.

It may well be that getting "good at school," especially for girls, is potentially toxic. When the obedience training takes, children in school are often indistinguishable from one another. They do the same worksheets in the same way in the same time frame as everyone else. They modulate their voices, discipline their bodies, perform their tasks carefully within the cramped boundary of "normal" that admits of very little deviance. It is as if, ushering students into a banquet hall of potential learning, educators hand them work book and activity sheet menus and say, "Here, eat this instead." (Kay 1995). As an ironic aside, in a technological age, Internet surfers headlong into the same dilemma. Told that the age of communication is upon us, that the Internet opens up the world of information at the click of a mouse, the intrepid adventurer on the Web is fed screen after screen after screen, not of text, not of real *stuff*, but of factoids and tables of contents. Devouring the hype that has grown up around electronic communication, people are in danger of starving on the *promise* of substance that so seldom actually materializes.

Unresisted, the story of the wilful child is a terrible one. Read as a metaphor of educational confinement, it begins to make a different kind of sense—particularly when we examine the mytho-poetic portrayal of the mother as the ultimate agent of subjugation and conformity. It is pedagogically worrisome that so much of children's experience in school is reduced to rote, meaningless activity. It is politically untenable to us that teachers, in the name of nurturing and caring, are cast into the role of mother. Primary teaching is almost universally regarded as the mastery of mothering: of zippers and caring and wiping noses and drying little tears. Rarely does someone champion the intellectual, spiritual and physical rigor that the job, thought of differently, demands. Early childhood teachers thus appear as institutional mothers—with all the attendant problems that accompany society's view of that calling.

Read within the context of "The Wilful Child", institutional mothering takes on a horrifying dimension that goes far beyond hugs and warmth and cookies at snack time. It is we, the mothers, who are called upon to smack little, resistant arms back into the grave. We, the mothers, are the vigilant ones, calling in psychologists, resource teachers, social workers, specialists of all stripes and hues the minute things go awry. It is we who pronounce judgment, who feed back to parents the first public assessment of their child: "is learning to cooperate"; "shares nicely at the Home Centre"; "is starting to take her turn properly"; "is beginning to sit still during group time"; "is learning to direct his energy in a more positive way". These assessments are often written in the careful code of "learning to", "beginning to", "starting to", recognizable in an instant to other teachers as a sign of struggle and trouble within the classroom; struggle and trouble that is often disguised from parents until it rears itself as irremediable, calling for a signature for special placement in a special class. Early childhood teachers are carefully trained both to spot and remediate troublesome abnormalities in a child's adjustment to school—and also how to cocoon those judgments in soft, modulated phrases that sound so *positive*, so attentive to the child's self-esteem and development.

However softened and euphemized, the blows to the eccentricities of the wilful child are sure and swift. The relentless, institutional job of normalizing falls to the mother-teacher whose professional competence is judged largely on the success of these efforts. Eccentric herself, refusing to normalize or subjugate little children in cheerfully repressive ways; refusing to hand out 30 pairs of scissors and 30 bottles of glue so that 60 little hands can glue identical woolly beards on 30 identical paper Santas by snack time, such a teacher can run into huge problems (Jardine, Graham, LaGrange & Kisling-Saunders 2006). For the institution has then to normalize *her*, bring *her* into line; cool her down; call in the professionals to adjudicate her failures of practice, her failures to conform; document her institutional failings and her peculiarity; transfer her out.

What the institution has done to wilful, eccentric children it must do first to its wilful, eccentric teachers. What we are taught to revile in children's inability to be institutionally normal we first learn to revile in ourselves. What we strive to modulate, dampen, tame and obliterate in children's energy, we first modulate, dampen, tame and obliterate in ourselves. And in that sense, our very success becomes our spiritual, emotional and intellectual undoing. It is the story of Lilith and the story of Eve, the story of Pandora. To win at the game of "ordinary", of subservience, obedience and silence is to lose the very best of ourselves—to lose passion, conviction, bloody-mindedness, curiosity, humour, intensity and joy. It is, as the old tales tell us, to become the spawn of demons and the mother of evil.

For the two of us, the story of the wilful child is partly a story of horror and repression—a story we lived in painful ways in the years we taught young children in eccentric and unusual ways. But it is more than that. It is also a story that contains the seeds of resistance, a story that points to the courageous possibility that any one of us—even the smallest and most nameless—can stick our arms out of the institutional grave over and over again, steeling our minds and bodies against the blows that inevitably follow yet another deliberate transgression. There are always ways to resist. We believe that one of the ways we can learn to resist is to read again, and differently, the stories of Lilith, Eve and Pandora—our foremothers in crime.

The Wilful Wives of Adam

In rabbinic literature, Lilith is sometimes depicted as the mother of Adam's demonic offspring following his separation from Eve and sometimes as his first wife, a wilful woman who assumed her equality with him, who "stood her ground, amazed/By the idea of differences" (Green 1991, p. 1). Undaunted like the traditional Eve whose eyes were downcast in the presence of her difference from Adam, Lilith had the audacity to presume, on her own behalf, that it meant something to be formed in the reflection of God.

As it turns out, Adam had some thoughts on the matter as well. To know the will of God did not mean, for him, taking joy in the dappled multiplicity of life; it did not mean celebrating difference and revelling in chaotic wonder and possibility. For Adam, to know God and to act in accordance with the will of God meant assuming the right of domination over a creature "as constrained and resentful/As he was" (Green 1991, p. 1). And God encouraged him to think this way, this version story goes. God *gave* him Eve to rule: a subservient woman whose existence on the planet became, in this story, a source of nagging irritation—a right royal pain in the ass.

And as for Lilith—her fate was to be cast out in disgrace. Her "disgrace thus defined/Good and evil" (p. 1) for all time, and she, herself, was condemned to roam, hungry, enraged and dangerous, on the margins of others' lives. Warnings were issued, signs posted, amulets crafted: beware this wilful, angry woman. She will ruin your children, destroy the good order of your constrained and resentful lives.

So what is to be made of this mythic oddity—this woman whose story is hardly known? What is to be made of our first mother, enchanted by difference and charmed by the power of inhabiting the spaces that difference opens? What is to be made of the Lilith by those whose simple, primal sin is delight? Well, we're not quite sure—for we, ourselves, have only recently stumbled on Lilith's story. We have learned that there was a cult of Lilith that existed until the 7th century A.D., and we puzzle over the way her story, her presumption of equality and her courage to stand ground have disappeared from the world. We grew up knowing about Eve and how *she* screwed up. We cut our mythic teeth on Pandora and her ditzy inability to follow even the simplest command, "Don't open the box, dummy." But Lilith was a stranger, and we have only begun to explore the contours of her expectations and her courage.

So what we offer here is just a beginning, just a feathery teasing out of some of the connections we sense between Lilith and the story of the wilful child with which we began. As teachers, the two of us are enchanted by the differences we see in children. We are intrigued by the pedagogical possibilities of creating spaces in which children will take up ideas, projects, issues and enthusiasms in ways we could never have imagined. We are committed to finding ways to organize our classroom so that the unexpected is the welcomest guest of all. We teach and write out of a conviction that the concept of childhood as it is currently constructed in both traditional and progressive theorizing and practice is repressive, driven by images of deficit and insufficiency that render much of the experience and the possibility of children institutionally invisible. We work the space of difference. And we stand our ground over and over again in the face of power politics that demand that we constrain, restrain, confine and pathologize difference.

Maxine Greene (1978, 1988) speaks of the malefic generosity of education: the "killing" that is done "for the child's own good". For too long, teachers have been like Adam, knowing the power of God through our own power to subdue creatures given to us to control. And for too long, we have been like Eve, "eyes downcast", embarrassed by the generative power of our difference, waiting to be shown and told what to do next.

But Lilith was right and her delight and simple insistence on the generative power of difference inspires us and gives us hope. Not that her story guarantees that life lived as Lilith will be safe or easy. It is not. Lilith teachers, thrusting unwelcome arms out of graves of conformity over and over and over again, find themselves often "on the outs" with the institution. Superiors may well try to beat them back into submission; colleagues may well fashion amulets to ward off the power of their presence. We know from hard experience that the Lilith in us is often enraged, ravenous and dangerous. We speak out, demand change, stir the pot, and keep on keeping on—calling from the margins when we must, but refusing, ever, to abandon the centre. For the power of Lilith is simple: it is the power of delight, passion, engagement, enthusiasm, wonder and tenacity. It is the power of equality, of voice, of standing firm and true in a world in which you claim the symmetry of your own creation. Lilith knows that the reflection of God is incomplete without her—however much Adam conspires with his creator to deny that simple fact. Somehow, and in ways that we have only begun to apprehend, we are inspired by the sheer audacity of her reminding the two of them that she, Lilith, is a force to be reckoned with.

Eve

But what of Eve in all of this? In the version of Eve's story we just told, and in versions that have come to all of us through the generations, Eve is a pathetic creature. Unable to resist the obvious temptation of Satan, Eve turns her back on God and implicates Adam—history's first unindicted co-conspirator—in a horrendous fall from grace that has condemned all human beings to suffering. Women are told the cautionary story of Eve in a particular, careful way: look what happens to you if you can discipline neither desire nor thought. And look what happens to you and all your children when you displease God. Disobedience, the primal sin, is the sin of woman.

Is it possible to understand Eve differently, to see something else in her simple act of transgression? We think so—and, once again, we find ourselves energized by new understandings of Eve's deal with the devil. What happens, we wonder, when women claim that first bite as a deliberate, mindful act of rebellion? What happens when we understand that Eve, ushered into the presence of knowledge—the banquet hall of learning—refuses to remain content to nibble politely at the corner of the menu and insists, instead, in taking a huge bite of the real thing? And what happens when Eve dares Adam to cut loose, too?

We think that such a reading changes everything. Adam cast Lilith aside for insisting on her own equality and difference. He married again, hoping the second time to find a creature who would not only start out, but who would also remain, with downcast eyes, obedient, maybe even playful in her ignorance and helplessness. Adam expected, in his second wife, a meek and compliant girl—one who knew and would stay within the confines of her place. He certainly did not expect a full-grown woman who would insist on knowing *everything*, and who would willingly share her desire to know with him.

What happens when we understand, as teachers, that in the Garden of Eden the compliant never eat?

Here is what happens, we think. First of all, as women and as teachers we are released from the mythic shackles that a repressive reading of the story of Eve impose. We come to understand the power of seeing, in Eve's transgression, a strong and deliberate choice. Life does not have to come to us as given, as inevitable, as predestined. Choices are possible. Simple, deliberate choices that change everything in an instant. For teachers sickened by the marginalization and pathologizing of children who do not or cannot conform, choices to live differently *are* within our grasp. Listening to voices other than the ones that control access to the garden, we *can* find new ways of seeing, new ways of being. However strong the institutional pulls to make us into malefic mothers, we can find within ourselves the courage and the means to resist.

And our resistance is crucial. First of all, it makes meaningful action possible for those of us who, like Eve, cannot accept the status quo. However comfortable it might be to inhabit orderly, idyllic classrooms in which we do things the way everyone else does them; in which we make no waves or ask no rude questions; in which all the lovely pictures line up nicely on all the lovely walls and all the lovely children line up nicely in all the polished hallways, we can resist. We can say no. We can also say Yes! Yes, there are other ways to think about our work. Yes, there are more generous ways of understanding why some children do not fit in easily. Yes, we can learn about ourselves and about our profession by attending carefully, thoughtfully, imaginatively to the lessons offered by children who do not color between the lines. Eve shows us how we can free ourselves. As we thrust our hands out of the graves of conformity, there is something out there beside the rod that would strike us down. There is also the fruit of knowledge. The knowledge of what the next right step into the unknown might be. The knowledge of pedagogical possibility. The knowledge of what is morally right to do for ourselves and for others.

For Eve did not act alone, however much partaking of the apple was *her* act, claimed by her. As the story goes, Eve took Adam and the rest of us down with her. She, herself, was conned by the serpent and she turned around and seduced Adam to follow her, against his better judgment. That, as we say, is one way the story goes. But that is not the only possible reading of Eve's transgression. Consider this possibility. In her defiance, Eve did not condemn anybody. Even though she and her daughters had to pay dearly for the freedom she bought, we think she rescued Adam and all of her children from the lives of conformity and order to which Adam might otherwise have condemned us all (Evetts-Secker 1994). What she took upon herself in both act and consequence she offered to others. "Follow me," she said. "I cannot promise that I will make your life easier, but I can certainly promise that it will be adventurous, dangerous, thrilling and wild. Your life is in your hands."

Before Eve, there was no choice in any meaningful sense of the word. She and Adam could play with anything else in the Garden—anything except the one thing that really mattered. Like children, they could color pre-drawn pictures, paste beards on fabricated Santas, chant the words to songs already measured out by someone else. They would have remained such children—sexless, docile, obedient, normal, never overstepping bounds laid out in advance; never shoving or pushing or calling out in big voices; never laughing too loud or too long; never questioning or wondering or imagining how the world might be otherwise than they found it.

In the Garden, as we say, the compliant never eat. Eve broke that anorexic chain, not only for herself but also for the generations of unknown children who followed her. Without Eve, the Garden would have remained a prison. Comfortable, yes. Pleasant, yes. Available to us all without toil or effort, certainly. But a prison, nonetheless. The Garden of Eden was like a perpetual kindergarten in which humankind could play and play all day long. Had we remained in Paradise we might have suffered the same fate as Peter Pan: we would never have had to grow up. Eve would have remained, perhaps, our perpetual Wendy-mother: sweet, warm, kind and nurturing. A good, Wendy kindergarten teacher. And the rest of us would have been her cheery, Lost Boys.

Instead, Eve's transgression allowed all of us to grow up. And in consequence, we have had to pay for that growth, generation after generation. So—is that the worst that could have happened to us, we wonder? However painful the consequences, Eve opened up possibilities. She teaches us that we can create both ourselves and the world quite differently. And she shows us what real power means. Born into a universe of givens, Eve found the one true act that would crack everything open and allow us to conceive and generate anything we could imagine.

Pandora's Tricks

In traditional readings of the stories of Eve and Pandora, all evil and suffering in the world derive from these two impulsive women. God, the story goes, gave us Paradise for our use, and we lost it. Prometheus, the kind benefactor, parceled up all the spites that might plague humankind into one jar to keep us safe. Pandora lifted the lid and turned it all loose in the world. Tempted beyond their strength to endure, we are told, these beautiful, mischievous, foolish and idle women condemned our race to the vicissitudes of old age, disease, pain, labour, war, insanity, vice and (Hesiod tells us) passion.

That is how our mothers come to us: as evil, foolish wantons who robbed us all of immortality. How not, then, to feel only scorn and anger for their daughters through whom successive generations of pestilence are born into the world? Why not, indeed, beat the arm of the wilful, disobedient daughter into the ground before she causes even more damage and destruction?

As we said when we began, if that is the way these stories continue to be told, we wish that they would simply disappear from the landscape. They are hopeless stories that justify the scorn and violence wrecked upon women generation after generation. They justify a blueprint for pedagogical repression and conformity that kills the spirit of eccentric children and teachers in the name of comfort, stability and order. They are vengeful and nasty, and we would wish such stories dead.

Read differently, however, the stories of Eve and Pandora offer exciting hope. They offer a chance both to heal old and horrid wounds and also the opportunity to look forward to new ways of thinking about what so many lament as the problems of educational practice: the learning disabled, the poor, the unruly, the severely gifted—all those eccentric children whose arms and legs stick out from the confines of the Procrustean bed of schooling. All those whose difference we pathologize and then attempt to "normalize" in the name of learning.

We see in the transgressions of Eve and Pandora a wonderful audacity that charms and energizes us. Led by their boldness, we propose to open up what Greene (1988, p. 128) calls "places for speculative audacity" that

> draw the mind to what lies beyond the accustomed boundaries and often to what is not yet. They do so as persons become more and more aware of the unanswered questions, the unexplored corners, the nameless faces behind the forgotten windows. These are the obstacles to be transcended if understanding is to be gained. And it is in the transcending, as we have seen, that freedom is often achieved.

Understood as audacious rather than foolish, Pandora has lessons to teach. In what, one might well ask, does this audaciousness consist? How is it possible to see Pandora (or Eve) as the people who secured our freedom?

Consider this: Pandora, conceived in Zeus' spiteful imagination as revenge for Prometheus's theft of fire, is intimately tied first and foremost to issues of knowledge. Zeus cared about the theft of fire because it was the theft, for humankind, of the most god-like power of all: knowledge. Having had the best of him stolen away, Zeus musters the other, lesser attributes of the immortals. "Give this creature your greatest glories," he orders the lesser gods. And so Pandora is given it all: beauty, music, everything. And from Hermes, she got a most curious and interesting gift. Hermes, the tricky messenger of the gods and inspiration of hermeneutics, gave Pandora voice: the power to speak her mind and heart. History is silent about Athena's gift to Pandora. But if each of the gods gave the gift most closely associated with them, then, we wonder, did Athena give Pandora a mind? If she did, whatever would be the use of giving someone a faculty if they could never exercise it?

In our schools do we perform the Zeus trick, the god trick (Donna Haraway, as cited in Bogdan 1992, p. 218)? Do teachers do to children what the gods did to Pandora? Do children with bright active minds enter the institution only to find themselves, given both voice and mind, forbidden to use either? When asked to name the sides of various geometric figures, children are encouraged to chant: "Triangles have three sides, squares have four sides" and so on. When asked, "How many sides does a circle have" children who answer "Millions and millions" are too often silenced. "Wrong," their zealous if uninformed teachers respond. "We all know that a circle has only one side, don't we?"

Whether we are stomping the life out of children with authoritarian rigidity or smothering it in gooey praise, we chill the life from the spirit and kill the soul of all but the most bloody minded, like the child in this poem:

> My auntie gives me a colouring book and crayons.
> I begin to colour.
> After a while she looks over to see what I have done
> and says
> you've gone over the lines
> that's what you've done.
> What do you think they're there for, ay?
> Some kind of statement is it?
> Going to be a rebel are we?
> I begin to cry.
> My uncle gives me a hanky and some blank paper
> do your own designs he says
> I begin to colour.
> When I have done he looks over and tells me they are
> all very
> good.
> He is lying,
> only some of them are.
>
> (Evetts-Secker 1994, p. 15)

Schools co-opt terms like critical thinking, creative thinking and independence without offering many genuine opportunities for students to exercise any of those faculties. It is the promise of the banquet and the reality of the menu. It is pedagogical bad faith. It is the god trick. After often it works.

But not always. In the face of her uncle's saccharine dismissal, the child holds her own counsel. She knows her mind. She knows he is lying. And she knows how to examine her works critically. She knows the difference. She will not be conned.

We see a similar bloody-mindedness in Pandora. Given faculties of judgment, she exercised them. Opening the jar was a mindful deliberate act of rebellion. Told to ask no questions, seek no answers, behave herself, be a good girl, color softly within the bold lines that others had photocopied for her, Pandora refused. She knew where the action was. It was shut inside that jar and she would not be denied. Life as she was living it was deadly boring. What did she have to look forward to: doing her nails, playing with Epimetheus, combing her hair, looking pretty for that foolish young man who could not see beyond the end of his own nose? What good is a mind if you can never use it? This is the question that the Pandora story insists we ask.

But what of the suffering? What can be made of the fact that Pandora's choice cost so much? Part of the answer lies in Prometheus's attempt to cushion human beings from the fullness of life. However well motivated Prometheus's attempts to bottle up all suffering, pain and sorrow, he was wrong. For life to fashion itself, it needs everything: gladness, joy, beauty, pain, suffering, war and sorrow.

Prometheus attempted to fashion his gift to humankind from all the beauty of the world: the clouds as round as pearls, light shimmering across an expanse of water, dew drops on grass blades (Gregory 1992). Having given knowledge with one hand, he tried to deny it with the other. Knowing what he himself would suffer for his transgression, he tried to protect humankind from the same fate. Prometheus was a kind and generous benefactor. He did what he could to protect us—but especially Prometheus would have known that the fabric would not hold. Prometheus, if no other, would have known with clear and absolute certainty that Pandora would open the jar. The hope that is there is the hope of our transgression and the courage to live out the consequences.

If teachers erect boundaries around learning that are rigid and unyielding they attempt another god trick. If we curtail children's curiosity, questions, and freedom of inquiry in the authoritarian belief that such freedom will lead to disaster, we are, like Zeus, jealous and stingy with our knowledge. Or if we wrap knowledge up in soft cocoons in the mistaken belief that children cannot handle big questions, abstract thought, passionate engagement, we are like Prometheus.

Either way, it makes little genuine difference. Both god tricks deny the power of children's minds and the power of their difference. Whether the motive is punitive or protective, freedom is denied. Genuine engagement with the world becomes impossible.

The pedagogical act that addresses the god trick is the transgression of Pandora. It is the act that creates spaces in which freedom, imagination, creativity, and possibility are created. It is our hope. Again we quote from Maxine Greene (1988, p. 129). Transgressive acts, like art:

> have the capacity, when authentically attended to, to enable persons to hear and to see what they would not ordinarily hear and see, to offer visions of consonance and dissonance that are unfamiliar and indeed abnormal, to disclose the incomplete profiles of the world. As importantly, in this context, they have the power to defamiliarize experience: to begin with the overly familiar and transfigure it into something different enough to make those who are awakened hear and see.

Should we be surprised that this is so? Not when we consider that Pandora, whose name means "all giving", was delivered to the world by Hermes.

And therein lies another story.

7

Landscapes of Loss
On the Original Difficulties of Reading

PATRICIA CLIFFORD AND SHARON FRIESEN

Fifty copies of our newly purchased novel, *I Heard the Owl Call My Name* (Craven 1973), sat in a box under the table beside our desk. It was an odd choice for a novel study. The book is nearly thirty years old. Written by a white woman, it is the story of a young priest's journey into a native village in a remote, coastal village of British Columbia. It is about dying: a dying community, a dying way of life, and a central character who has no more than two years of active life left. Other than the dying, nothing much actually happens. Not exactly the fare that comes to mind for Grade Eights in a large, urban, high-needs junior high—but a book that we had nonetheless chosen with care for these students, and whose use in this setting we wanted to make an explicit part of our own action research. We let the books sit under the table for a couple of weeks, watching out of the corners of our eyes as the kids pushed at the edges of the box with their feet.

"We're not going to read that book!" several kids moaned as they walked past.

"Oh, have you read it before?" we asked, fakely innocent.

"Well, no, but like, it's a book. Why do we have to do a book?"

To the students, this unknown text was suspect by the mere fact of its being a book purchased, in bulk, by teachers. Our students seemed quite certain of what they were in for, and just as certain that they would hate it, and detest everything we had planned to do with it. Over coffee, we talked about Pat's years as a senior high school English teacher, and her students' perennial frustration with doing what one of them called "that shit" with books: those predictable teacher questions about plot, theme, setting and character; about how little that shit actually had to do with the real reasons anybody reads, anyway; about the stupefying round of worksheets and teacher questions that seem to mark so many students' experience of reading. We talked, too, about what had happened in Grade Seven when we had asked this same group of students to start Response Journals when we launched into that year's novel study: "Response Journals? No way. We hate Response Journals. Why do teachers always make us do those Response Journal things?" While our students' complaints were less scatological than those of their senior high school fellows, the grumbling was just as heartfelt, and we were taken by surprise. For our students, reading had become a school task, defined and regulated by school activities. It was what teachers expected, not what you, yourself, would choose to do. And it was so slow, they told us. Couldn't we just watch the video instead?

We were on dangerous ground. In opening conversations with them about school reading, which was part of our own research interest, we invoked some powerful old ghosts. It would have been snappier and trendier to have set their minds at ease with a menu of fun activities designed to deflect their attention from the difficulties of intense engagement with the text: "We'll watch the movie, we'll make posters and carve masks and have a potlatch and write song lyrics. Everyone can read a different book and dress up and do television interviews. You'll see, you'll love it."

But that's not at all what we had in mind. What we wanted to do was far more difficult: we wanted to exorcise those ghosts by moving farther into the very territory that students wanted so desperately to abandon. We wanted to take up residence together in a reading landscape whose very topography is formed by the inherent, original difficulty, not only of particular books like this one, but also of the whole business of reading itself. We were all going to read the book. Together. Out loud. Twice. We were going to work with Dennis's idea of a commonplace text, "the cumulative and collective intertextual relations among readers, other texts, other experiences, and the present context of reading" (Sumara 1995a, 107).

As teacher-researchers, we had already pushed our own understanding of reader response in the direction of what we were now learning to call "focal practices" (Sumara 1995b) designed to take students beyond the teacher questions, and even beyond the more seemingly-generous Response Journal into more hermeneutic, interpretive spaces where knowledge and understanding are created through the vibrant life of a community of relations (Palmer 1993). We wanted to learn more about helping students understand that through common engagement with this book, here and in this place, we would come to know ourselves and one another differently. We wanted them to understand that reading together matters. We wanted them to see that their response to text was not some kind of mopping up activity (Richardson, as cited in Sumara 1996, 46) orchestrated by teachers to test whether they had somehow "got" the book. We wanted to show them that genuine understanding is always self understanding, a matter of becoming worked out in relation to particular situations, particular places, in community with others.

As we began our work, that is, we thought mainly about the ways in which this novel and our approach to it would broaden and deepen our students' experience. That was the direction in which we cast our gaze, and in important ways that we are still in the process of trying to understand, we were successful. But that initial attention to the significance of focal practices for students is not the subject of this present paper. What we want to talk about here is what happened, not so much to the students, but to us as we came to know that what we wanted our students to understand about reading this book was just as true about our own emerging understanding of teaching and research. We came to learn that our own research and writing were not mopping up activities added on to the end of a busy day. They were integral parts of the experience of reading *I Heard the Owl Call My Name*. A hermeneutic involvement with this text, these students, and our own situation as their teachers touched the students, certainly. More surprising to us, however, was how it touched the two of us as teachers and as researchers in fundamental ways.

Lost in a Book

Right from the opening pages of the novel, there were rich moments in which many students found themselves, almost beyond their "wanting and doing" (Gadamer 1989, p. xxvii) drawn into the dilemmas, the images, the world of this novel and of their own experience. But as we proceeded, we felt as well a strong sense of resistance, of unhappiness and complaint: "What a dumb book. When's something going to happen? Like, nothing's happening in this book. We hate it. We're lost."

Lost. That was it, exactly: in the unfamiliar world of this novel, our students were losing their way, as they so often lost their way at the start of new books. Something in the word "lost" called to us. There was something bountiful in the particular way they pleaded with us to abandon the book and return to familiar ground, something that led us to wonder whether getting lost was less a problem that we needed to solve with this book than an inherent part of the reading experience itself. And it was this ineffable something that led us into unexpected places in our own research. Beginning by focusing on what happens when teachers open up an interpretive space, we had stumbled onto fundamental aspects of the reading experience itself. While we continued to explore the themes and characters of the novel, we also began to talk with our students about how reading feels.

For us, as experienced readers, there was only charm in the phrase "getting lost in a book". We loved that feeling of abandoning the everyday reality of our lives, forgetting "about the doorbell, the shopping that needs to be done, the house that lies in a clutter" (Hood 1996). We actively sought out what Birkerts calls the reading state, "a gradual immersion . . . in which we hand over our groundedness in the here and now in order to take up our new groundedness in the elsewhere of the book" (Birkerts 1994, p. 81), a state in which time is foreshortened as if "the whole of my life—past as well as unknown future—were somehow available to me . . . as an object of contemplation" (Birkerts 1994, p. 84).

But that is not how the kids felt. They seemed more like Hansel and Gretel, terrified in the underbrush, avoiding confrontation with the gingerbread house and the witch by refusing to move. They were like literary agoraphobics, para-lyzed by fear as they ventured out beyond the confines of familiar walls of experience. Their trepidation fascinated us, but so did their courage. In what at other times we might have heard as a contrary refusal to engage with the text— "We're lost and we hate it"—we began to hear a cry for direction. We took up their complaints as a serious topic. Could it be, we asked them, that as readers we are like Mark, the central character? Would it be helpful to think of our-selves, like Mark, thrust into a place we know nothing about, surrounded by strangers who make demands of us that we barely understand? Are we all like Mark, unable at first even to tell the difference between one villager and another, yet forced by chance to make sense of them, anyway? Is that what reading this book is like? We discussed the only other white person in the village, a teacher "serving time" for two years, and hating every minute of it. Was there any difference, we wondered, between Mark's dilemma, which seemed to be to find a way into the life of a village he understood so little, and the dilemma of the teacher, which was clearly to get out as soon as he could? Might those two characters tell us something about different kinds of readers?

As experienced readers, we knew and delighted in the necessary sense of loss that accompanies the opening of any new book. We read for exactly the kind of experience our students were finding so difficult to endure: the vertiginous sense of alienation and self-loss that permits the boundaries of the familiar to "waver and tremble" (Caputo 1987, p. 7) as we enter into other worlds. We knew, because we had done it so many times before, that the adventure of read-ing books in this way always holds, ironically, a promise of self-discovery. Let-ting go of the hard-edged protocols of the normal, of the taken-for-granted, of the ordinary aspects of everyday life, we had learned, through imaginative engagement as readers, the hermeneutic lesson that the world is interpretable; that things can be other than they seem; and that "when we read we not only transplant ourselves to the place of the text, but we modify our natural angle of regard upon all things; we reposition the self in order to see differently" (Birkerts 1994, p. 80).

As experienced readers, we knew that the other-wise space of imaginative possibility was a space in-between: in between the familiar and the strange; in between self and other; in between the text of the story and the texts of our lives. We knew that one of the addictive delights of reading is its power to invite us, "without expectation into one of those moments that is suspended between time and space and lingers in the mind" (Craven 1973, p. 58). As teachers, we knew as well that letting go and learning how to live in between can be very scary, indeed, for a change in the natural angle of regard holds always the terrifying, exhilarating possibility that everything will be different because we have read.

As teachers, then, we knew that part of our task had to be to help students give themselves over to the world of the text. We did not want to abandon those

scary, in between places by reducing our explorations of the story to the grotesque certainties of worksheet questions that treat the landscape of text as
inalterably given: "Is . . . [the author] using metaphors or similes? Define each
term. Why did . . . [the author] choose to use metaphors instead of similes, or
similes instead of metaphors?" (Postman 1995, p. 173). Neither did we want to
substitute the seemingly open-ended and seemingly more generous version of
stock questions that appear in as Reader Response posters and Journal
prompts: "I think . . ., I wonder . . ., I feel. . . ." The banality of such questions
seemed to us to be an abandonment of another kind: not to the intractability of
text-as-given, but to the "chill structures of autonomy" (Greene 1988, p. 478)
that erect "shells of privatism" around the experience of reading, reducing it to
a private, interior interaction between the solitary reader and the personally
constructed text.

We wanted questions that were more true to that in-between space: questions that required conversation; questions that demanded both a careful attention to the text, an exploration of self, and attentive listening to the voices of
others. We wanted our students to begin to see light filtering through trees—
both the trees on their own street, and in the park across the way—as well as
trees on the page "that take on outline and presence" (Birkerts 1994, p. 81) as
they read. We wanted students to experience the ways in which small details
and large events could speak directly and powerfully to them, not as what
they were, Grade Eight students in our classroom, but as who they were:
diverse, unique individuals bound together in a web of relationships created
through the work that we did with one another. And so, in all our talk and
writing about the novel, we asked them to pay attention to "good bits": lines,
images and phrases that called out to them, for whatever reason. In conversation and in our response to their writing, we helped them learn how to
explore those good bits, connecting them with feelings and ideas, asking
questions, drawing parallels between passages in the novel and issues in the
world around them; listening for echoes of other books they had read; arguing with the text and with one another whenever they took issue with the
point of view of one of the characters, of one of their fellows, or of the
author herself.

And we let the good bits from one day's conversation propel the next day's
work so that their talk made a difference. It worked. We found increasing numbers of our students coming to care about what happened to Mark and the
villagers, and more and more of them willing to enjoy the time it was taking to
read to the end of the book. We delighted in their delight in compelling
passages, and we enjoyed our explorations with them.

For many students, the reading space opened up a more reflective, inwardly
directed part of themselves. But what we want to pay attention to here is that
we found the same thing happening to us. Parts of the book began to open
unresolved dilemmas in our own lives that we had not expected to see

addressed in a schoolbook. And that opening helped us understand our own action research as a quality not only of teaching, but also of living.

Even as we write that we had not expected to see parts of our own lives as teachers addressed in this novel, we know that is not quite what we mean. In learning, over the years we have taught together, to pay attention to our choice of books, we have learned that the best choices are those that contain, usually without our knowing it, lessons that we, ourselves, need to learn. Again and again, we have found ourselves, with one book or another, stopping dead in our tracks. "Oh my God," we would say, "is that what this is all about?" And we would talk and talk about what this new book told us about our lives as teachers. We would read parts of the stories over and over again to one another. And on bad days, long after all the children and all our colleagues had gone home, we would sometimes cry.

Being touched in particular and powerful ways by stories and by students' questions that created connections and touched parts of our lives that they could not know, we had experienced many times before the generosity of those in-between spaces: in-between us and the story, in-between the story and our engagement with our students. And here we were, once again, moving into spaces where we, as teachers, were most strongly addressed (Gadamer 1989, 299) by the text. Teaching the novel, we were once again claimed by the work we were doing. Writing about that teaching, the book came alive for us. It spoke directly to us and to our engagement with the classroom, the school, the community in which we had come to live: the hardest school in the city, the poorest community, the most difficult and chaotic of children.

Until we began our work in this junior high, we had always worked in middle-class schools. As we read about the central character, Mark, being sent to Kingcome, to the hardest parish in the diocese to learn what he needed to know in the time that remained to him, we realized that, like Mark, we had come to a difficult place, to one of those schools that people often try harder to get out of than to move into.

So Short a Time to Learn So Much . . .

In *I Heard the Owl Call My Name*, characters wait. From the beginning we puzzled over passages like this on page 37: "It was always the same. The sad eyes. The cautious waiting. But for what? How must he prove himself? What was it they wished to know of him? And what did he know of himself . . .?" From the beginning, we tried to get our students to talk about all this waiting. They were not interested. What puzzled us, made us highlight our own copies, and raised questions for us, did not speak at all to them. For them, waiting was not an issue.

But it was for both of us. Here we were, in our difficult parish, teaching the same group of students with whom we had begun the year before. What was there in our situation that made waiting such a puzzle? As we talked about the story with the students, with colleagues, and between ourselves, we recalled how we had arrived, committed, eager to make a difference in a school most defined in the public mind by its needs. Two years have gone by, and we are only now able to face squarely the dark side of the missionary-like zeal that had fuelled some of our early months in the school: our determination to give the best of what we had to offer, our hopes that we could make a difference with these students, make their lives richer, our good intentions to involve them with us and with each other in compelling work.

And when, by October of the first year we had made almost no headway at all, we were devastated. Going head-to-head with angry, rebellious teenagers who refused to follow our plans for them, we learned the awful power of Mark's observation about the Kwakiutl: our students had no word for thank you in their language. Even if we left the classroom, broken, they would not thank us for our coming. Teachers come, teachers go, they had learned, and there was no reason to think that we would be any different from any other. We offered story after story, problem after engaging problem, and they refused all of it. They fought with us and with each other, turning whole days upside down with an awful, defiant energy. "Where on earth are we?" we asked ourselves again and again, "and why the hell do we think we belong here?"

In retrospect, we think we were like Mark, wondering what we could possibly do to prove ourselves. It was such a difficult, difficult time. We desperately wanted to break through the hard shell of rebellious indifference that met us day after day. We wanted to re-create what we had had before, a classroom community sustained by work that was rich enough to encompass all. We had no way of knowing then what students have only decided to tell us now, a year and a half later: they had no intention at all of being saved by us or by anybody else. Only after all this time will they talk to us about their previous school experiences. Only now will they tell us their stories, the myths that were the village of their experience. When we breezed into their lives, sitting them at tables, reading stories out loud, coaxing conversations and exploratory writing and problem-solving, they were sure it would never last, and neither would we. They knew they could wreck every single thing because they had done it before. In elementary school they had sat at tables for a couple of days once, they now tell us. Their teacher had been so horrified at how they behaved when they were let out of straight rows that he quickly moved all the desks right back again. They had already plotted successfully how to do teachers in. We remembered their boastful warnings from the year before: this teacher had had a heart attack, that one had had a nervous breakdown. "We caused it, you know," and they looked us straight in the eye.

As we sat with the novel and with these students well into our second year together, we read words like these in a way made possible by the trials we had all endured together:

You'll see a look that is in the eyes of all of them, and it will be your job to figure out what it means, and what you are going to do about it. And . . . [they] will watch you—they will all watch you—and in . . . [their] own time . . . [they] will accept or reject you.

(Craven 1973, p. 11)

As we look back to those first difficult months, we see written here the truth of our experience with these students: it was in their hands to accept or reject us. They would do it on their own terms, and we could not know in advance, could not even know in the present moment of any action, any decision, whether we were making ourselves more or less acceptable to them. We dug in our heels in the face of their intractability. We refused to bring in desks and straight rows. We refused to run off worksheets or dictate pages of notes to keep them busy and quiet. We insisted, day after day, of meeting as a full group to talk. We tossed them out of class for fighting, would not let them swear or scream. And we insisted that they do good work, turning back half-hearted and slap-dash attempts and insisting, instead, that they take their time, rewrite, plan. We would sit with first one and then another, revising, talking, taking their reading and writing seriously. Met with fierce adolescent stubbornness, we gave as good as we got most days. It was as we remember it now, an ugly battle of wills, waged without the least assurance that we were even doing the right thing fighting fire with fire and insisting on having our own way in creating a work space dedicated to thought and genuine exploration.

And yet there was more to it than just stubbornness, for even in the early, difficult days we knew that what we had been told about these kids was somehow very wrong.

"They're experience deficit," some would say, meaning that the kids knew little of middle-class virtue.

"They haven't got any work ethic," others would insist. "Don't expect any homework out of them. They'll never do it."

"Fully a third of them are functionally illiterate. They need remedial work, basic skills to build a foundation."

"Aw, fuck the curriculum when you work with these guys. They can't learn anything until you civilize them."

Even then, we knew that all of this was wrong, for through all the struggles we also saw glimmers of something different, something breathtaking breaking through in odd moments and small, precious ways. We knew, that is, what Mark himself had learned when he wrote to the Bishop:

"I have learned little of the Indians as yet. I know only what they are not. They are none of the things one has been led to believe. They are not simple, or emotional, they are not primitive." The Bishop wrote back: "Wait—you will come to know them."

(Craven 1973, pp. 55–56)

Cast so often as problems, our students reminded us about the true nature of pedagogical problems. They were on sure and certain ground in their dealings with us. They knew what they wanted to do and how to do it. It was we who actually had a problem; we who were uncertain about whether it was possible to make any headway at all in this strange, new place. It was we who would have to wait to see whether it was possible to know them differently, to know them as we now do, as people who write wonderful things like this:

> When Mark says the old ways are reflected on the faces like the glow of a dying campfire, it shows that he can sense the joy and importance of the old ways. Yet he knows that it is only a faint glow and it flickers on and off. He knows that one day it is going to die out unless someone lights it again.
>
> (Student response)

Or, in response to their own "good bits", this:

> "They were six years old perhaps, a little girl and boy. They had entered without knocking and they stood like fawns, too small to be afraid. They stood absolutely still, and they smiled, slowly and gently." When I read this passage I . . . thought about a little girl and a little boy with large, wide-open eyes. They stood still to look at strange things. How beautiful it was! I like the sentence "They had entered without knocking." I do not think that this means they are bad kids. It just means they do not know that they should knock because no one had taught them. In the Indian land, there is probably no one who knocks. . . . The kids have grown up in the Indian land and have been taught the Indian ways. People here are probably shy. I remember my country, Vietnam. The kids who live in the country, not in the city, are very shy. They are afraid of everything. Whenever you talk to them, the first action you get is a smile, a shy smile. They use the shy and gentle smile to begin a dialogue with strangers.

Or this:

> "The young women found an imminent need to exchange crochet patterns, and they met like a huddle of young hens and whispered about his looks, his manners, even his clean finger nails." Whether or not this is meant to be a good passage, it reminds me of my friends and I checking out the new guys . . . or still looking at the old guys from last year. We all make our huddles and whisper, and look at their bums. All the little things we girls do. I kind of laughed to myself listening to this.

We are not sure that we could have identified what we were doing as a kind of waiting if we had not read *I Heard the Owl Call My Name* with these students, in this place. Were we waiting for these students to reveal their true, but hidden, selves to us? Not really, for what we saw emerging in their engagement with the novel, with us and with one another were selves constituted and known in the particularity of our situation, studying this book, at this time, in the second year of teaching and learning together. The character of which we became to one another through the reading of this book was not lurking in the underbrush awaiting discovery. The distinctiveness of the complex web of relations that connected us through this book would have emerged differently if we had chosen a different novel, or if we, ourselves, had been claimed by a different set of issues and ideas. The novel mattered. The good bits the students chose mattered. It mattered that the issue of waiting called to the two of us from start to finish. And it mattered that all of the strands of our knowing took time to weave.

"Wait," we remember the Bishop saying to Mark, "you will come to know them." What Mark is left to figure out for himself is the tactful, mindful quality of the waiting that will make it possible to weave a fabric of care with the people in his charge. It is, we think, precisely the kind of waiting and weaving that teachers must learn to do.

But if, while we were struggling to get to this point with our students, someone had said to us, "Just wait, it will be all right," we would probably have become quite angry.

"Wait?" we might have shot back. "We can't afford to wait. There's too much to be done. We don't have time to wait."

In the ordinary, passive sense of waiting, we would have been right.

We have learned, certainly, that waiting is not a kind of idleness. If, for example, we had sat on our hands, had given in or fallen apart in those early, difficult days nothing at all would have happened. Things would have been, if not well, at least ordinary and recognizable to the students. And we would have left the school, as Mark knows he might well have to leave the village, broken and soon forgotten.

There was much to be done, and we set about doing it regardless of whether anyone would bless our efforts or not. We mobilized caretakers, tossing out broken chairs and insisting on tables rather than the slant-top desks that made group work impossible. We painted all the bookshelves, scrubbed the carpet and washed stains off the cindercrete walls. We lugged in more than fifty cumbersome boxes of books and four computers by ourselves, covered bulletin boards and bought flowers. We could not have known it then, but we were like Mark who, faced with a falling-down church and vicarage, rolls up his sleeves and fixes things up himself, prepared to accept help if it were offered and prepared to do without if it were not.

Mark recognizes the seductive danger of beginning "where every man is apt to begin who is sent to hold some lonely outpost. He was going to begin by begging, 'I want this. I need that . . .' " (Craven 1973, p. 35). In fact, he sees such exactly this kind of begging in the school teacher, the only other white person in Kingcome, who "accosted him on the path, asking that he intervene with the authorities that he be given proper supplies. Even the smallest villages were given more pencils and pads. Also, he was expected to pay for the paper tissues which he dropped so generously for the sniffling noses of his pupils" (Craven 1973, pp. 38–39).

We have thought a great deal about that teacher and his vast unhappiness in the village of Kingcome. Having chosen to come there solely for "the isolation pay which would permit him a year in Greece studying the civilization he adored" (Craven 1973, p. 33), the teacher is miserable. "He did not like the Indians and the Indians did not like him" (Craven 1973, p. 33). Nothing suited him. The children, runny-nosed and inalterably other, were a constant disappointment. There wasn't enough of anything: not enough money, not enough pencils, not enough resources, not enough support, not enough recognition. His litany of complaint was uncomfortably familiar to us. Was that what we were doing when we said, "These broken chairs have to go. No rich kid in this city has to sit on a broken chair." Or, "We won't have these desks in here. They're no good. How can anybody do lab work on these things? Their stuff will slide right off onto the floor." Were we being as whiny and obnoxious as that teacher? Is that how our insistence on better chairs, better tables sounded to others who had lived for so many years without? We were tempted to read fast over these bits about the teacher, tempted to peek at him only between our fingers, for he warned us of the seductive hubris, of the dark side, the shadow of our own commitment. In some way, the teacher is on a colonial mission to the village, a mission on whose edge the two of us often skated.

Mark is different from that teacher, and we sensed a lesson in his difference. For Mark, the derelict church and vicarage are, indeed, unacceptable. He does not expect the villagers to worship in filth and neglect, nor is he, himself, prepared to live that way. But neither does he expect another person in the village to do for him what he refuses to do for himself. While the villagers look on in amusement (and while our own colleagues dropped by to comment on the domestic enthusiasm of the new guys on the block) Mark simply does what he does, expecting nothing in return. We sensed in him a subtle tact needed by all of us who move into the lives of others. Throughout the novel, the teacher remains aloof, apart from the village and its essential life. He lives like a colonial expatriate, like the British of the Empire among whom it was a virtue not to feel touched by the natives. Even at the very end of the novel, when Mark's body is brought home to the village for burial, the teacher stands behind his closed door, refusing to make himself part of the funeral procession, for "to join the others was to care, and to care was to live and to suffer" (Craven 1973, p. 158).

To Join the Others

To care is to live, and as we think about how we have come to care for the students we teach, we realize in ways that would have been impossible without the experience of reading this novel with them, how fully we have come to live in our work with them. Now, years after all the furious scrubbing and cleaning, after the battles and the relentless insistence, day after day, of doing things other-wise, after the joys of precious moments when we broke through the walls that had been keeping us apart, we overhear one of the girls say to a friend in another class, "Look, if you want to talk, you've got to come to this room. I'm not going to your classroom. I like my own room". We grin because we know her stubbornness is only partly about paint and wallpaper and the sun streaming through the window. It is also about the spirit of the place, about the sense of belonging to one another through the hard work and, indeed, the suffering, we have endured together.

We asked a great deal of our students when we asked them to read *I Heard the Owl Call My Name*. We asked them to lose themselves so that they could find themselves transformed by the experience of reading. We worked with them to make the edges of their known worlds waver and tremble. And we did that with a particular kind of mindfulness, we think, because what we asked of the students we also demanded of ourselves.

We said to the kids at the very beginning that teachers could be guides through the mysterious forest. "All the trees are going to look the same for a while," we told them, "but we will help you learn to tell oak from aspen. It will be okay." What we now know is that there are at least two kinds of guides. There is the guide who can show a path because she had traveled it many times before. This is the kind of teacher-guide who has puzzled through all the known difficulties of the text and can help students short cut or at least endure the underbrush.

But there is another kind of guide, we think, and that is the kind of guide we strive, through our research, to become.

Connected to the landscape of loss, we want to be like Mark, doing our own work even as we wait for others to begin theirs. Asking students to immerse themselves in the difficulty of the novel, we ourselves embraced anew the original difficulty of all reading. Refusing to remain aloof, imprisoned behind the closed door of pedagogical certainties, we ventured out with them, experiencing in our own ways how bloody hard it is to do the work that we daily ask of them. We promised not only with our words to help them find their way. We also promised with the deepest possible commitment to stick with them as they—and as we—lost our selves together.

And somehow, even though we never talked to them about the specifics of our own struggles to understand what waiting is all about, they seemed to know that we were with them in powerful ways. Less strange to one another than when we began, we came to know each other through reading this book together. Less strange, we all were better able to understand more about the place we inhabited together, about its beams of light and dark, frightening shadows. Less strange even to ourselves, the two of us came to know more deeply and more fully who we are in this world.

For us, action research is not just one more thing to add to our lives. It is, instead, layered way of living that embraces the very difficulties, ambiguities and suffering that so much teaching practice seems determined to eradicate. We began with a practical concern for teaching students through a more interpretative approach to shared texts and experiences. However, our own thinking, reading and writing about these particular texts and experiences soon became far more than a report on what we did with the novel. Rather, our own interpretation, itself a hermeneutic act, moved us, as teachers, into new spaces in which epistemology and ontology, knowing and being, lost their distinct and sometimes lonely character. It moved us into a space in which the teaching of a novel became the text, itself, of our lives as teachers.

8

"Because It Shows Us the Way at Night"
On Animism, Writing, and the Re-Animation
of Piagetian Theory

DAVID W. JARDINE

> Let us imagine the *anima mundi* neither above the world encircling
> it as a divine and remote emanation of spirit, a world of powers,
> archetypes and principles transcendent to things, nor within the
> material world as its unifying panpsychic life-principle. Rather, let
> us imagine the *anima mundi* as that particular soul-spark, that
> seminal image, which offers itself through each thing in its visible
> form. Then *anima mundi* indicates the animated possibilities pre-
> sented by each event as it is, its sensuous presentation as a face
> bespeaking an image, in short, its availability to imagination.
>
> (Hillman 1982, p. 77)

I

Does the sun know anything?
  Yes, it heats.
Does the moon know it shines?
  Yes.
Why?
  Because it shows us the way at night.
              (Jean Piaget, 1974, pp. 205–6, in conversation with "Vog,"
                                             age 8 years 6 months)

Jean Piaget explored the ways in which such animistic thought was true of a
certain stage of the development of objective, scientific (mid-20th century)
conceptions of physical, mechanical causation.

There is a fascinating, mysterious sense in which "Vog's" words can also be
treated as somehow true of the sun and the moon.

What if we entered the imaginal realm and allowed "the sun" and "the
moon" to no longer be literal designations of univocal objects? What if we took
"the sun" and "the moon" to be multivocal ciphers, holding in their hearts all
of the ways that they have arrived here, in our fleshy, human lives, through the

105

pores, as the gods, in the tales, on the tongue, in the leafy-chlorophyllic gobbles of sugar production, and in the tumbles of burning gases and their reflected light that shows the way at night?

So that sun and moon "bear witness to [themselves] in the images [they] offer, and [their] depth lies in the complexities of [these] image[s]" (Hillman 1982, p. 78), and not just in the tales that the sciences have to tell about literal, objective states of affairs:

> I am not anthropomorphizing. It's more like a thing is a phenomeno-logical presentation, with a depth, a complexity, a purpose, in a world of relations, with a memory, a history. And if we look at it this way we might begin to hear it. It's an aesthetic appreciation of how things present themselves and that therefore they are in some way formed, ensouled, and are speaking to the imagination. This way of looking is a combin-ation of the Neoplatonic *anima mundi* and pop art: that even a beer can or a freight car or a street sign has an image and speaks of itself beyond being a dead throwaway object.
>
> (Hillman 1982, pp. 132–3)

But we must delve deeper here: even "dead throwaway objects" now *bespeak themselves, show* themselves as what they are. Thus, science and its tales of the world becomes *a living part* of these imaginal complexities, not an exception to them, a thread among others, needing to find its proper place and needing, as we all witness, to learn how to conduct itself with more grace and care and generosity in relation to all its kin.

Thus, interpretively taken up, "Vog's" words must be understood in their address to the full range of these phenomena of sun and moon in our lives, as evoking true, real relations uttered by one of our kin, and not simply as immature developmental precursors to the texts of the sciences. "Only in the multifariousness of such voices do [the sun and moon] exist" (Gadamer 1989, p. 295).

What happens in bypassing the monotheistic (Hillman 1983) canons of non-contradiction and giving up the hope that Piaget expressed, that "a single truth alone is acceptable when we are dealing with knowledge in the strictest sense" (Piaget 1965, p. 216–17)? What if we gave up Piaget's suggestions that children's tales are odd "deformations" of the truth (Piaget 1974, p. 50), that children often become "duped" (Piaget, 1972 p. 141), "victims of illusion" (p. 141), where the tales they tell become "traps into which [they] consistently fall" (Piaget, 1974, p. 73) to the extent that "the whole perspective of childhood is falsified" (Piaget 1972, p. 197)? What if, instead, the truth were to be had in the spaces "in-between" (Gadamer 1989, p. 295) all our kin—ourselves, our chil-dren, our shared and contested ancestors, and the Earth that holds us all here in relations of kind?

What if we were to look at the life of these words, their animating spirit, allowing ourselves to be drawn into the wondrous cosmologies they bespeak, drawn out of our selves—a "momentary loss of self" (Gadamer 1977, p. 51), a type of self-dispersal out into the ways of things, out into the voices beyond my own, out into "all my relations" (King 1992)?

II

Of course, the most fruitful, most obvious field of study would be reconstituting human history—the history of human thinking in pre-historic man. Unfortunately, we are not very well informed about the psychology of Neanderthal man or about the psychology of *Homo sinien-sis* of Teilhard de Chardin. Since this field of biogenesis is not available to us, we shall do as biologists do and turn to ontogenesis. Nothing could be more accessible to study than the ontogenesis of these notions. There are children all around us.

(Piaget 1971, p. 13)

Thus, for Piaget, "the child is the real primitive among us, the missing link between prehistorical men and contemporary adults" (Voneche & Bovet 1982, p. 88).

When Piaget (1971, pp. 12–14) speculated that ontogeny (the stages of growth of the individual) might recapitulate phylogeny (the stages of growth of the species), he was not deliberately contending that our ancestors were like children, or that those of cultures other than Europe might be full of the naiveties and simplicities and immaturities and petulance of childhood.

He was not deliberately demeaning the great tales of sun and moon and stars and gods and demons that still hold us spell-bound in the tales we still tell our children (and this despite the fact that we and they are "destined to master science" [Piaget 1952, p. 369] somehow instead). The alert ears that come in the moonlight when vision fails, the deep, darkening woods and the messages housed and hinted in Coyote's moony giggle—these things still trickle thick in our blood and in the blood of our children, despite our seeming destinies.

Let us give him this much, even though speculations such as these were rife in the spirit of the times (Eliade 1968, 1975; see Jardine 2005). Such tales were understood as:

belonging to a different mentality [than scientific discourse]: savage, primitive, underdeveloped, backwards, alienated, composed of opinions, customs, authority, prejudice, ignorance, ideology. Narratives are fables, myths, legends, fit only for women and children. At best, attempts are made to throw some rays of light into this obscurantism, to civilize, educate, develop.

(Usher and Edwards 1994, p. 158)

Much has been made of such parallels as those very "un[der]developed others" read our Eurocentrism and its colonial presumptions back to us (Nandy 1987; Minh-Ha 1994; Le Guin 1987, 1989).

Let us give him this much, reading him perhaps more generously that he could have read himself (Jardine 2006c); let us give up talk of what readings his legacy might angrily deserve and take up the task of making his work speak whatever truths it might hold—its openings, its portals, its wounds, its ways.

Let's grant him what we wish that he might have granted "Vog" and his tales of the moon and the sun.

III

> In that land of beginnings spirits mingled with the unborn. We could assume numerous forms. Many of us were birds. We knew no boundaries. There was much feasting, playing, and sorrowing. We feasted much because of the beautiful terrors of eternity. We played much because we were free. And we sorrowed much because there were always those amongst us who had just returned from the world of the Living. They had returned unconsolable for all the love they had left behind, all the suffering they hadn't redeemed, all that they hadn't understood, and for all that they had barely begun to learn before they were drawn back to the land of origins.
>
> (Okri 1991, p. 3)

When Piaget speculated that ontogeny (the stages of growth of the individual) might recapitulate phylogeny (the stages of growth of the species), he was certainly not deliberately contending that our children might somehow be our ancestors, potential clarions of what our prized 19th century hallucinations of "development" may have somehow forgotten. Children as reminders of past lives, as holders of memory, living nearer-by old springs that have lasted, that still nourish, nearer to remembering old tales that objectivism has dispersed, dispelled or demeaned as not really telling of the ways of the Earth.

What if we were to give up picturing "development" as a line in which one stage is replaced by another, in which one is more precious than the other, where we must somehow make a moral choice between youth and age and the tales each might tell? What if we were to imagine "development" as an open field of relations, in which each voice, each tale, each breath requires all the others, all its relations, to be full and rich and whole and healthy and sane? What if we were to understand development thus ecologically, full of Earthy relations of the flesh? So that, in fact, the old never replace the young but live *with* them, so that one does not fulfill any destiny in aging, but simply becomes who one becomes, generous or not, able to live well with all the voices of the Earth, or unable, disabled, desperate.

The articulations of adults and children might thus each protect and cradle the other from the mortalities that entwine us (see Chapter 9 on the idea of "intergenerationalness").

This is *almost* what Piaget contends, that the "concepts and categories of established science" (Inhelder 1969, p. 23) require genetic grounding, and that science—what Piaget took to be an unquestionable sign of "maturity"—is not comprehensible without delving into its genesis, into its arrival. The ways of age are not properly understandable in isolation from the generations that have brought them to be what they are. And again, whether this means that ancestors, and our current attraction, in curriculum, to the old tales, the "old ways" (Snyder 1977), are child-like or our children are ancestral becomes alluring again, far more interesting than Piaget might have been able to imagine.

If we pursue a study of the child and her "course" (curriculum), we cannot presume the presence of logico-mathematical knowledge and turn children and the coursing of their lives into our object. *It is that very presence of logico-mathematical knowledge, that very presumption, which is drawn into question by genetic epistemology;* but it is, *at the very same time,* left in place as the method genetic epistemology uses to give answer to that question. Piaget was unwilling to risk this much, not because of cowardice or malice, but because he believed that to produce a science of children was to raise children up into their truth and, at the very same time, to ground that very scientific truth in its fragile, intimate genesis.

However, he need not have feared quite so much. If we are to engage our children—meet them as our kin and not just as our object—we must allow our ways of proceeding to come into conversation with them in such a way that their ways and ours "converse"—turn around each other, each becoming different in the movement, each held in place, held in check, by the other.

Dead ordinary, this. We live in a world *with* children, and we live in it as adults who are defined in concert with our kin. When we read these books full of spooks and spirits, we ourselves are drawn down into deep entrails of belief that work in the guts, that perk the sensuousness and sonorities that ring and hum through our throats (Abram 1996), and that haunt in the "sedimented layers of emotionally resonate metaphors" (Fischer, 1986, p. 198) housed in our language. Resisting the ascendancies of "development" (Piaget's stages are always pictured as ascending, like a spirit rising up in the flesh, finally becoming free and pure in the fleshlessness of the pure operations of logic and mathematics [Jardine 2005]), we plunge down into worlds that are alive beyond the mechanisms allowed by logico-mathematical reasoning, beyond what is allowed by our feigned "maturities."

In such an interpretive descent, logico-mathematical reasoning *itself* becomes full of life as well, haunted, as Piaget *almost* suggests, by old family ties that bind it to our living: "part of the history of the human spirit" (Gadamer 1989, p. 283), and not some abstract, other-worldly exceptionality cut loose from the ways of the flesh.

Youth or age and the tales they have to tell—each without the other loses its sense of place and proportion and relation. Each without the other becomes monstrous (Jardine 1998a; Jardine & Field 2006). And, as hinted with the sun and the moon, perhaps these too, "youth" and "age," are themselves ciphers that ought not to be pinned squarely and solely on certain chronologically specifiable objects.

IV

> The whole leap depends on the slow pace at the beginning, like a long flat run before a broad jump. Anything that you want to move has to start where it is, in its stuckness. That involves erudition—probably too much erudition. One wants to get stuck in the history, the material, the knowledge, even relish it. Deliberately spending time in the old place. Then suddenly seeing through the old place.
>
> (Hillman 1991, p. 154)

If one pursues a hermeneutic study (say, into Piagetian theory and his work on the animistic child [1974]), it is not enough to write about different things than are common in curricular discourse. I must also *write differently*, in a way that acknowledges, attends and waits upon the agency of the world. Hermeneutics is therefore akin to the opening up of "animating possibilities presented by each event" (Hillman 1982, p. 77).

Hermeneutic writing is premised on the eventful ("Understanding proves to be an event" [Gadamer 1989, p. 309]) arrival of animating spirit. This is why its name is the name of a god of arrival, of youth, of fecundity and fertility and agency. It is premised on the belief in a resonant, animate world, full of voices and spooks and spirits which require a form of attention that extends beyond one's self, out into the living ways of things.

It is premised on the arrival of the young boy Hermes, flitting and flirting. Little wonder that Piaget identified animism with the young child, for the young child, in fact, is one of its gods. It is premised on "the [animated/animating] leap" beyond the old and established; in a sense, an enlivening leap *into* the old and established. Hermeneutics represents a conversation with the old borne on the breath and in the face of "the new, the different, the true" (Gadamer 1977, p. 9). This is not precisely a leap that I *do*, even though I must prepare myself through immersing myself in the voices of the ancestors, spend time in the old place, the "resting place" (Ly 1996, p. 1). I must, for example, carefully read Piaget's work down into all its meticulous details; it must become familiar, cellular, memorable, at the tip of the tongue in immediate ways. And then, "the leap"—some insight arrives, it seems, from elsewhere, a "provocation" (Gadamer 1989, p. 299) carrying its own agencies and consequences and desires.

"To understand . . . hermeneutically is to trace back what is said to what wishes to be said" (Grondin 1995, p. 32)—just imagine, things *wishing* to be said.

Thus, when the issue of animism is posed to Piaget's work as a hermeneutic task, a question is posed to what is left unsaid and unheard in this work and, in such posing, "the whole" of it wakes up by being called to account from elsewhere than it has come to rest. "The whole" of it seems somehow new and different and true. Piaget's work suddenly becomes visible as in the sway of age-old tales already told. Piaget's decision to focus on scientific knowledge and its genesis is suddenly recast, suddenly visible as a profoundly spiritual, even cosmological decision to cast the gods and ancestors as children.

A way therefore opens to carry on a conversation with this elder, but it is a way that is beyond his intent in his work, beyond his wanting and doing (Gadamer 1989, p. xxviii), and, insofar as I pay careful attention as well to the lessons he leaves, beyond mine as well. Something, so to speak, happens (Weinsheimer 1987) and this happenstance of meaning—a "breaking forth" as Gadamer (1989, p. 458) describes it—is revivifying, re-generative, "fecund" (Gadamer 1989, p. 32). "It has to be epiphantic. [It has] to come forth and surprise us." (Hillman 1991, p. 50). This is the first condition of hermeneutics, that "something addresses us." (Gadamer 1989, p. 299).

V

The Idea is an organism, is born, grows, and dies like organisms, renews itself ceaselessly. "In the beginning was the Idea," say the mysterious words of the Christian cosmogeny.

(Piaget 1977, p. 27)

The calm of the Idea . . . brings [us] closer to God.

(Piaget 1977, p. 28)

The good is life. Life is a force which penetrates matter, organizes it, introduces harmony, love. Everywhere life brings harmony, solidarity in the new and vaster units that it creates.

(Piaget 1977, p. 31)

Life is good, but the individual pursuing his self-interest renders it bad. Every individual instinctively, unconsciously serves its species, serves life. But self-interest may lead the individual to keep for himself some of the vital energy which he might bring to others. One day intelligence appeared, illuminated life, opened new domains to mankind, and through him God thought to attain his ends. But here again self-interest appeared, now armed with reason. Life is threatened, instinct evolves and is transformed into a sacred feeling which sets man on the right path again, and brings him back to God. But man, having tasted of the fruits of the tree of life, remains caught in this conflict between self-interest and renunciation.

(Piaget 1977, pp. 29–30)

The individual can only attain true life . . . by sacrifice, by force of the Idea, harmony with life.

(Piaget 1977, p. 30)

It is the Idea, which is the engine of life, it is the Idea which will animate our corpse. Let us restore the Idea!

(Piaget 1977, pp. 32–3)

Piaget's work originated in a mystical, near-ecstatic image of "life itself," an identification of "life" with Christ as the *eidos* of the Cosmos. In his later claims regarding the "self-organizing principle inherent in life itself" (Piaget 1952, p. 19) are hidden evocations of a biogenetic vision of the Living Word and a vision of humanity and human development as a progressive, developmentally sequenced shedding or renouncing of one's self-ishness (egocentrism and the individual, psychological subject), and the progressive participation in the pure functioning of life itself. The functioning of "life itself" in earlier stages of development is encumbered by the body, by the flesh, by the animate corpse, and the progression of development is a shedding of such encumbrances.

Underwriting development and all the multifarious changes one undergoes in becoming an adult, is the "absolute continuity" (Piaget 1971a, p. 140) of the functioning of "life itself." Development, therefore, is a matter of the slow, sequential achievement of a state in which such functioning is expressed purely (even though it is present from the beginning of life). It becomes clear from this why a single truth alone is acceptable: under the monotheistic rubric of Christianity, the pristine principle of identity in mathematics (A=A, which, for Piaget, underwrites the concepts and categories of established science as a pure expression of their functioning, their operations, their "methods") becomes entwined with God's self affirmation of the "I am that I am"—and, in Piaget's genetic epistemology, such pure (self-)identity is properly called an *operation*, i.e., a *function* which represents in a pure form the self-regulating or "autoregulatory" (Piaget 1971a, p. 26) character of life. Development is a process of life "coming to" so that the highest stages represent perfect self-identity, where the operations of logico-mathematical knowledge, and the objects of such knowledge are the same.

In such knowledge, one has an experience akin to a re-union with God.

And again, this work frees the animate spirit, the fiery *logoi*, of the disciplines of logic and mathematics. The purity and self-enclosure and pristineness and anonymity of logic and mathematics to which Piaget's work attests becomes visible as full of old, familiar, oft-told tales of ascendancy beyond our fleshy, human countenance, images of purity, of purification beyond the putridities of the bowels and the blood (see Chapter 19).

But here is an odd twist. Piaget's earlier works are concerned with the animistic realm in which "life itself" is still deeply embodied—bodily reflexes, bodily functions, language, cosmology, imagination, play, dreams, images, clouds and sun and moon. As his work progressed, it became more and more fixated on issues of logic and mathematics. His earlier work, then, is more childish in its concerns. His work as a whole, then, betrays the very movement of development that his work is about at its core: the struggle of the animate sprit, the breath of the world, to escape its mortality and free itself.

VI

> The sole work of *La Loba* is the collecting of bones. She is known to collect and preserve especially that which is in danger of being lost to the world. . . . [H]er speciality is said to be wolves.
>
> She creeps and crawls and sifts through the *montanas . . .* and *arroyos . . .* looking for wolf bones, and when she has assembled an entire skeleton, when the last bone is in place and the beautiful white sculpture of the creature is laid out before her, she sits by the fire and thinks about what song she will sing.
>
> And when she is sure, she stands over the *critura*, raises her arms and sings out. That is when the rib bones and leg bones of the wolf begin to flesh out and the creature becomes furred. *La Loba* sings some more, and more of the creature comes into being; its tail curls upward, shaggy and strong.
>
> And *La Loba* sings more and the wolf creature begins to breathe.
>
> And *La Loba* sings so deeply that the floor of the desert shakes, and as she sings, the wolf opens its eyes, leaps up, and runs away down the canyon.
>
> (Estes 1992, pp. 27–8)

Clarissa Pinkola-Estes' re-citing of the tale of *La Loba* can be read as an expression of the deep experience that hermeneutic writing entails. It is a mytho-poetic evocation of the life of those who, in some sense, gather together the dry bones of a particular topic (snippets, passages, citations, references, suggestions, turns of phrase, hints, clues and page numbers, all the bones of the old place, the resting place) and who must carefully and patiently sing over them, hoping that they will come to life, hoping that the song sung, this enchantment, will result in a re-enchantment (Berman 1983) and a reanimation of the world—a wonderful twinning of the formative power of the living Word and its profound helplessness (Gadamer 1989, p. 390) before the ways of things.

Helpless, of course, because we must wait upon the things to arrive (in hermeneutics, truth is epiphantic, it *arrives*). Fearful, too, provoking "all these deeper fears of the spontaneous and eruptive. The *invenio*: the coming-in of something" (Hillman 1991, p. 68). A hermeneutic reading of Piaget is a deliberately creative act of reanimation. Like *La Loba*, breathing, sitting firm on the ground, resting in the old place, abiding, waiting upon the Earth for the leap of life beyond the singer.

And look where we have ended up—in a giddy, fearsome place. Who would have imagined that underwriting our dull and dusty images of curriculum development was such a whirlwind of ancestral voices, such a living world, such mystical hallucinations and hope.

VII

> All things show faces to the world. Things are not only a coded signature to be read for meaning, but a physiognomy to be faced. As expressive forms, things speak; they show the shape they are in. They announce themselves, bear witness to their presence. They regard us beyond how we may regard them, our perspectives, what we intend with them, and how we dispose of them. This imaginative claim on attention bespeaks a world ensouled. More our imaginative recognition, the childlike act of imagining the world, animates the world and returns it to soul.
>
> (Hillman 1982, pp. 77–8)

What breaks here is the closed seal of constructivism which places the making of all things in our hands, in which Piaget envisaged the development of the young child as a progressive move from the chaos of early experience to the construction of a cosmos (Piaget 1971b, p. xvi). Things regard us beyond how we regard them, and however active our knowing might be, it must rest in the grace of things—"entrusting ourselves" to the ways of things (Gadamer 1989, p. 378)—if our knowing is to not be ecologically and spiritually insane. A fearsome insight. A world re-enlivened, where all the old alignments shift and flutter.

VIII

Recently in a Grade 1 class, the children were learning the science curriculum requirement of living and non-living as part of "science." As the University supervisor, I arrived and the student-teachers handed me an 8½ × 11 sheet of paper, divided in half with a black line, with the words "living" and "non-living" at the top of each column. This large double classroom of children were then divided up between eight adults, myself included, and, after a brief discussion, we were sent out onto the playground to search for objects and decided where they might be placed on the chart we were given.

Our group quickly checked out cars and dogs walking by. One child then picked up a Popsicle stick.

"Non-living," one child insisted.

Another said, "That's not non-living. It's dead. That's different."

"Write that down," I insisted. "Here, I'll help." The children had been encouraged as well to simply make drawings on the paper if they had trouble with the writing, whatever might help remind them when we gathered to talk later in the classroom.

Later, all of us gathered together and the student-teachers, on a large version of our worksheets, started taking down children's discoveries, probing for why they chose to put things where they did. I nudged a child in my group.

"We couldn't decide where to put a Popsicle stick. She said it's 'non-living' and I think it's dead."

"They were in *your* group, right?" the student-teacher said, smiling at me, and we had a good laugh with the kids about "university teachers" and the odd questions they can bring.

Then, one child said, "I don't know where to put the sun." A *huge* debate broke out, with questions and counter-questions, examples and counter-examples.

"It keeps us alive so it *has* to be alive."

"It's just a big fire." And on and on.

So, for now at least, "the sun" was printed on the line between.

There is little room to move in many schools, and we do not want to confuse our children. But a door opened here that is at the heart of education: a moment of age-old indecisiveness, an indecisiveness that holds some truth about "all our relations" (King 1992; see Chapter 5) and how we have come to be who we are. What about this sun on the line in between? What does it do? What are the Helios tales of its arcing across the sky? How do these green leaves feed on its gifts? Where does it fit in this precious Earthly life we live? What have the old ones said of it? How are our lives placed and positioned by its heat? The Tropic of Capricorn, and the Sun's turning in the heavens, Old Sol static for a moment, turning (*tropos*) in the sign of the Goat.

And, too, it heats. St. Francis called it brother, and such calling was not simply foolishness. Such calling called up some truth.

Why do this? Because, interpretively treated, the issue of the life of the sun is not new, not trivial, not easy, and not yet decided once and for all times. The line between living and non-living is an age-old *decision* that was made, that it could have been made otherwise, and that we sweet humans divide purposefully. And this dividing in the Grade One curriculum guide is a profound cosmological choice that hides great wisdoms that are left unaddressed if we simply place objects where they unthinkingly and obviously belong.

Our children, in such dull-minded placing, are robbed of their relations if we do this.

Piaget's decision to trim the narrows of contemporary scientific discourse is a profound spiritual and mythopoetic decision to take up the world a certain way, and, as the late 19th century warranted, he splayed all other beliefs in developmental sequences of great progress towards our own age.

And that the decision to drain the agency, drain the daimons from the Earth and take it up as mere mechanism, not as our home, our brother, our lover, our guide, our fearsome teacher—these are tales far too archaic to map out here in full. But, oddly, as Piaget discovered in his searching of the child's animism, the spirits and faces of long-forgotten ancestors remain. Children still place the sun "between" in an odd imaginative space full of many more "animated possibilities," much more "sensuous presence" than the lesson-as-planned allowed.

There is something beautiful here. Something *shows*.

IX

One need only think of the great effort that structuralist poetics has put into shedding some light on myth—and yet without even coming close to realizing the aim of letting myth speak more clearly than before.

(Gadamer 1995, p. x)

But what is animism? It's *esse in anima*. It's living in the world via the soul and sensing the soul in the world . . . feeling the world as personified, as emotional, as saying something. [We] live in the *anima mundi*, in a world full of figures, omens, signatures.

(Hillman 1983, p. 91)

Things have skins and faces and smells. Now that would be a revolution. It would give the world back to its soul, and let the soul out of our private personal subjective idea of it. We might then love the world and not be in terror of it.

(Hillman 1982, p. 145)

It is not enough to simply replace a literal take on science and its voices with a literal reading of animism. This opens up nothing at all, and engulfs interpretive work in paradigm wars premised on the very literalism that is killing us. What a serious, playful fugue on animism does is attempt to breathe life into our work, even the often brutal works of an old crank like Piaget. His work is full of spooks, full of spirit, full of animated possibilities beyond the hard-edged readings of curriculum development.

As I hope my own child will know, the world is full of wonder, full of agency beyond our own, and we need not be in terror of it, although its fearsomeness can sometimes cause the breath to halt. We need not simply learn about animism. This is not what the mythologies of curriculum hold. We need to learn from it.

Let us end by dedicating a little word to "Vog" and the moon and sun he knew.

9

Meditations on Classroom Community and the Intergenerational Character of Mathematical Truth

SHARON FRIESEN, PATRICIA CLIFFORD,
AND DAVID W. JARDINE

I

"Sometimes my teachers try to make things so simple that they don't make sense any more. I need to know where I am going to know where I am."

These words of a 13-year-old boy, full as they are of wonderful geographical/topographical images, hint at an unintended pedagogical consequence of developmentalism: the overcompensation for children's "developmental levels" to the extent that any particular activity or event or understanding starts to become incomprehensible because it no longer occurs within a large, patterned, disciplined space of relations and possibilities. Developmentalism has, in some quarters, unintentionally become a excuse to fragment children's learning in the name of developmental appropriateness or in the name of the child's individuality and difference. Often, teachers narrowly "target" children's needs and activities, and in the process can, however unwittingly, damage or undo the deep communities of relations that make various bodies of knowledge whole, comprehensible and sane and that make the child's learning coherent and true.

Many student-teachers often lament this situation, rightly claiming to be overwhelmed by the fact that there are so many individual developmental needs in their classroom, and that each child's needs must be individually met. This image of the pedagogic requirements of the classroom quickly becomes monstrous: 25 individual students, each with their own life and history and abilities and troubles, suddenly becomes multiplied times the number of desired learning outcomes, times (in Alberta, for example) 107 mandated curricular-developmental strands in language learning alone, times multiple curriculum guides for each developmental area.

Teaching with any sense of coherence or continuity or community begins to appear to be virtually impossible in the midst of such developmental proliferation.

In response, the ability and willingness of teachers, student-teachers and university education faculty alike to learn about the discipline of, say, elementary mathematics, becomes fragmented. Talk of mathematics as being constituted by a deep community of relations becomes vaguely incomprehensible, too "theoretical" and not really, as one student-teacher said, "hands-on practical, like what I can actually *do* with the kids." A sense of mathematics as a community of relations becomes replaced with a flurry of unconnected, hyperactive "activities" frantically pursued in the name of meeting student's individual needs and keeping students' interest. And, as the child cited above hinted, in any particular activity, students and teachers alike very often no longer know where they are because all of the topographical relations that provide a sense of direction and place have been severed or dispersed.

As a consequence, everyone involved in classroom life (students, school teachers, student-teachers and university teachers) becomes extremely *busy* and extremely *active*, and no one feels that they have any time (or energy) to do any real work. Worse yet, sometimes it seems as if "the surface is all there is" (Smith 1999, p. 177) and that there is no real, abiding community of work even possible, let alone required. The community of mathematics, like the community of the classroom, becomes dispersed into the odd and unintended isolationism of developmental difference.

When we were in the process of having conversations about writing this chapter, Sharon gave a compelling picture of how, especially in mathematics education, something like memory loss figures in this dispersion:

> The problem with math in particular is that all the work you do, all the ins and outs of conversations, little details—it can easily collapse and condense. As the next generation enters, it has to try to pick up all the conversation all over again that has since collapsed into one clear equation. Math collapses like that all the time and all the work that gets you there, all the community memory you've built up in the class, gets lost and the next generation try to simply memorize the equations. What the memorized equation loses is all the memories, all the sense of membership. It loses all its relations and acts like its got none. In many classrooms, you can't get in on the conversations about all the relations of math because *there aren't any such conversations*. Instead each child gets shoved into all these separate, "appropriate" activities. There is no place to *meet*.
>
> It's not just that teachers don't like math; they don't know what's happening because they can't remember what the real work really is. All they remember of math is the equations and the rules and the facts they've memorized the surface activities with all the relations forgotten. Teachers always talk about children "showing their work," but unless you base serious mathematical conversations on that work, children end up

believing that the answer, the clear equation or just following the rule, is all that counts, and the activities just become stupid distractions, entertainment. Just for "show." For *all of us.*

As a consequence of such a loss of memory and depth, not only does the community of the classroom become frayed into what Dressman (1993) describes as a place not unlike a shopping mall, where everyone comes together only to mind their own business. The community of relations that constitute mathematics itself never comes forward as a generous and alluring "place" in which children and adults might meet and might do real work together. Mathematics becomes simply a place where everyone can come together to mind their own "developmentally appropriate" business.

II

We wish to directly confront this (however much unintended) legacy of developmentalism. We have been involved in reading the work of Jean Piaget differently from the schooled, "curricularized" version of developmentalism (and the consequent version of mathematics pedagogy) might allow. We suggest that Piaget's work, if read interpretively rather than literally, does not so much lay out a developmental line along which children's abilities might be strung, as much as it opens up a large, generative space full of rich, interdependent, co-present relations. For example, Piaget shows how bodily and concrete manipulations of objects in the world, like the footfalls of the young child on a staircase counted out with each descent, bear a "family resemblance" (Wittgenstein 1968, p. 32) to the operations of logico-mathematical knowledge. *Each of these* seemingly particular, discrete phenomena, helps open a space around the other, making the other more comprehensible than it would have been without the co-presence of all its "generations," all its multiple "relations." Each is thus potentially "fecund" (Jardine 2006). Therefore, the halting steps of the young child do not need to be conceived simply as in need of maturation, refinement and eventual replacement, or as some sort of proto-mathematics. Rather, these steps are steps paced out by one of us, one of our kin, and they articulate mathematical kinships and relations in ways that are irreplaceable in a full understanding of the whole of mathematics. This young child's steps thus have the power to keep logico-mathematical knowledge in place, in relation. They have the power to prevent logico-mathematical operations from becoming simply self-referential and self-enclosed and all the consequent memory loss that ensues in the collapse into clear, memorizable (but not especially memorable) equations and operations. The young child's presence, if carefully and generously read, helps keep mathematics open to the arrival of renewal, of difference. If educators forget how our children might be raised up into this logico-mathematical knowledge and how their work is thereby a real, irreplaceable part of mathematics as a *living* tradition, our knowledge becomes worse than dangerous. Under such conditions, education becomes crazy-making, because it begins to work against the real conditions under which it might go on. We can, it seems, too easily forget that the traditions and disciplines of mathematics live, not in fixed, self-enclosed rules and equations, but in the living conditions that constitute its being *passed on*. This is how we might understand Piaget's (1970, p. 731) invocation: "How, *in reality*, is science [for example, the science of mathematics] possible?"

In this odd sense, then, pedagogy, as openness to the arrival of young, becomes inscribed into the heart of mathematics. Pedagogy is not simply a conduit or vehicle for the inculcation of a knowledge that is already finished and complete. It is, rather, part of the very renewal of mathematical memory that makes mathematics, *in reality*, possible.

This sort of reading of developmentalism therefore suggests something similar to the premise of genetic epistemology: that mature adult thought requires genetic grounding (Piaget 1968, pp. 116–17; 1976, p. 143; Piaget & Inhelder 1976, p. viii), or, as he playfully puts it, "the child explains the man as well and often better than the man explains the child" (Piaget & Inhelder 1969, p. ix).

One way of reading this notion of genetic grounding is that the discipline of mathematics cannot remain simply self-enclosed and self-referential. Even though such enclosure might describe "an ideal, perhaps a hope" (Piaget 1970a, p. 7) of a structuralist *theory* regarding the ways in which this community of principles and operations gain their sense in reference only to each other (such that the messy ins and outs of mathematics as a living tradition can be formulated as simply "extraneous elements" [p. 7]), in reality, as the life of the classroom attests, mathematics also requires something else. It requires the arrival of the young into that community of relations and the inevitable difference that such an arrival of new relations (and therefore new ways of seeing old relations) makes. It requires attesting to the fact that, if it is to continue making sense as a living, human enterprise, the "others" to which mathematics refers must include all its *real* relations. Or, to use Piagetian terminology, "the concepts and categories of established science" (Inhelder 1969, p. 23) require genetic grounding.

This different reading has profound pedagogical consequences. It suggests that the child's understanding of a certain mathematical nuance must be read for the ways in which it is true of mathematics, for the ways in which it has a real, abiding place in the community of relations that constitutes mathematics. It must not be abandoned or trivialized or, as Piaget suggested in an early work, understood as an "exceedingly suggestive deformation of true conceptions" (Piaget 1974, p. 50), conceptions that are developmentally "destined" (Piaget 1952, p. 363) to be replaced through maturing.

Through an interpretive turn in Piaget's idea of genetic grounding, children's work must be ushered into the real world and real conversations about real mathematics and that it must be understood as such if teachers are to act in a pedagogically responsible way and students are to be allowed to participate in pedagogically viable work. This does not mean simply affirming "the child" and their efforts. It means carefully reading the child's *work* out into all its mathematical relations, finding ways to help make it strong, stable and *true of mathematics*. It means reading the stubborn particularity of child's work in relation to the sense of the community of relations that constitutes mathematics that is building in the classroom—*these* children, remembering in *these* ways what *this* thread of mathematics is about (see Chapter 11 and 12). It means, for us as teachers, taking on for ourselves the task of deeply understanding the geographies and topographies of mathematics, so that we can hear the child's comment, not just as indicating something about her or him, but as indicating something about her or his presence, place and orientation in the world of mathematics itself (and therefore, indicating something about mathematics which would have been lost without that presence).

Interpretive work contests Piaget's suggestion that "a single truth alone is acceptable when we are dealing with knowledge in the strictest sense" (1965, pp. 216–17). Rather, interpretively understood, the truth of mathematics is found *within* the conversations that ensue *between* its multiple relations, *within* the conversations *between* multiple generations of understanding (both in the sense of mathematics' traditions and histories and in the sense of the co-presence in the classroom and in the discipline of mathematics of the old and the young, the experienced and the less experienced).

We are suggesting, therefore, that the truth of mathematics is *intergenerational*.

But we are suggesting something more than this. We are suggesting that the truth of mathematics is also inherently *generative*. That is to say, the arrival of *this* child in the classroom, and the odd and wonderful way that he or she has formulated some mathematical theme, does not signal the arrival of simply one more formulation of some mathematical concept that can be simply added to all the rest or that can be shelved because we have heard this before. Rather, as we have often witnessed as teachers (and as we show by example below), such arrivals can sometimes precipitate the transformation and regeneration of what all members of the class have heretofore understood this theme in the field of mathematics to mean. *This* child's work can cause our understanding of the whole of mathematics to "waver and tremble" (Caputo 1987, p. 7); it can open what was previously closed, make questionable and provocative what was previously a given, cause us to re-read and re-think what was previously obvious. It can make the brutal clarity of an equation or a previously merely memorized rule something about which we might now have a real *mathematical* conversation. Each new arrival has the potential to rattle through the whole of our previously established relations and can make our understanding of the whole (however slightly) different than it would have been without this arrival.

As with the arrival of a new child in the class, this arrival is not just "one more." And, as our example below attests, even though the clarities of the mathematical principle of cardinality might suggest that such arrivals can be counted as simply "one more," the actual taking up of cardinality in its full meaning as a topic in the classroom requires treating children's responses as more generative and difficult than this merely additive notion allows. For cardinality to become comprehensible, we must break below its clean, clear surface definition and remember all the difficult ins and outs that make it possible to understand, possible to pass on. This is the messy work of teaching the young and the equally messy work of making mathematics teachable.

In terms of classroom practice, this process of taking the truth of children's work seriously requires something different than the ever-narrowing targeting of developmentally appropriate activities (and the consequence hyperactivity that often ensues in the effort to "keep up" [see Chapter 12 and Jardine 2006b]). It requires pursuing deeply disciplined classroom work ("*real* work" [Snyder 1980]). This work must be open and generous enough to embrace the full multiplicity of understanding in the classroom and create a sense of a real, mathematically devout community. And it must be strong enough to hold together as well the deep communities of relations that constitute the disciplines of mathematics.

This pedagogical commitment to intergenerational community includes a deeply ethical and ecological act. It requires of all concerned simply saying "no," refusing those classroom activities or philosophies that trivialize, flatten or fragment the real work we do as teachers.

III

We now begin an exploration of this notion of the classroom as a community of relations in which children's work is taken seriously in its claims to truth through exploring an "individual case" (see Jardine 2006a). This classroom experience hints at a sense of generous, intergenerational, conversational space in a concrete way. This experience began in a large Grades 1–4 classroom of 70 children. It has since spilled over into our work with student-teachers and with a large group of Grade 7–8 students in an inner-city setting. It thus involves the deliberate, difficult work of building both individual and collective memory and the deliberate attempt to open a *mathematical* space that can bear such memory, that invites exploration at many levels and in many ways. Rather than developmentally delaying some of the questions and patterns of mathematics, we looked for ways to inscribe into each classroom venture the possibility of moving back and forth between the simple and the profound.

We had been working with the origins of counting. We had imagined ourselves as shepherds tending our master's flock at the time when numbers had not been thought of. We wove together a story that involved all of us as characters. Only through a story was it possible to put aside what we knew or assumed or had memorized about the number system to think of a time when there was none. Only stories have the imaginal power to place us elsewhere (Bogdan 1992; Bruner 1990; Clifford & Friesen 1994; Egan 1986; Hillman 1983).

Children added to this tale as we kept the plot line moving along. Even for Grade 1 children, it was almost impossible to put aside what we knew about the number system to think of a time when there was none, to put ourselves into that other space. The Grade 4 children, too, found this tale compelling. They faced the real question of what one would do without the mathematical knowledge that they had come to learn so well (which, implicitly, is similar to the pedagogical question of what one does with the young child who does not yet know how to count, or who is just beginning the work that we ourselves thought we had finished—see Daniel's story below in the *Concluding Remarks* of this chapter).

We, as adults, were ourselves taken: what is it, in what we have assumed about these seemingly simple events, that we actually know? When the habits are stripped away, and when the memorized surface clarities of mathematical definitions and equations no longer suffice, what, after all, *is* counting? What is it about the world to which counting might have provided a sensible response? And how can a real conversation about counting ensue *for us all*, children and teachers alike?

We needed to devise a way for keeping track of the sheep we were to care for each day. Each sheep needed to be accounted for at the end of the day. Eventually, we decided that we would use pebbles to represent each of the sheep we took from the master's house and into the field. At the end of the day we would return and the sheep and the pebbles would be counted and if they matched, we would be allowed to continue to live and tend sheep for another day.

We employed the principles of cardinality in these conversations. The children understood that the two sets of sheep and pebbles could be considered equal in number if they could be put into one-to-one correspondence with each other. (Some student-teachers later balked, at first, at the suggestion that musical chairs might itself be *real* mathematics.) Our counting went like this: we have one, and another one, and another one, and so on. And for each one, there was a matching pebble until all the sheep were accounted for. We saw how easily we could make the leap to a tally but we still had no way of describing an ascending set of quantities. We had no way, yet, of denoting any sequential relationship.

We continued to work, over several days, with various counting systems. We moved from our system of ones to a system employing two numbers (one and two). With two numbers, we could count: one, two, two and one, two and two, two and two and one, two and two and two, and so on. Our sequence did not need to include "one and one," because, of course, one and one is two. But now, this "of course" which everyone in the class knew before we began our tale is no longer so simple, now that we have seen it *arrive* up out of real work and real questions. Or, differently put, its simplicity becomes suddenly *brilliant*. We didn't only have a counting system with two numbers. We also had emerging the understanding that there is a *relation between these two numbers* and that two stands in for one *and* one.

At this point in the class, Alex rose onto his knees on his table and started to rub his hands together: "but you can make five by two and one and one and one. And you can make five by one and two and two."

The rest of the children in the class caught Alex's excitement. A space had opened and questions rushed in. Just how many ways were there to make five? What if you were not limited to ones and twos? We were *in*, and the glances between us told the tale. As Daniel (Grade 4) once said about a similar moment in the classroom, "I can always tell we've hit something because you two [Sharon and Pat] look at each other in that way."

Witness, too, was given when this activity was shown to student-teachers at the university. They, like us (children and teachers alike), gasped with delight when they, too, "got" it. It was clear that what they "got" was not simply "here's a bunch of hands-on activities for the children in my practicum class." What they "got" was the feeling of a generative rush of insight, the rush of opening. Their gasp (and ours) was caused by a sense of vertigo caught in Alex's excitement. The space he opened for us all was larger than just his particular questions. It was as if we had come with him over a rise and that just these few particular steps, taken seriously and followed, had opened up a huge horizon of possibilities around *all of us*. And it was not simply that we now had new territories to traverse. We also now came to understand territories already traversed in a new way.

Clearly, *no one* present could experience or understand every possibility. But even the youngest or least able of us (sometimes this was, of course, the adults involved) knew that what had arrived had to do, somehow, with the work that we ourselves were somehow already in on. Even if we did not fully understand all of the implications, we knew that we were *there*, with these others, doing part of the real work. Even the child (or adult) who did not initially "get it" at all could now be *understood* better and more generously treated, and could experience the classroom as having such generosity, such openness and sense of possibilities, even if the work is not yet especially understood.

It was our obligation as teachers to take this opening seriously. We gave each of the children a 10×10, 2 centimetre grid and asked them to color in all the different possible patterns of adjacent squares they could in order to make five.

What occurred here was important: even the youngest or least able of children, if they could count and color, could find a way into the real work that was now going on in the class. And our work with the youngest or least able child was still the same: to help each of them with the work that was now necessary in this common place. If necessary, their classmates or we helped them to count out five or to make a pattern on the paper. Some children were given small blocks to use at first. Some children simply needed initial encouragements or the detailed one-on-one talk of counting and patterns and coloring and "how many do you have now?" Some needed only the example of the questions and wonderings of child next-door whose work they might imitate or whose questions might propel new lines of work and wondering. But these individual "needs" were not allowed to fragment or disperse, because each of them was taken up as necessary for the full range of the work of this place to be done, for the full range of the community of mathematical relations to be seen and understood.

Some of the children coloured in five squares in a row. They decided that they could represent these by $1 + 1 + 1 + 1 + 1$. When they grouped the five squares like this:

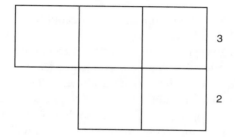

those who knew the mathematical designations wrote $3 + 2 = 5$. Those who didn't were able to write 3 beside one column and two beside the other, so that when talk of "+" occurred, they were able to experience their work as *already in that space*—that this "+" referred to what they somehow already knew, familiar territories and terrains.

And, of course, some children, using the very same figure, wrote $2 + 2 + 1$, as such:

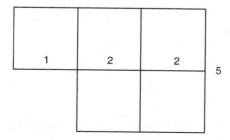

With a lot of good talk, it was clear and obvious that both of these were correct. And—this is vital—not only were both of these each individually "correct." Each of them makes the correctness of the other more comprehensible than it would have been without the presence of that other. With each other, each becomes not simply an isolated "actual" answer, but a possible answer which could have been answered otherwise. Paradoxically, then, one piece of work makes the individuality and difference of another piece of work appear, each giving the other dimensionality and depth. Without the other solution, each solution loses its sense of topography and place and relation. Without this sense of place, each becomes less fully *mathematical.* The nest of relations continued: some children, from this figure, decided that five can be understood as two times two plus one only if you do the two times two first and *then* add the one, thus opening up the whole issue of the order of operations and how $2 \times (2 + 1)$ is not equal to $(2 \times 2) + 1$. Other children struggle to make these five shaded squares into a rectangle and raised questions about the workings of prime and composite numbers.

Some of the children found the challenge of counting out five squares and coloring them in and recording their way quite sufficient for now, and opportunities were provided for these children to remain in this place and explore it more deeply, all with an eye to the broader relations inscribed, but not yet visible, in this place. However, it wasn't long before some of the children seemed to exhaust all the possible ways in which to make five.

Several children began wondering what would happen if we included zero, thus expanding our number system to include whole numbers. It didn't seem to make much difference, they concluded, but it certainly led to some interesting conversations about the role of zero. "What kind of number is zero?" they wondered. "It doesn't add anything. What's it *for?*"

"Zero is a number and a place holder and the centre on the number line between positive and negative numbers" answered Alex.

Some children pictured six as follows:

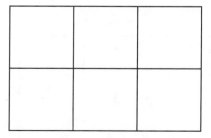

In the conversations that followed, they glanced up against how it is that six is two threes, or three two times, and how three times two is two times three, and both of these are two and two and two (and, of course, three and three).

By this time, small groups of children began to form around different places of work. Onlookers from different tables joined in with these groups—with the groups that offered a mathematical place they could inhabit themselves, with the groups that were asking the questions they understood and that compelled them. Because this activity was not targeted to meet individual needs, it allowed precisely those wonderful, alluring differences to come forward, often in specific, meticulous ways that we could not have anticipated, however careful or well-informed our targeting and developmental planning might have been. Moreover, because of the space created, these differences came out also *in relation to each other* and to the whole community of the classroom. "Individual difference" came forward, now, as *mathematically instructive* for us all, rather than as pathological conditions of isolated individuals. Differently put, we were able to experience the individual differences, not just of these children, but *of mathematics itself.*

"What if we don't limit ourselves to whole numbers? What happens then?"

For some children, out came the rulers and a small group of students started to divide the squares into halves. Justin (Grade 2), who understood what was happening, ran into his own inability to handle a ruler and pencil well enough to draw from corner to corner and ended up, for a few moments, standing full height on his table, pointing down at the paper, crying in frustration. Sharon helped him back in to the work, and helped the student-teachers who were present at that point to understand that it wasn't helpful to see what occurred with Justin as a "management problem." It was better, more pedagogically sound, to take it up as a *mathematical* problem, and to deal with the child's frustration by going back, carefully, with love and attention, to the mathematical work that caused the trouble in the first place. What was so clear with Justin was the absolute physical intensity that occurred. He did not want to be rescued from his dilemma. He deeply wanted to learn how to do this because he knew that was the work that needed to be done.

The group (which Justin soon rejoined, now standing on his chair, beaming, full of "I told you I could do this!") became determined to find all the ways in which halves (and, eventually, quarters and smaller) could be used and their equations were getting longer and longer (meanwhile, concretely, less able children were easily able to see how you need two halves to make a whole and how, if one colors only one half, you have one out of a total of two, how, then, you have something that could be represented as 1/2).

Some children spun off into issues of how many different patterns "5" could make, and children were encouraged to cut out the different patterns, fitting them together, turning them around. Talk of tessellations ensued with some as did talk of how "two squared is just two in a square."

With the following work, one child made it so obvious to us how the equation for the area of a right-angled triangle works. The child coloured in "four" as follows (to his shape we have added our letters):

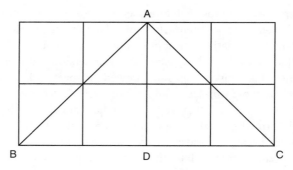

He then cut out the triangle ABC, cut it along the line AD and placed the new triangle ABD so that the line AB became adjacent to AC:

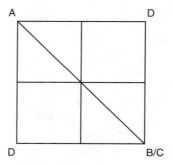

clearly showing us all something that had become a too clear equation: that the area of this right-angled triangle is half of the base (DC) times the height (AD): $2 \times 2 = 4$.

Then came the work of Cartesian planes which laced together this 10×10 grid with earlier, meticulous work on the number line and lovely questions about the existence of negative integers. This, of course, is not exactly another story, but it will have to wait for now.

Concluding Remarks on Daniel's Return

Long after travelling the Cartesian planes, Daniel, Grade 4, went over to look at a Grade 1 child's work and remarked that he could have never done that stuff when he was in Grade 1, and that they were so smart, doing such hard work.

This is a wonderful image of an older student returning to work that he had, in fact, done, now with a broad and generous knowledge that allowed him to see the depth and hidden detail in the simplest of events, allowed him, a Grade 4 child, to see something that Piaget couldn't quite see: that the world of "other generations" is more than simply exceedingly suggestive deformations of the truth. This is a wonderful image, too, of the experienced older boy treating the young so graciously, letting them and us know that they are doing real work.

Daniel was correct. The Grade 1 children were doing hard work. And, as we talked, he also came to understand this work differently than he did when he himself undertook it. Because of the continuing presence of the younger children in the classroom, he was able to remember this work he thought he never did because now, he could see where it belonged and where it was going.

This, again, bears witness to the intergenerational character of mathematical truth because, of course, the younger children engaged in such hard work because of Daniel's presence to them. They knew—each as they were able—that the work they engaged in was real work.

10

A Play on the Wickedness of Undone Sums, Including a Brief Mytho-Phenomenology of "X" and Some Speculations on the Effects of Its Peculiar Absence in Elementary Mathematics Education

DAVID W. JARDINE AND SHARON FRIESEN

The memories of childhood have no order, and so I remember that never was there such a dame school as ours, so firm and kind and smelling of galoshes, with the sweet and fumbled music of the piano lessons drifting down from upstairs to the lonely school room, where only the sometimes tearful wicked sat over undone sums.

(Dylan Thomas, from *Reminiscences of Childhood* 1967, p. 13)

Car ride to school. And I'm (D. J.) quizzing my 14 year old son, Eric, about how mathematics is going lately, what they have been doing, whether he understands. The class has just entered in to the nebulous beginnings of algebra, and Eric offhandedly says, "I don't really get this stuff about 'x'."

Suddenly I am drawn away. I have been working since 1992 with Sharon Friesen and her teaching partner, Patricia Clifford, who have been working both in elementary and middle-school classrooms. Sharon is a brilliant mathematics teacher, and part of her brilliance is how she is able, even with the youngest of children, to maintain the integrity of the discipline of mathematics and help children find ways into its real work, underneath the burgeoning and often seductive trivialities that pass for some elementary school mathematics "activities."

Our conversation, now so oddly coincidental with Eric's quandary: no mathematician would ever write "$5 + 3 = \_\_$." They would always write "$5 + 3 = x$." If you do not write in the "x," you turn what is, mathematically speaking, an equation into an unanswered question, as if you are saying "five plus three *equals*?" with a rising pitch of voice at the end.

More disturbing still, without the "x," equality is turned into an *operation,* something you have to now *do.*

We talked through all those long lists of so-called "math facts" that children are given in school, each one missing an "x."

And how each one becomes filled with an odd and inappropriate form of anticipation and suspense, as if, with "5 + 3 = __," a pendulum were pulled over to the left-hand side, tensed, unable yet to let go, needing our concerted intervention in order to achieve its blessed release.

Once the "x" is returned to its proper place, this suspense is not fulfilled but lifted. Equivalence becomes, not a question but a state, a point of rest.

It loses some of its compulsiveness.

With "5 + 3 = x," we can finally admit that *there already is* equivalence (even though *what it is* may be undetermined). Equivalence is now no longer an operation. It no longer longs or waits or demands to be *done.* It no longer needs us to *do it.* We need no longer be actors or manipulators or constructors drawn into the frays of action and manipulation and construction.

As this once-taunt pendulum now rests in equivalence, we, too, can now rest *in it.*

Without the "x," vision becomes narrowed and singular: answer it, *make* this equivalence (in school talk, "five plus three *makes?*" is commonplace). With the reappearance of "x," a wide field of movement and choice and decision and consequence flowers open. What was once made narrow and singular by the absence of "x" is now an open topography of relations, a "space," a "place" with relatives and kith and kin.

So now, a new pleasure arises to replace the tensed pendulum jitters. Now that we know *that* there is an "x," we ourselves can rest with some existential assurance in a given field of equivalence, with all of the multiple possibilities involved. Against such a background of possibilities, manipulation becomes careful, measured. We can (carefully!) manipulate the equation "5 + 3 = x," into "5 + 3 − x = 0" or even "−x = −(5 + 3)," and so on.

Without the "x," the very idea that you can do anything to one side of an equation as long as you do the same to the other side is not simply meaningless.

It is impossible.

Without the "x," children can come to believe that subtraction is one more damn thing to be done (and teachers can come to believe that subtraction is one more damn thing to be taught).

With the "x," it is possible to see that *subtraction is already co-present in the givenness of "5 + 3 = x"* as an implicate relation living at the very heart of addition.

With such existential assurance *that,* we can now safely ask "What is 'x'?" We are safe, now, because our actions and manipulations and constructions are no longer necessary to the very being of things: *that* is given, it is already assured, even though *what* it might turn out to be still suffers the indeterminacy of "x."

Constructivism, we might say, has found its limit.

A "that there is" of implicate family resemblances flowers open without us.

Alethia: the word hermeneutics invokes for truth as uncovering, opening up.

"5 = 3 = __," we might say, is lethal, deadening. Nothing can open up.

Truth in this hermeneutic sense is not possible without an "x" which throws open a field of relations and revelations that we can now *come upon* and cannot simply "construct." With such a field of relations, we must be careful, considerate, quiet sometimes, sometimes full of vigour and ebullience. Our actions are held in place.

We are no longer little gods, and the stories of mathematics are no longer stories only about us and our heroic deeds of construction. We are *in a place*, and our deeds become heroic only if we do what is needed, what is proper to this place.

What is regained with the re-placement of "x," then, is a hint of the deep pleasures that mathematicians experience in entering into open play-fields of possibilities, feeling the exhilarating rush as relations rattle open like the furls of wings, the heartpump sense of potency and option and quandary and challenge and difficulty and adventure and arrival *within* a still place.

Without an "x," the walls close in and smother movement and breath.

Trapped.

Spotted in sights.

The Teacher's Question: "5 + 3 *equals*? David? *Well*?! You weren't listening, were you?"

("No, actually, I wasn't.")

Clearly, some young children (and many adults I know) would not be able to or interested in doing the work of opening up this mathematical field and exploring it, taking its paths, seeking its ways, its patterns, its semblances, its seasons, its quandaries and comforts and thrilling perfections.

However, with the systematic early absence of "x" in mathematics education, *there is no such field*. The systematic early absence of "x" is thus akin to an ecological disaster, and the image of the Child-as-Constructor-Without-Limit is ecologically ruinous. Without an "x," mathematics loses its openness. It loses its truth. It becomes distorted into monstrous little "equivalence as operation" math-fact-question-lists in the early years.

Deadly.

And our children become distorted into little manipulative monsters roaming the landscape without regard.

So, back in the car, I asked Eric to recall all those addition and subtraction questions that, in his earlier grades, were written "5 + 3 = __".

"It should have been '5 + 3 = x'. The 'x' should have never been left out."

A moment's silence.

"Okay, so, algebra. Right. I get it. Why didn't they tell us this in the first place?"

Speculation: that the systematic and deliberate absence of "x" in early mathematics education turns the learning of mathematics into something more desperate than it needs to be. Perhaps worse yet, it turns mathematics itself into something that cannot fully make sense, that is distorted, misrepresented, flattened out, often lifeless, robbed of the truths of family resemblance and topography. It becomes "the solving of problems," and loses its character as an open world of relations. It becomes "unworldly"—nothing more than mental operations in the omnipotent, manipulative charge of a thinking subject whose competence is bewilderingly beyond me and, let me admit it, frightens me to no end in its confidence and blindness.

More than once, I have written the word "mathematics" on the chalk board in my Early Childhood Education teaching methods classes, and have turned around to tears, looks of panic, like deer caught in headlights, transfixed, unable to move or speak.

Horror, if you will, at the spittlefear smell of something awful impending.

Lifelessness: *lethia.*

This is the lifelessness these students experienced in their own mathematics education and the lifelessness that they are now dreading to pass on to their own children, as part of their professional responsibility.

So much of this because of an odd absence of "x."

11
Math
Teaching It Better

SHARON FRIESEN

Many years ago a trustee for a large Canadian school district took the Board statistician to task: why were math results on provincial examinations lower than those of a neighboring jurisdiction? Frustrated by what he perceived to be a long-winded analysis, he cut the statistician off. "Look," he said, "what I want is simple. I want all the students in this district to score above average on all these exams—and if they don't I want to know the reason why."

That's an odd little story, good for a chuckle at the trustee's mathematical expense. But it is also telling. People worry about math, even when they don't fully understand what all the fuss is about. Politicians, policy makers, teachers, and parents pore over local, provincial, national, and international test results in the ways old soothsayers scrutinized the entrails of chickens to assess the alignment of critical forces for future success and disaster. They want to know who's making the grade, who's not—and what can be done to make sure *their* students are the ones on top.

People believe mathematics is important. It is taken for granted that numeracy is one of the basics of a sound education. Poor math skills are a worry all over the world, and there is growing consensus around a few key beliefs:

- Math "skills" involve more than memorization of number facts and formulae.
- Teaching for understanding is important.
- Being good at math means being able to solve problems.

The difficulty is that there is little agreement about what all these fine statements actually mean. *Why*, precisely, is mathematics important? What should a fully numerate person in today's society be able to do? What mathematics should be taught in school, and how should it be done? If competence involves more than quick recall of number facts and algorithms on command, what precisely is that *more* that we should be teaching? What does understanding in mathematics actually look like? And does the ubiquitous dilemma of one train leaving from Chicago and another leaving from Toronto really count as a mathematically worthwhile problem anyhow?

More of the Same

These are pressing questions in the current climate of mathematics reform. A number of large international research studies (TIMSS, 1995, 1999, 2003; PISA, 2003) have helped the mathematics education community address the task of improving mathematics learning and achievement for all students through teaching better mathematics and teaching mathematics better.

But the contemporary urgency of this task should not blind us to how old the fundamental questions of mathematics reform actually are. Setting these new initiatives in their historical context may help us understand the complexity of mathematics reform—and this "long view" may also help us appreciate why easy answers are usually wrong.

The first significant reform in Western mathematics teaching and learning was led by Gerbert d'Aurillac more than a thousand years ago. He believed that students needed more than explanations and lectures in order to understand abstract mathematical concepts, and so his teaching relied heavily on the use of teaching aids and manipulatives he designed and constructed to meet needs that he perceived. It is said that he "broke with all tradition by devising charts, models and instruments for demonstration to his students and for handling by them" (Lattin, 1961, p. 18). The use of such devices had been around since the time of Quintilian, a Roman educator living in the first century, but "Gerbert's innovations extended far beyond the utilization of teaching aids" (Buck, 2000, p. 80). He used models to assist learners to grapple with abstract and difficult ideas, particularly difficult and messy mathematical ideas. And he was an early supporter of what others have come to call "learning by discovery."

Gerbert was dedicated to improving his students' understanding; he was an exceptional pedagogue who was fully attentive to his students' increasing ability to reason and explore in mathematically sound and creative ways. Because of his success, many of his contemporaries attempted to copy his methods and devices. However unwilling or unable to learn the pedagogy required to foster student learning and understanding with these technologies, they failed to produce the learning and deep understanding that Gerbert's own students experienced. The result was "poor instruction at best, or dissemination of incorrect information at worst" (Buck, 2000, p. 84). What started as creative and effective new ways of teaching mathematics ended in a failed bandwagon, undermined by "ignorance and suspicion [that] helped ensure that Gerbert's innovations were not used or adopted" (Buck, 2000, p. 86).

In 1100, William of Malmesbury declared that Gerbert's devices, early examples of the use of new technologies in the classroom, were "the work of the devil"—somewhat bewildering since in AD 999 Gerbert d'Aurillac had become Pope Sylvester II.

Three lessons emerge from Gerbert's unfortunate experience:

1. Among all subjects taught in our schools, mathematics seems to

present a unique problem. There is no other discipline in which the gap between the curriculum presented to students and the body of knowledge that constitutes the discipline is so great. Gerbert was a solitary and puzzling voice in calling for students to understand mathematics, and not just perform routine computational tasks presented to them. His insistence in immersing students in complex, messy, difficult mathematical problems was strikingly different from the pedagogy of colleagues—and, indeed, of much contemporary teaching in Canadian schools. Ask anyone on the street what they think mathematics is. You won't wait long until someone says it is a logical discipline where you have to learn basic things first in order to prepare for more difficult math later on. Adding and subtracting are easier than multiplication, and algebra is *way* too hard for little kids. Being good at math means getting right answers fast. And you have to memorize a lot. It is unlikely that many would use words like "messy," "creative," or "imaginative" in respect to mathematical thinking— even though wonderful math reformers have been trying to introduce these ideas for a millennium.

2. The secret of teaching mathematics well does not lie in borrowing teaching strategies holus-bolus. Even those of Gerbert's colleagues who admired his results and tried to emulate his success in their own classrooms had terrible difficulties. There is a simplistic and all-too-common view of curriculum as something to be "delivered." Teaching, it is felt, means just adopting better delivery methods. But Gerbert's peers found it almost impossible to do that—and teachers today have the same problem with methods imposed from away. Even when they are anxious to improve their own teaching, it is not immediately clear what kind of support they need in order to keep good ideas from degenerating into failed experiments.

3. Nobody's neutral about changes to the teaching of mathematics. Turf wars are fierce and personal, with sides lined up, lances at the ready, prepared not only to do battle over ideas, but to attack and even vilify opponents. "All's fair in love and war" should also include the climate into which mathematical reformers must move. While few might be as colorful as William of Malmesbury in dismissing serious efforts at reform as diabolical, the history of attempts to change the mathematics taught in school, and how that mathematics is taught, exacts a considerable toll on those willing to wade into the fray. Nowhere, it seems, is the status quo defended with such fervor.

Fast Forward

Most of us have heard about "the new math"—a short-lived effort to reform mathematics in the wake of the Soviet launch of Sputnik on October 4, 1957.

The United States, humiliated by the Soviet victory in space, launched a major math reform:

> Over the ensuing months, as policy makers stopped blaming other policy makers, they began to argue that our apparent lag in science and mathematics was, in part, the product of an outdated school curriculum in those subjects. Greatly increased amounts of government money quickly became available to reform school mathematics and science, and a new era began.
>
> (Kilpatrick, 1997)

The new math reforms were intended to bring mathematics education in K-12 more in step with the mathematics that was taught in the universities:

> Because the university mathematicians who dominated the modern mathematics movement tended to be specialists in pure rather than applied mathematics, they saw pure mathematics . . . not only as the content that was missing from the school curriculum but also as providing the framework around which to reorganize that curriculum.
>
> (Stanic & Kilpatrick, 1992)

So what was new about the "new math"? Well, one thing was a switch from teachers telling to students learning through investigation, discovery, and hands-on learning. Sound familiar?

Math educators once again tackled the problem of teaching abstract mathematical ideas in ways that would develop sound understanding:

> One focus of the new math was set theory, where students were encouraged to think of numbers in a new, hopefully more concrete way. Students would take a set of four items, and add it to another set of five. Yes, the result was still nine, but the emphasis was on the concept of addition, rather than the answer per se. Using this technique, students were hoped to discover that the sets would yield the same number regardless of their order (the commutative property), and that taking one original set from the combined set would yield the other original set, thereby discovering subtraction, the inverse of addition. Other aspects of the new math including using number bases other than base-10 and introducing more abstract number theory concepts such as prime numbers earlier in the students' careers.
>
> (Cecil's Mail Bag, Straight Dope Science Advisory Board)

Before the ink was dry on the new math reforms, mathematicians started to line up on either side of a fierce debate. Morris Kline, a preeminent mathematician and an ardent critic of the math reforms, led one charge. He believed that the efforts of the reform were " 'wholly misguided,' 'sheer nonsense,' attempts to replace the 'fruitful and rich essence of mathematics' with sterile, peripheral, pedantic details" (quoted in DeMott, 1964, p. 55).

Except for the mathematicians and mathematics educators who worked on creating the "new math," few people greeted the reform with enthusiasm. Teachers ran into problems trying to teach the new curriculum. Parents, too, had difficulty with it, frustrated that they could no longer help even a second-grader with their homework. Hands-on mathematics just didn't look like real math to teachers and parents who had learned so much of their own mathematics by rote. By 1965 the new math reform had already disappeared from most Canadian classrooms, and in 1970 the US National Science Foundation withdrew funding from the reform initiative, thereby ending it officially.

During the late 1960s, 1970s and 1980s, "back to the basics" quickly replaced the failed "new math" curriculum, returning mathematics education to familiar approaches that everyone recognized: rote recitation of facts, memorization of algorithms, and solving of routinized word problems. As familiar as these conventional approaches to the teaching of mathematics were to teachers and parents, they left essentially untouched the actual problem of teaching better mathematics, better. A 1983 report, *A Nation at Risk*, signaled the lack of satisfactory outcomes and student achievement from this conventional approach, and mathematics reformers were back at the drawing board again. This time it was the mathematics educators who stepped forward, and what began as a grassroots movement turned into a mathematics reform based on standards articulated by the US National Council of Teachers of Mathematics (NCTM).

Current Reform Initiatives

The principles and standards articulated by NCTM provided the basis for the development of many mathematics curricula worldwide, including Canada's:

> *Principles and Standards for School Mathematics* describes a future in which all students have access to rigorous, high-quality mathematics instruction, including four years of high school mathematics. Knowledgeable teachers have adequate support and ongoing access to professional development. The curriculum is mathematically rich, providing students with opportunities to learn important mathematical concepts and procedures with understanding. Students have access to technologies that broaden and deepen their understanding of mathematics. More students pursue educational paths that prepare them for lifelong work as mathematicians, statisticians, engineers, and scientists.
>
> This vision of mathematics teaching and learning is not the reality in the majority of classrooms, schools, and districts. Today, many students are not learning the mathematics they need. In some instances, students

do not have the opportunity to learn significant mathematics. In others, students lack commitment or are not engaged by existing curricula.

(*Professional Standards*, 1991)

While NCTM Standards and Principles have had both detractors and supporters, they appear to have developed a staying power that earlier reform efforts lacked, and that have provided a base on which findings from international testing and research are now building.

Learning to Improve

Lessons learned from these latest reform efforts are only now emerging as tentative findings rather than as prescriptive recipes for change. Among the most promising are these:

1. Not all teaching methods are equal. While every country has its own way of teaching mathematics, there are features that exemplify methods of teaching that help students achieve well (Hiebert, 2005, p. 6).
2. When relationships between facts, procedure, concepts, and problem solving are attended to and made explicit in the mathematics classroom, student achievement increases (Hiebert, 2005, p. 6).
3. When students grapple with and solve challenging problems, their mathematics achievement increases (Hiebert, 2005, p. 6).
4. Reform recommendations disseminated through curriculum documents and delivered to teachers are insufficient to improve the teaching and learning of mathematics. So is simply issuing edicts that teachers will be more accountable. However necessary solid standards, excellent curricula, innovative materials, and accountability, they are not sufficient to ensure that teachers increase students' mathematical understanding and achievement. Nor do they ensure quality math teaching for all students.
5. Mechanisms must be built into the teaching profession to permit teachers "to improve gradually over time" (Stigler & Hiebert, 1999).

Improving over Time

One of the most promising differences between earlier reform efforts and those being developed today is the emphasis on professional development. Meaningful mathematical reform must start with the classroom. If change is to take hold, teachers and students alike have to accept, understand, and enact it within the context of what they already know about mathematics. Thus, new ways of working cannot be so alien as to be unrecognizable to teachers. Rather, they should connect in meaningful ways with what teachers already know, and then work to extend that knowledge in significant ways.

What teachers know and understand about mathematics makes a difference to the quality of their teaching. This means more professional development dedicated to:

- improving teachers' knowledge of mathematics;
- improving the ways in which they know and understand content so they can teach it better; and
- improving their knowledge of how students learn particular concepts and topics.

And finally, we have come to understand that reasoning and problem solving have to be the focus of mathematics instruction in the classroom. This last point is important and tied strongly to all the others. Reasoning and problem solving require students to learn how to generate, evaluate, justify, and revise mathematical models while solving problems. They also require teachers to involve students in activities that require generalizing and justifying various solutions to problems. The teaching practices that embody modeling, generalization, and justification in order to sponsor mathematical reasoning and problem solving represent a fundamental shift in the ways that many teachers now teach mathematics—although Gerbert would probably have found such practices exciting.

Conclusion

History has shown us that mathematics reforms of the past have never quite lived up to what their creators and supporters wanted, nor to what their detractors and opponents feared. While the task of creating classrooms in which students understand abstract and difficult mathematical ideas, see relevance in the mathematics they are learning, and achieve mathematical competence seems daunting, as a mathematics community we are further down the road in knowing what to do to achieve these goals. We have made demonstrable progress by working together—mathematicians, mathematics educators, and teachers who understand that mathematics reform is a complex matter. There are no easy answers.

As we move our efforts into the place where people learn, and teach, and do mathematics—the classroom—we also need to be mindful and open to the next question: Are we teaching the right mathematics content to achieve goals of numeracy, or the qualitative literacy required for meaningful participation in democratic societies?

This is a profound and difficult ecological point. Our lives and actions are sustained in part by what is beyond us, beyond what we know, experience, or construct (see Jardine, 2005, 2006a). Another child "just knows the answer" but cannot articulate the operations she performs. Another gets caught up in such articulations and takes on the task of filling out all the permutations of operations embedded in the question at hand, verging, for a moment, near calculus and the formulation of functionally defined sets.

What occurred here was a wonderful but also rather disorienting phenomenon for many student-teachers in this class. They began to see that being stuck in the present tense with the three surface samples and then rushing to accumulate more and more in order to understand "the whole child" (or in order to "cover the whole curriculum") was somehow potentially misguided and unhealthy. Such however-well-meant pursuit skitters over the deeply experiential "ecology" of *just this*. "Underneath" (this term is troublesome and interesting—"surrounding"? "implicit in"?) the surface of each stubborn particular was an almost overwhelming richness, diversity, hitherto unnoticed communities of relations. But more than this, once opened up, we could begin to see how each stubborn particular—*this* child's work and this child's work—becomes reflected and refracted through all the other stubborn particulars, giving all the others shape and place and sense. Differently put, once *this* "5 + 3 = 8" becomes *interpretable,* it is no longer an isolated given which simply is what it is independently of everything else, like the unread work samples found in the children's files. It becomes "readable" as a multivocal *sign* which portends a whole nest of sustaining relations that are always already wholly at work and without which this stubborn particular would not be what it is. Each stubborn particular thus becomes placed within a nest of possibilities that house and sustain it. It becomes, in this deeply ecological sense, *whole,* through the slow, meticulous, disciplined working out of its relations. And, to push this one step further, each child can come to understand their own work and its particularities *as* a way into a whole world of relations which their work incarnates and summons and responds to.

Here we have a wonderful inversion of the metaphysical assumption of the urban sprawl version of curriculum integration. Each curricular fragment is what it is only *in relation* to the "whole," a whole now readable in and through the stubborn particulars of our lives.

It is important to add that this does not mean that every child should be relentlessly inundated with relations, possibilities, and articulations at every turn. This would simply turn our interpretive efforts into another version of urban sprawl that acts irrespective of where we are and what particular relations are at work "*here* and *here.*" This is the profound sense in which the particular is "stubborn": there is no way that we can replace the exquisiteness of *this* particular (child's work, for example). *This* work—*this* "5 + 3 = 8"— occurs at an irreplaceable intersection between the world of mathematics, this child's life and breath and attention and experience, the life and relations of the classroom, the hopes and actions and experience of the teacher, the working out of our curriculum and our culture in and through the institutions of schooling, and so on. Differently put, *this* work—the delicacies of this child's slow counting out of "5"—is the "centre" of "the whole" of these relations. It is, in its own way, a sacred place where the whole of the Earth comes to rest in relations of deep interdependency.

However (and this cannot be overemphasized, given our culture's tendency to inflate "child-centeredness" to ecologically disastrous proportions), *this* work is, at the very same time, peripheral to (yet still housing of) the work of this next child and this one. This stubborn paradox is at the core of curriculum integration. On the one hand, "the universe is a fabric of interdependent events in which *none* is the fundamental entity" (Nhat Hanh, 1986, p. 70): curriculum integration is not child-centered or teacher-centered or subject-matter-centered, but rather gives up the fundamentalism that underwrites such centration in favor of a *world* of relations. And yet, at the same time: "*The centre is [also] everywhere*. Each and every thing becomes the centre of all things and, in that sense, becomes an absolute centre. This is the absolute uniqueness of things, their [stubborn] reality" (Nishitani, 1982, p. 146).

The arrival of each new child in one's class, the arrival of each new piece of work, is thus potentially fecund. Each stubborn particular carries the potential of re-opening and thus re-vitalizing what I have heretofore understood the whole web of delicacies surrounding "5 + 3 =__ " to mean. This particular child always counts by twos and seems stuck there in a loop. She disassembles "5" and "3," re-sorts them and adds them two by two by two by two by setting out pairs of small wooden blocks in rows in front of her. This child brings a uniqueness and individuality and irreplaceability to this activity. But her actions are not just that. Her work cannot simply be accumulatively added to "the whole" of what we have heretofore understood "5 + 3 = 8" to mean. Rather, because of her work, that whole now "waver[s] and tremble[s]" (Caputo, 1987, p. 7). This fecund new case refracts and cascades through each particular relation that we took to be a given, giving each one a renewed and transformed sense of its relations and place in the whole. Without the arrival of such fecund new cases, and the portend of transformation and renewal that they bring, mathematics would become simply a given set of memorizable (but not especially memorable) facts and rules and would lose its sense of potency and possibility. It would thus lose its integrity as a *living* system.

What we have come upon here is an understanding of what is basic to mathematics as a living discipline. It is both open and closed, new and established, young and old, if you will. It has its own patterns and structures and operations, its own arrays of possibilities and potentialities, its own shared and contested conversations and contestations, but it is renewed and made whole by the arrival of the young (see Chapter 19). If we pay attention to the stubborn particularity of *this* "5 + 3 = 8," this arrival need not be caught up in an onslaught of accumulation and acceleration. Our attention to *this* "5 + 3 = 8" is slowed and held in place by the wisdoms and disciplines and sustaining relations of this "place" called mathematics. Conceived as a living system (one hopes that this is a warrantable image for our curriculum), mathematics is not a fixed *state* (whether already achieved or yet to arrive). It is not a dead and lifeless corpus, a body of knowledge that is no longer a living body. It is, rather, a *way* that must be *taken up*, whose life and living must be taken on in order for it to be a living whole.

There is thus this deeply ecological point, that there is a *way* to mathematics, and this not in spite of but because of the fact that this way needs the questions and arrivals of the young in order for it to remain a living way. Learning its ways means entering into these ways, making these ways give up their secrets: making these ways *telling* again, making them more generous and open and connected to the lives we are living out. Understanding mathematics thus becomes a type of ecological intimacy which always already contains images of children and the passing on of the wisdoms of the world to the young. Consider this passage as describing the "world of mathematics" and all its sustaining interdependencies:

> Some people are beginning to try to understand where they are, and what it would mean to live carefully and wisely and delicately in a place, in such a way that you can live there adequately and comfortably. Also, your children and grandchildren and generations a thousand years in the future would still be able to live there. That's living in terms of the whole.
>
> (Snyder, 1980, p. 86)

Living in terms of the whole requires somehow making the world of mathematics *livable*. As such, it is not enough to simply delve into its indigenous operations and patterns; nor is it enough to simply abandon children to their own devices and, so to speak, let them have their way with mathematics and not teach the difficult lessons of how to pay attention to where they are and what mysteries this place offers.

It is here that we encounter a paradox: making the world of mathematics livable requires going beyond mathematics itself into the deep, patterned relations of the world which house and sustain the possibility of pursuing mathematics *at all*: patterns of experience and breath and bone and blood. It is in this deeper, fleshier discipline of repeated patterns of operations and structures and doings that mathematics becomes integrated. It becomes whole.

Interpretive Descent and the Mathematicity of the World

The patterned doings of mathematics are themselves not simply isolated facts. Rather, we find in the patterns and structures of mathematics "an anciently perceived likeness between all creatures and the earth of which they are made"

(Berry, 1983, p. 76). Consider how the following passages describe the patterned doings of the human body (pulse, breath), the patterns of our Earthly lives (daily and seasonal cycles and rhythms) and the structure of language itself. Consider how these passages show that each of these refracts through all the others:

> The rhythm of a song or a poem rises, no doubt, in reference to the pulse and breath of the poet. But that is too specialized an accounting; it rises also in reference to daily and seasonal—and surely even longer—rhythms in the life of the poet and in the life that surrounds him. The rhythm of a poem resonates with these larger rhythms that surround it; it fills its environment with sympathetic vibrations. Rhyme, which is a function of rhythm, may suggest this sort of resonance; it marks the coincidences of smaller structures with larger ones, as when the day, the month and the year all end at the same moment. Song, then, is a force opposed to speciality and isolation. It is the testimony of the singer's inescapable relation to the earth, to the human community, and also to tradition.
>
> (Berry, 1983, p. 93)

Or, even more mysterious:

> Rhyme leads one no doubt to hear in language a very ancient cosmology. Rhyme is not only an echo from word to word. Arrangement for arrangement, the order of language evokes and mimes a cosmic order. In realizing itself, rhyme is tuned in to [this cosmology]. Rhyme and meter are praise. An indirect theology.
>
> (Meschonnic, 1988, p. 93)

Given this, we can see how curriculum integration cannot involve concertedly *adding on* language or science or history simply alongside mathematics or vice versa. Rather, it requires delving, for example, into the mathematicity of language itself—its patterns and structures and rhythms and tones and operations and grammars. And, once we crack the literalist surface of mathematics that might render it an isolated discipline, a cascade of implications ensues: the rhythm of mathematics, mathematicity of language, the language of music and rhythm, the music/patterns/rhythms of the world and, in the end, the profound mathematicity of the shifts and flutters in a bear's gait as it breaks from a walk into a run. Differently put, deep in the underworlds of "$5 + 3 = \_\_$" we find a strong and sustainable integration of mathematics into a "bear theme." Or, better, we find the integration of bears *and* "$5 + 3 = \_\_$" into a "whole" which embraces them both, each in their own way, and refracts each through the other—structure, pattern, rhythm, operation.

This is an exhilarating movement—a type of meditational and imaginal descent into the crawling underworld of the particularities of our lives. *Every thing*—even just this red wheelbarrow, or that child's holding five tight in her fist for fear of losing it—abounds with connections, dependencies, relations. Every thing, every word, every curricular fragment is a potential opening into "the whole"—"*this* and *this*" (Wallace, 1987, p. 111). More strongly put, only *through* a deliberate and disciplined attention to the "stubborn particulars" is "the whole" anything more than simply a floating and, in the end, unsustainable *idea* (see Chapter 15).

However, there is also a fearsomeness attached to the realization that the world is not a flat, clean, literal surface and that our sanity and wholeness/health cannot be had by skittering across such surfaces, however safe and secure such surfaces might appear at first glance. There is a fearsomeness attached to the realization that the world is interpretable, alive with implications and complicities that are always already at work in the intimacies of our everyday experiences, and that we cannot always control and predict what relations we might stumble on in the dark, no matter how well laid our (lesson) plans might be.

But none of this goes quite far enough. The mathematicity in the gait of a bear as it breaks from a walk into a run is, in the end, a topic which still simply "floats." We could just as easily have mapped out the parabolic curve of its shoulders or counted its toes or graphed its offspring or lifespan in relation to other animals. The sort of interpretive descent that curriculum integration requires of us is far more fearsome and more experientially immediate than this allows.

In dwelling upon the mathematical changes in the gait of a bear as it moves from a walk to a run, I cannot avoid coming to reflect on my own living involvement in such Earthly rhythms, an "anciently perceived likeness" (Berry, 1983, p. 76) that embraces us both and makes the life of each complicit in the other. In walking up this hill and feeling the fluttering mathematical patterns of breath and pulse and steps, I come to better understand this creature and its mathematical being *in place*, housed by flesh and humus, housed by a mysterious immediacy. And, in understanding this creature in this way, I come to understand myself and my own living involvement in the ecological conditions under which this creature lives and which I live with it, pulling hard at this same air as it curves up the steep valley sides. It is the fleshy mysteries of my own life and my own wholeness and integrity that this bear and its steps pace out. And, it is mathematics—the very mathematics which I now teach my child—which has underwritten technological images of severance, fragmentation, commodification, and mastery that have ravaged this place, this bear's life, and thereby mine along with it. To teach mathematics in an integrated way, therefore, requires more than simply dwelling in its indigenous intricacies and patterns. I must help children (and myself) place mathematics back into the embrace of the Earth (into the embrace of its kin, like the symmetries of these pine branches). Such embrace will help make it more generous and forgiving and livable than it has become in the severities of our curriculum guides and the severities and violences of our unsustainable beliefs in its dominion as a "Father Tongue" (Le Guin, 1987) which silences all others.

It will help make it (and ourselves, and our children, and this bear, which paces out a life beyond our dominion) whole.

Concluding Remarks

> It is impossible to divorce the question of what we do from the question of where we are—or, rather, where we think we are. That no sane creature befouls its own nest is accepted as generally true. What we conceive to be our nest, and where we think it is, are therefore questions of the greatest importance.
>
> (Berry, 1986, p. 51)

Just as it is my own wholeness and integrity that this bear and its steps pace out, so too it is my own wholeness and integrity that are foretold in whatever actions I do here, with these children in the classroom. In another Grade One classroom, children are completing subtraction equations on a white sheet of paper. When they are done, the rectangles, each with one equation, are cut out, curled up, pasted on Santa's beard, and posted for parents to see during the Christmas concert and classroom visits that surround it.

If we meditate for a moment on this activity, there is a sense in which it is, frankly put, insane. This is not to say that some children might not enjoy it. It is to say that fostering such enjoyment abandons children to a flickering, hallucinatory vision of the Earth, of mathematics, of the events surrounding Christmas that is, in the end, an ecological and spiritual disaster that no amount of acceleration and accumulation can outrun. Such activities suggest that we no longer know where we are. Such activities, too, are disturbingly suggestive of where we might *think* we are.

In this chapter, I have been suggesting that curriculum integration requires a concerted, thoughtful resistance to such skittering hallucinations. To prevent the woozy visions often associated with such matters, curriculum integration and the wholeness it portends must not sidestep a disciplined, mindful attention to the "stubborn particulars of grace." But there is another suggestion here: these examples of math facts on a teddy bear's tummy and Christmas subtraction equations bear witness to a terrible logic that many teachers and children are suffering *on our behalf.* This is one of the agonies of ecological mindfulness: my own life is implicated in these very examples—"*this* and *this*"—as is my son's. This difficult knowledge, more than anything, is at the heart of curriculum integration and the ecologies of experiential education.

13
Birding Lessons and the Teachings of Cicadas

DAVID W. JARDINE

I went birding last summer with some old friends through the southern Ontario summer forests where I was raised, crackling full of songbirds and head-high ferns and steamy heat. It was, as always, a great relief to return to this place from the clear airs of Alberta, where I have lived for 20+ years—academic, Faculty of Education, curriculum courses, practicum supervision in the often stuffy, unearthly confines of some elementary schools.

As with every time I return here, it was once again a surprise to find how familiar it was, and to find how deeply I experience my new home in the foothills of the Rocky Mountains through these deeply buried bodily templates of my raising. It is as if I bear a sort of hidden ecological memory of the sensuous spells (Abram, 1996) of the place on Earth into which I was born. How things smell, the racket of leaves turning on their stems, how my breath pulls this humid air, how birds' songs combine, the familiar directions of sudden thundery winds, the rising insect drills of cicada tree buzzes that I remember so intimately, so immediately, that when they sound, it feels as if this place itself has remembered what I have forgotten, as if my own memory, my own raising, some of my own life, is stored up in these trees for safe keeping.

Cicadas become archaic storytellers telling me, like all good storytellers, of the life I'd forgotten I'd lived, of deep, fleshy, familial relations that worm their ways out of my belly and breath into these soils, these smells, this air.

And I'm left shocked that they know so much, that they remember so well, and that they can be so perfectly articulate.

I became enamored, during our walk, with listening to my friends' conversations about the different birds that they had been spotting. They spoke of their previous ventures here, of what had been gathered and lost, of moments of surprise and relief, of expectation and frustration. Their conversations were full of a type of discipline, attention, and rich interpretive joy, a pleasure taken in a way of knowing that cultivated and deepened our being just here, in this marsh, up beside these hot, late-afternoon, sun-yellowy limestone cliffs.

Updraughts had pulled a hawk high up above our heads. We spotted a red-winged blackbird circling him, pestering, diving.

Sudden blackbird disappearance.

Hawk remained, over a hundred feet overhead, backlit shadowy wing penumbras making it hard to accurately spot.

Where had that blackbird gone?

"There. Coming down the cliff face."

Sudden distinctive complaint around our heads. He had spotted us as worse and more proximate dangers to this marsh than the hawk that'd been chased far enough away for comfort.

My friends' conversations were, in an ecologically important sense, *of a kind* with the abundance of bird songs and flights that surrounded us—careful, measured, like speaking to like, up out of the hot and heady, mosquitoed air. And, standing alongside them there, sometimes silent, certainly unpracticed in this art, involved a type of learning that I had once known but, like cicadas, long since forgotten.

I had forgotten the pleasure to be had in simply standing in the presence of people who are practiced in what they know and listening, feeling, watching them work.

I had forgotten the learning to be had from standing alongside and imitating, practicing, repeating, refining the bodily gestures of knowing.

I had forgotten how they could show me things, not just *about this place*, but about how you might carry yourself, what might become of you, when you know this place well.

Part of such carrying, such bearing, is to realize how the creatures of this place can become like great teachers (see Chapter 17) with great patience. Such a realization makes it possible to be at a certain ease with what you know. It is no longer necessary to contain or hoard or become overly consumptive in knowing. One can take confidence and comfort in the fact that this place itself will patiently hold some of the remembrances required: like the cicadas, patiently repeating the calls to attention required to know well of this place and its ways.

So we stood together in the bodily presence of this place. Listening, watching, waiting for knowing to be formed through happenstance arrivals and chance noticings. Seeking out expectant, near-secret places that they knew from having been here before, often evoking slow words of fondness, remembrance and familiarity—intimate little tales of other times. Repeating to each other, with low and measured tones, what is seen or suspected. Reciting tales from well-thumbed-through books that showed their age and importance. Belly-laughing over the wonderful, silly, sometimes near-perfect verbal descriptions of bird songs: "a liquid gurgling *konk-la-ree* or *o-ka-lay*" for Peterson's (1980, p. 252) version of the red-winged blackbird.

Then settling, slowing, returning, listening, and looking anew. Meticulousness: "at the edge, below the canopy of the oak, there, no, left, there, yes!"

These are, in part, great fading arts of taxonomic attention, and the deep childly pleasures to be had in sorting and gathering and collecting (Shepard, 1996). There is something about such gathering that is deeply personal, deeply formative, deeply pedagogical. As I slowly gathered something of this place, it became clear that I was also somehow "gathering myself." And as I gathered something of the compositions of this place, I, too, had to become composed in and by such gathering. And, with the help of cicadas, I did not simply remember this place. Of necessity, I remembered, too, something of what has become of me.

A birding lesson: I *become* someone through what I know.

This little lesson may be the great gift that environmental education can offer to education as a whole. Coming to know, whatever the discipline, whatever the topic or topography, is never just a matter of learning the ways of a place but learning about how to carry oneself in such a way that the ways of this place might show themselves. Education, perhaps, involves the invitation of children into such living ways.

This idea of a knowledge of the "ways" (Berry, 1983) of things and the immediacy, patience, repetition, persistence, and intimacy—the "attention and devotion" (Berry, 1986, p. 34)—that such knowledge requires, is ecologically, pedagogically, and spiritually vital. It suggests that a knowledge of the ways of red-winged blackbirds is not found nestled in the detailed and careful descriptions of birding guides. Rather, such knowledge lives in the living, ongoing work of coming to a place, learning its ways, and living with the unforeseeable consequence that you inevitably become someone in such efforts, someone full of tales to tell, tales of intimacy, full of proper names, particular ventures, bodily memories that are entangled in and indebted to the very flesh of the Earth they want to tell.

It was clear that my friends loved what they had come to know and what such knowing had required them to become. They took great pleasure in working (Berry, 1989), in showing, in listening, in responding to the simplest, most obvious of questions. There is a telling, disturbing, ecopedagogical (Jardine, 2000) insight buried here. Because a knowledge of the ways of a place is, of necessity, a knowledge webbed into the living character of a place and webbed into the life of the one who bears such knowledge, such knowledge is inevitably fragile, participating in the mortality and passing of the places it knows. A knowledge of ways, then, must, of necessity, include the passing on of what is known as an essential, not accidental part of its knowing. It is always and already deeply pedagogical, concerned, not only with the living character of places, but with what is required of us if that living and our living there are to go on.

Another birding lesson: if this place is fouled by the (seeming) inevitabilities of "progress," the cost of that progress is always going to be part of my life that is lost.

Some days, it makes perfect sense to say that all knowledge, like all life, is suffering, undergoing, learning to bear and forbear. Because of this fearsome mortality that is part of a knowledge of ways, we are obliged, in such knowledge, to cultivate a good, rich, earthy understanding of "enough" (Berry, 1987). We are obliged, too, to then suffer again the certain knowledge that in our schools, in our lives, in our hallucinations of progress and all the little panics these induce there never seems to be enough.

Sometimes, in bearing such knowing, I feel my age. I feel my own passing.

At one point we stood on a raised wooden platform in the middle of a marsh just as the sun was setting, and the vocal interplays of red-winged blackbirds' songs, the curves of their flights and the patterning of both of these around nests cupped in the yellow-and-black-garden-spidery bulrushes—audible but invisible sites bubbling full of the pink, wet, warbling smallness of chicks—were clearly, in their own way, acts of spotting *us*.

"Ways" bespeaks a thread of kindredness with what one knows, a sense of deep relatedness and intimate, fleshy obligation (Caputo, 1993). But it betrays another little birding lesson: that we are their relations as much as they are ours, that we are thus caught in whatever regard this place places on us:

> The whole ensemble of sentient life cannot be deployed except from the site of a being which is itself visible, audible, sensible. The visible world and the eye share a common flesh; the flesh is their common being and belonging together.
>
> (Caputo, 1993, p. 201)

Or, if you like, a more drastic mosquito lesson about living relations: "flesh is . . . a reversible, just insofar as what eats is always edible, what is carnivorous is always carnality" (p. 200). So just as these mosquitoes eat up my sweet, sweaty blood skinslicked under the lures of CO_2 that drew them near, I get their lives in return, gobbled up into liquid gurgling *konk-la-rees*. This is the meaty, trembly level of mutuality and interdependence that crawls beneath all our tall tales of relations. This common flesh is the fearsome limit of our narrativity.

In a knowledge of ways, I do not simply know. I am also *known*. These cicadas and I turn around each other, each forming the other in kind, "both sensible and sensitive, reversible aspects of a common animate element" (Abram, 1996, p. 66). Even more unsettling than this, *as* we know this place, so are we known by it (Palmer, 1993). That is, the character of our knowing and how gracefully and generously we carry what we know reflects on our character.

One final birding lesson for now. Catching a glimpse of a blue heron pair over past the edge of the marsh, tucked up under the willowy overhangs.

Shore edge log long deep bluey sunset shadow fingers.

Sudden rush of a type of recognition almost too intimate to bear, an event of birding never quite lodged in any birding guides:

"It's *that* pair!"

What a strange and incommensurate piece of knowledge. How profoundly, how deeply, how wonderfully *useless* it is, knowing that it is *them*, seemingly calling for names more intimate, more proper than "heron," descriptions richer and more giddy than "Voice: deep harsh croaks: *frahnk, frahnk, frahnk*" (Peterson, 1980, p. 100). Such knowing doesn't lead anywhere. It is, by itself, already always full, already always enough.

Perhaps this irreplaceable, unavoidable intimacy is why our tales of the Earth always seem to include proper names ("obligations require proper names" [Caputo, 1993, p. 201]), always seem to be full of love and heart, always seem to require narrations of particular times and places, particular faces, particular winds, always seem to invite facing and listening and remembering.

It is squarely here that a great deal of my own work has come to rest: how to carry these birding lessons home, back into the often stuffy confines of elementary schools, back into the often even stuffier confines, for example, of elementary school mathematics (see Chapters 9–12), back, too, into the archaic, often literal-minded narrows of academic work and the forms of speaking and writing and research it allows.

Just imagine: mathematics conceived as a living discipline, a living topography, a living place, full of ancestors and kin and living relations, full of tales told and tales to tell. And imagine, too, mathematics education conceived as an open, generous invitation of our children into the intimate ways of this old, mysterious, wondrous place.

14
The Surroundings

DAVID W. JARDINE

I

Beginning meditation: There is a robin singing out straight south of our house, high up in one of the spruces or pines, out of sight but echoing off the hill to the west. Bursting full of the sunlight spring that has finally arrived after a terrible winter (dark cloud brain stem cabin fevers and all, wanting, at times, to scream out of my skin).

This is the third morning I've noticed him singing. He is there. But he is also there *again*. A brief little pitter-patter, but not the sort of thing I'll report to others, because what would I say? How odd such saying would seem.

"Why are you telling me this?"

So, what is the character of such knowledge, and how does it differ from what usually passes as knowing?

How is such knowledge obtained?

To what does such knowledge obtain? That is, what, precisely, is it that is known in such knowing? In these days of meaning making (socially constructed or otherwise), can we tolerate believing that what is known here is, in any sense, *there*? somehow *of* the Earth *even if* I hadn't noticed? Can we imagine, in these days of hyper-consciousness, living as we academics do under the terrible burden of hyper-literacy, that human experience breaks out beyond the envelope of flesh? That such breaking out might not require a Foucaultian sadistic hyper-experience, but just might require quiet, rest, some attention spent to robins, some time spent beyond the confines of this weird, new, addictive god of post-modern urbanity?

How fragile, we might then ask, how long-lasting, how vital, how telling, is such a knowledge, not only of robins and their habitualities, but of *that one, its* having returned, *there* up in *those* trees, in these failing days of May?

What is the goal of such knowing? What is it for? Where does it lead and who does it lead there?

What is the good of such knowledge? What good does it do to know this, and to pass it on in these written words?

What becomes of me in this sort of knowing? What becomes of me in attempting, here, to cite it in words on pages?

What does such knowing require of me in its obtaining, in its having and holding?

I'm sure I've experienced such robins before, but something, this time, is striking about having such experience.

Noticing that this pattern of living exists is odd enough.

Finding it, this time, so thrilling, is especially odd.

But there is something almost fearsome: finding that it is not only a noticing of patterns of robins, but a noticing *there*, of *that one*.

Noticing those things means conceding something else. If it is just there, just that one, then I am just here, just this one, in just this spring, under just this sun, and, after this horrible winter, feeling my age, feeling the passing of my days.

(Last fall, right in the middle of carrying wood in panics against the coming cold, something dropped. I will never finish this wood gathering. I will gather the wood I gather. Then I will be dead. What a relief!)

I *feel* something in such knowing. It trickles out into the higher sunarcs, into the clearing overhead, into the evidential bursts of living that are around me, the smell, the longings, the greenywhite plantdriven upwardness, spring. This knowing is, in part, a felt connectedness to all the small times humans have raised their heads and paused their breath and noticed the faces of the Earth.

It is a felt connectedness to the way these yellow dandelions raise their heads to sunlight and turn and nod at its passing.

This one just this, and that one just that.

All the times of prayer over small foods, of thanksgiving and relief over sun's returning, of the bodily pleasures of fires from woodpiles cut and stored last summer. A sense of pleasure and gratitude and grace in hearing that robin return, especially after this winter.

Deeply felt connection to all those hesitations.

Like the place of meditation, like the place of breath, this noticing is always *right where I left it*.

It is always The Same, even without my attention, even though each breath makes all the difference.

II

The smaller the surroundings become, the more vital and irreplaceable and necessary I seem to become to the character and continued existence of those surroundings.

Not just smallness.

Speculation on theory and geography: that constructivism and its dark twin of deconstruction were born in the city, where I and others like me are rightly understood as vital and irreplaceable and necessary to such surroundings and their senses and significations and continuances. There, everything ultimately signifies us, as Makers of the World, and constructivism and deconstruction orbit each other in the turns that are proper to that place.

III

Elbow River walk, winter 1997, −40 degrees Celsius, with icefog swirls rising up off the stillpatch water.

Brilliant Alberta Big Sun Blue Sky Blue. Past a low hill covered in three feet of snow. The unmistakable signs of a deer having humped its way down, two deep round fronthoof punctures and a huge ass-and-back-feet rumpprint, clunked downhill every four feet or so.

I have taken hundreds of these walks and never noticed such prints before.

This is so humiliating! *Where have I been?* And a cascade of feeling a sort of shame, a sort of nakedness before this hill, before this snow, before just these signs of just that deer, signified and now absent, and just me and no one else, with my own tracks trailed behind, standing here, stock-still, breathing hard.

I sometimes so wish that these prints could just be prints and not a comment on my life. But as soon as they become deer prints, they point to what is absent, what is signified, and as soon as this first breakout appears All Beings Innumerable show up to bear witness to these prints, myself included and this single life. Yes. These Beings Innumerable are a comment on my life and I don't really wish it otherwise.

So, where *have* I been? And how shall I answer to these Beings Innumerable? How shall I repay the debts of my lack of attention, seen in the pretty rainbow oilslick oozing from the road overpass I've just driven to get here?

And who is this "I" that's been missing?

And how could it be that I could go missing in this way?

And what does all my writing rest upon with this gone unnoticed?

What are the geographies of these words you are reading?

Our epistemologies don't serve us especially well in such questions.

IV

... the order and regularity in [what] we call *nature*, we ourselves introduce. We could never find [such orderliness and regularity] ... had not we ourselves, or the nature of our mind, originally set them there.

(Kant, 1767/1964, p. 147)

If order and regularity we ourselves introduce, without us the whole of things disassembles. Thus, theory and geography. A suspicion: deconstruction operates within the limits of human construction, *but there is no limit*, because, in Hegel's little horror show, any knowledge of such limits is always beyond such limits.

Hyper-consciousness: how could there be a world without us? And paranoia: what if there is!?

We could not find anything in the world if we had not put it there ourselves.
All knowledge is construction.
All intimacies are discoursed.
All care and love are simply hidden wills empowered.
All learning is caught in the sway of busi[y]ness.
All breath is measured.
All deadlines precisely that.
All reliance is slavery.
All naming is colonial.
All dependencies are to be treated with irony, cynicism, and condescension.
(No longer three "R"s!)
Let's finally admit these as the real outcomes of post-modernism.
Perhaps these moods are not necessary to post-modernism. Perhaps it is not depression. Perhaps it is not cabin fevers.
But it must find more of a belly heaved beneath its crowns of words.
I need more of a belly heaving beneath my crowns of words.

V

A sweet friend took a group of people up into the Rocky Mountains, and sat them in a circle, enticing them, in an ecological exercise, to breathe this place, to recollect themselves and their relations, here, to "re-connect."
A sudden muffled CA-COOM of heavy pawprints lifted off a low spruce up the hill above their heads.
Cougar.
And the footloose giddy rockstumble run as fast as possible that resulted. And in the puffy airgasp, in the bloodypump redness, in the nickelspittle of mouths dried to tears, belly laughs of a deeply felt and fearsome connectedness that had broken the spell of heady thoughts of Mother Earth.
Edibility.
Here, then, sits the fallacy, but it is no longer an epistemological fallacy. It is no longer a quarrel about concepts and subjects and objects and patterns and schemata and structures and where they are located and who is who and what belongs to which.
Surely we all bring our lives to bear on what we see, how we live, what we think, how and when the heart warms.
Just as surely, we "construct"—that is, we "make" something of—what comes to meet us.
And just as surely, the paw thumps of that cougar were "read" as "signs" of "something."
But it is not a significance we can endlessly postpone at our leisure, toying with it, and finally hating it for its obviousness.
Crawling underneath these sureties is the certain knowledge that these makings are also *the problem* we face in our humanity.

The chattering monkey is always narrating, so that any attempt to rest in the ways of things and to allow what is beyond us to have *its own* ways, *its own* Dharma, is haunted by the bareteethed chitter-who-who-who of this is this and that is that and what if and when and then and therefore.

Monkey mind.

And a bit of a hint about the geographies of these theories I hold so dear.

VI

I just imagine the cynical post-modernist caught and felled by that cougar. And as its teeth begin to pull bloody human thigh muscles from their place, we see the final grinning sneer at the cougar for being so obvious, so foundationalist, so bereft of the twittery insight that my leg might not signify food at all! Ha ha!

VII

I'm not sure if this is a dream: walking to Lakeshore Public School through the powerline field in spring just after a big rain, and seeing the trembly beginning of a small stream, big elementary-school-yellow-Crayola sun, big blue smile of sky, and moist, fleshy eye-corner water runoff snaking through the newly lifted white brightygreen blades.

Today, spring runoff trailing through aspens that have just opened and cast green parabolas under the sun's airblue arch over foothills. Yes! Sunlight and the teeth of lions.

Entering the powers and potentialities of this place through damming up water with sticks, or cutting shoeslide mudtroughs for letting water flow faster.

Damming and letting go. A swinging gate.

Down on my hands and knees 46 years old (just got a soaker!) prodding at the sticks holding the organic bubbly surfacefroth of fastrunning overflow stream wanting to feel the breathrush of release working to no end then squatting, sunshine, meditation, breathmeasures, after, hard, walk, in, fog, steaming, up, off, weeks of woody rain.

Fatsquat. Bellytilt. Breath. Looking upstream and knowing that something was slowly coming downstream out of the yellowy lightturns of water.

Close to awe.

Not awe of the eyes and brains and ascendancy and visions. Eyes drawn down. The crawly awe of muscles and shit and wormy Earth smells.

Just around those little bends.

Coming this way.

Under the purposeless warbles of robin haloes overhead.

15

"In These Shoes Is the Silent Call of the Earth"

Meditations on Curriculum Integration, Conceptual Violence, and the Ecologies of Community and Place

DAVID W. JARDINE, ANNETTE LAGRANGE,
AND BETH EVEREST

Introduction: "Sounds like an Interesting Unit"

The following is a portion of a recent e-mail exchange:

> Forgive the cross posting; I'm looking for a variety of points of view. I'm looking for lesson plans (or ideas that I can make into lessons) for teaching art in math (or math in art). Specifically, what math can I see in any work of Van Gogh? This will be a workshop for 5/6th graders.

One response received to this request was:

> How about the spirals in Starry, Starry Night and the sunflowers in picture of same name? Both can be connected to math and/or science. Spiralling procedures can be written in Logo teaching the concept of stepping. Estimations of number of sunflowers in head as well as patterns created by seeds while still in head are other ideas. You could sprout sunflower seeds and collect data: How many days average to sprout? What percentage of seeds sprouted? Does size of seeds affect sprouting speed? etc. etc. Sounds like an interesting unit.
>
> (Lugone 1996)

The authors' interest in curriculum integration is, in part, a response to an unsettling sense of fragmentation that can be found, not only in this example, but in much of our work with teachers, student-teachers and schools. We believe that the above-cited example is typical of what counts as thinking about curriculum integration in elementary schools. It betrays an almost random surface skittering over topics which casts the oddest of things together. The brilliant sunflowers in Arles in the south of France and how they bore Van Gogh's agonized attention in his final years are linked, in the imagination of those who frequent early elementary classrooms, to rows of white Styrofoam cups with masking-taped names and dried soils and neglected, dying sunflower seedlings drooped on hot Grade 1 classroom sills. Reading this e-mail exchange produced in us a strange sense of restlessness, displacement, and homelessness, a sense of no longer knowing where we are or what is required as a proper, generous, but honest response to this well-meant pursuit of "curriculum integration."

Curriculum integration poses hard questions to those involved in the educational endeavour. What does it mean to teach with integrity? What does it mean to treat one's topic of study with integrity? How might school classroom and university teachers alike teach in a way that respects the character and integrity of the lives and experiences of children and the work undertaken with them?

We suggest that part of the answer to these far-too-large questions is ecological in character. Curriculum integration has to do with keeping things in place, nested in the deep communities of relations that make them whole, healthy and sane. We are intrigued by Berry's (1986) reminder that an orientation towards integrity and wholeness has something to do with health, healing, and the mending of relations, and, therefore, that pursuing curriculum integration in our classrooms has something to do with "choosing to be healers" (Clifford & Friesen 1994) in relation to ourselves, the Earth, the topics taught in our schools, and the children invited into those topographies. We are intrigued as well by how such difficult, disciplined work is much more deeply *pleasurable* (Berry 1989) for adults and children alike than the panic of "activities" that consumes so much of educational practice.

We must be generous enough to hope that the clashing together of Van Gogh and mathematics in this e-mail exchange was done in good faith, and that real, substantial, integrated, heartening work has resulted. Even if these teachers did not find their way into such work, we cannot deny that the oddness of this example is not precisely *their* problem. School teachers and university teachers all, in their own ways, are living out a deep cultural logic of fragmentation and we (for we must include ourselves here, as the authors of this chapter) have all participated, directly or indirectly, in the strange efforts at curriculum integration that sometimes result.

This exchange still stands, however, as a sign or a warning that issues of curriculum integration still need our attention. This continuing need for attention is almost too obvious: in a living system, health and wholeness and the cultivation of good relations are never simply givens, because the young are always still arriving again, ready to call what we have taken as given to account in their own lives. The Earth, too, is beginning to have its say about our character and our conduct and our ignoring of its ways.

"One after the Other"

A few years ago, a teacher mentioned on an Internet listserve called "Kidsphere" that she was thinking of doing "shoes" as a "theme" or a "unit" in her classroom. Over the course of nearly two weeks, the net was inundated with dozens of responses from all across North America—different types of shoes, different styles and preferences, different materials that shoes are made of: "There was an old woman who lived in a shoe," indoor and outdoor shoes, Hans Brinker's skates, shoes and boots, cobblers and elves, different professions and their footwear, snowshoes, skis, and such, different countries and their shoes, different ways to secure them (laces, velcro, buckles, slip-ons—leading to numbers of eye-holes and lengths of laces and the idea of "pairs"), Puss and his boots, sizes of shoes, graphs of shoe sizes, graphs of shoe colors, graphs of shoe-lace colors, dismissing children by shoe color as a management technique, shoeprints and footprints in paint, tracks and animals in science, and perhaps a detective game that has children tracking something by its prints.

And so on.

We can all understand the giddy rush of such exchanges, and we have all participated and taken some pleasure in them. However, despite their earnestness and good will, and the conviviality with which they occur, such exchanges seem to treat each moment, each particular, with haste and a lack of careful attention. Of course, such a "continuity of attention and devotion" (Berry 1986, p. 32) to particulars is not what such brainstorming sessions and subsequent "webbings," "mappings" or "theme-ings" are for. They are intended to give a broad and quick picture of surface similarities, surface connections, surface relations under the name of "shoes."

However, because none of the nodes in the web is read for its rich textures and patterns and hidden discourses, none of the connections seem especially strong or robust or well-rooted. What results are connections that sometimes seem forced and trivial, betraying a rushed, ultimately unsatisfying lack of attention and care to anything in particular (see Chapter 21 for thoughts on how time itself changes character in such matters). Rather than providing a picture of some integrated patterns of the world or serving as a prelude to the work of settling oneself somewhere, it is as if these themes or webs of ideas concede, aggravate, or even sometimes create the very situation of fragmentation and alienation that they are meant to remedy.

Consider these words of a Grade 6 teacher:

> When you mention an idea, it's so typical of teachers to graciously share everything they can. And they start throwing ideas at you, all meant to help out. You really don't have time to think about anything. Nothing gets a chance to soak in. You get so overwhelmed by all the bits, and, after all, you don't want to leave any out now that people have offered them, so that all you can do is just present them one after the other.
>
> (Research note, December 1996)

In their own way (and this may be especially aggravated by the existence of Internet and the possibility of hundreds of comparatively instantaneous responses), such brainstorming flurries seem to work against, or at least make more difficult, settling down *somewhere*, doing *something* well, treating *something* with the integrity it warrants.

It is as if these flurries start out as emulations of the giddy rush of life, of newness, freshness and ebullience that we find so pleasing in our children. However, in many elementary school classrooms (and so much of the work done in Faculties of Education), we let loose rushes of thin, restless activities not one of which warrants much attention or work. We then end up producing, in turn, fading attention spans both in our children and in ourselves. And such a loss of attention is most frequently then blamed on our children. We call their shortness or lack of attention "a characteristic of young children" and we excuse our own lack of attention to the work at hand by citing the attention each individual student needs from us.

After witnessing the activity of her cooperating teacher for a semester, one student-teacher recently said something we found quite telling regarding the tempo, attention and activity level in elementary school classrooms: "My teacher is busy all the time but she never seems to do any work" (Research note, December 1996).

Curriculum Integration and Conceptual Violence

What is lost in many efforts in curriculum integration is precisely the *topography*, the *ecos*, the place of any particular thing. Many webs or themes proceed in a "heady" fashion: each particular gains "wholeness"/integration only through the concerted intervention of a *concept* (e.g. the *concept* of "shoes"). It is the *concept* that brings the particulars together.

Pursued in this way, curriculum integration can become a sort of *conceptual violence* that tears particulars out of their intimate, particular places and re-sorts them "away from home" under general, abstract, anonymous categories. These categories are not sensuous, bodily, indigenous, and immediate, but oddly cold, ideational, fleshless, and alien. The very act meant to heal and restore communities of real, integral relations and patterns thus becomes complicit in their unwitting destruction and replacement with conceptual structures that are cleaner, clearer, and less Earthy and alluring than those living communities. The very act meant to help us attend to the integrities of our experience in a whole and healthy way becomes a form of interpretive deafness, an inability to hear what words and worlds of implication might be *already at work* in the stubborn particulars (Wallace 1987; see Chapter 12) that come to meet us, before our conceptualizations take hold. As one teacher put it so poignantly, "the water of chemical composition and the water in which my child has drowned *don't belong together*" (Research note, December 1996), in spite of their conceptual affinities. The *world* of hydrogen, oxygen, and their combinations is not the same world as the agonies of the loss of a child, or the mysteries of the water that washes away sins, or a tall cool glass stippled with condensation on a hot summer's day. Each of these bears *its own* memories, relations, obligations, its own tales and topographies that make it whole, healthy, and livable.

The intervention of a *concept* of "water" into these worlds in order to "integrate" them is simply tactless and unbecoming—disintegrative, in fact, of the integrities of experience that are already at work without such intervention.

Narrative Integration and the Recovery of the Particular

Our growing concerns over this portrayal of the situation of curriculum integration as a sort of thin, conceptual surface picture and the ensuing loss of the topographies of the particular, gave way to the recollection of a passage in Martin Heidegger's *Origins of the work of art*, in which he meditates on a Van Gogh painting of a peasant woman's shoes. This meditation, in all its convoluted twists and turns (and despite its tone of high German Romanticism), provided us with a way to begin reconceptualizing the nature of curriculum integration:

> As long as we only imagine a pair of shoes in general, or simply look at the empty, unused shoes as they merely stand there in the picture we shall never discover [them]. A pair of peasant shoes and nothing more. And yet from the dark opening of the worn insides of the shoes the toilsome tread of the worker stares forth. In the stiffly rugged heaviness of the shoes there is the accumulated tenacity of her slow trudge through the furrows of the field. Under the soles slides the loneliness of the field-path as evening falls. In the shoes is the silent call of the earth, its quiet gift of the ripening grain and its unexplained self-refusal in the fallow desolation of the wintry field. This equipment is pervaded by uncomplaining anxiety as to the certainty of bread, the wordless joy of having once more withstood want, the trembling before the impending childbed and shivering at the surrounding menace of death.
>
> (Heidegger 1971, pp. 33–4)

There is a profound familiarity in these words, one that recalls all the years of early childhood. Stopping, with a sort of interpretive mindfulness, over *this* pair of shoes (and not skittering past it in a brainstorming session) might itself reveal a way that our course (*currere*/curriculum) is whole/integrated in some deep, ecologically sane and sustainable way.

We can recall moments of passing by our father's or mother's or grandfather's shoes tucked by the front door or left tumbled on balconies or verandas, seeing the deep imprint of their tracks inside, the places of shiny imprint, traces of the lives they have lived and the work they have done, and how, in slipping these on our own small feet, it was not just these particular things that we engaged but a whole world, their world and its deep familial intersection with our own. We can all recall, too, how we may have warily avoided those shoes and the life they stamped on us or others.

All of us understand, somehow, that *these* shoes are not capturable with any integrity and wholeness on a web under, say, "different types of shoes" or "shoes and types of work." Rather, *these* shoes gain an integrity and place in a world full of rich memory and familiarity and use, a world full of the intractable particularities of experience, whether for good or ill or some troubling mixture of the two.

These shoes—the black boots my neighbour Harry wore in our trudging work of installing furnaces in people's basements—are not understandable in an integrated way by simply placing them alongside others in a list of different types of shoes from around the world. They do not belong alongside others, except perhaps those of his wife when he arrives home, or mine as we rested at lunch, and then how those age-old boots fit with the thermos and lunchpail worn thin from use, like his tools, bearing the marks of his hands and the marks of age and work and craft. The world in which one might produce a web of different types of shoes is a different world than the world evoked by dark stains and smells of oil and coal dust, or the knotted pieces of broken lace as signs of Harry's odd frugality.

Understood conceptually and in general, "shoes" bear no history, no memory, no continuity, no dependencies, no place, no communities of relations. They are not *someone's, here, in this place*, and, in this sense, they are simply an *idea* of shoes, not fleshy and warm and curved just so. Despite all its calls to integration, categorizations, or thematizations such as "different types of shoes" breaks apart the very small, intimate threads of familiarity, obligation and relation that actually hold *these* shoes in a real, integrated place. Such small, intimate threads and the worlds they evoke get replaced with a concept that cannot provide any of the comforts, the common strengths, of the place the particular has left behind in such severances.

Sticking with such particularity has an interesting effect. Rather than simply bogging us down in the burden of specificity, the particular takes on a certain buoyancy and lightness. It becomes a node on a web of real sustenance and import. It becomes an "opening" out into something rather than closed in on itself. It is, so to speak, "held up" by all of its relations, lightened of its isolation and pathology, and experienced, somehow, as "fitting" (Bly n.d., p. 13). The language, here, of course, is bizarre and groping as befits the attempt to express in general terms the outward burst of a fecund individual case.

What emerges from taking these particular shoes seriously in their wholeness is a sense that things have integral places. Things themselves, in their very particularity, issue a sense of belonging somehow, in intractable relations of materiality, obligation, community, history, memory, and so on. The integration or wholeness that ensues, therefore, is not just about these particular shoes. Rather, the phenomenon of integration or wholeness itself, as involving an attention to place and memory and relations and community, starts to come forward.

What starts to come forward is not a bluster of activities for the classroom, but a way of taking up the world that breaks the spell of the consumptivism, exhaustion and the panic of activities into which so much of our lives is inscribed.

This does not leave us with a "great idea" that we can now directly address or directly "apply." We now have, in its stead, *a serious, immediate, ecological obligation*, to treat things that come to meet us with integrity, to heal the ways that things have become fragmented and displaced and unsettled and dispersed into the ethers of good hearted but ecologically suspect internet exchanges.

Endbit: Particularity and De-Romanticizing "Place"

In circulating the idea of this chapter to colleagues and students and friends, an odd thing began to emerge, something typical as a response to interpretive work. What arrived were particular tales of particular shoes that were, in each case, wedged deeply in the flesh and breath of the teller. As this paper proceeded, it became clear—although still somewhat mysterious—why shoes are so frequently a topic in Early Childhood Education. It seems that they always already bear a fleshy familial intimacy that we all recognize at some deep, gutty level and that belies and resists our efforts at conceptual thematization. It may be that our initial attraction to shoes reveals some mute recognition of an integrity of children's (*our* children, and therefore our own) experiences that is then unwittingly betrayed in our subsequent conceptualizations.

It may be that our curriculum-integration-conceptualizations are unintentionally teaching a horrible lesson.

Consider one particular response we received as we wrote and spoke of shoes and curriculum integration. A poem that brings particular shoes to life:

> David is talking about shoes, about some
> paper he is writing about shoes, & I am
> thinking about Dad's rubbers, the black
> rubber oversoles/overshoes that he always
> wears in the rain & the snow. old man's
> shoes. things that he must wear. the stamp of
> him. the mark that he makes in the snow, in
> our lives, in my own life. his father wears
> them too

> & I think that i cannot really find the shoe
> that fits my mother; perhaps it could be the
> high heels that are in the dressup box, the
> things that are left over from some other
> life that we as children never knew, can
> never know. but she does not wear these now &
> i must imagine her long legs sliding into

white silk stockings. the garter belt that
she throws on her wedding day

all of these scenes i must imagine, as now
most often i remember her in sneakers, but
this is not the right word to describe my
mother's footwear. ked's? tennis shoes? sensible
flats? the glass slipper?

my father wears rubbers, overshoes, like he
has always done because he has always been
old, but my mother i cannot define so simply.
nor can i explain her passion for shoes, stored
in her closet. winter shoes: oxfords, smooth
soled, vibram soled, patent leather, navy, black,
brown, dark green, khaki. summer shoes:
red, white, yellow, orange, stored in boxes

I hear the water running for her bath. imagine
the dressing gown folded. her blue
nightie. the large white towel. a new bar
of soap. her legs. still slender, she
steps into the bubbles. her feet, narrow,
bumpy. her voice is soft.
i cannot hear her step
on the stair.

(Beth Everest)

We wish to end with a plea for forgiveness that we ourselves require. We are all living out a deep cultural logic of fragmentation that distracts attention, that is cynical about devotion or depth, and that mocks any talk of good work, that identifies settling and quiet and meditation with passivity, and that cannot imagine how one could want anything but business in our classrooms.

What we are alluding to here is not simply another great idea for the classroom. It is not merely an issue of *teacher knowledge* or adequate *information* about a topic or a child:

One thing we dare not forget is that better solutions than ours have at times been made by people with much less information than we have. We know, too, from the study of agriculture, that the same information, tools and techniques that in one farmer's hands will ruin land, in another's will save and improve it. This is not a recommendation of ignorance. To know nothing, after all, is no more possible than to know enough. I am only proposing that knowledge, like everything else, has its place, and that we need urgently now to *put* it in its place.

(Berry 1983, pp. 65–6)

This place into which knowledge must find its way, Berry suggests, has to do with care, character and love—surprisingly antiquated words in the current educational milieu. Integration and wholeness have more to do with the *way* one knows, the *way* one is, the *way* one hopes children will become and how we and they will carry ourselves, and how light and careful our footfalls will be on this Earth.

The examples we have cited are from the good-hearted work of teachers who are bearing an old logic of fragmentation and distraction on our behalf. We cannot pretend that their distraction is simply *their* problem, as if our own lives were somehow precious and exempt from questions of how to proceed with integrity, as if we might pretend to have somehow solved this problem in our own lives. Each new topic we address in our work with colleagues, with children and with student-teachers requires that we raise these questions of integration all over again. Although it might initially result in frustration, we have deliberately resisted the false promises of "yet another model" of curriculum integration sold to the highest textbook bidders.

One thing, however, is certain. We, as teachers, as parents, find ourselves at an especially difficult juncture in this cultural logic that we are all living out, facing the possibility, but not the necessity, of passing it on to our children.

16

American Dippers and Alberta Winter Strawberries

DAVID W. JARDINE

I

> In the seventh month the Fire-star declines,
> In the ninth month winter garments are handed out.
> The eleventh month comes with the blustering wind;
> The twelfth month, with the shivering cold.
> Without cloak or serge
> How are we to see the year out?
> (from "In the Seventh Month," compiled in the *Shih Ching*,
> 7th to 12th century BC, China [in Lui and Lo, 1990, p. 9])

The American dipper is a small black bird, half way in size between a robin and a sparrow, L-shaped, with stubby upright tail and head balanced high. These dippers are common all year long along the Elbow River that winds out of the Rocky Mountains and through Calgary, Alberta. Walked this past winter, in –40 degree winds, along the Elbow and its swirls of ice fog over rare still patches of open water, most of the river steeply hurrying east.

Dippers. Swim underwater upstream about 10 feet at a go, feeding on water-carried food. Then standing there dipping up and down while waiting for the next dive. Or rush to low water-surface flights full of a distinctive twittery warble. Like the muskrat in the steaming cold beaver pond nearby, remaining here as I leave. Remaining here, –40, what little left low-riding sun setting.

Leaving, under the darkening air-blue arch of what I hope is a gathering chinook, caught in bitter cold that breaks your bones.

> The twelfth month comes with the chopping of ice—clanging stroke after
> stroke
> The first month comes—we bring ice to the cold-house for storage;
> The second month comes—we rise early
> And make offering of garlic and lamb.
> In the ninth month comes the severe frost.

(p. 11)

Home, eating freshly bought fresh strawberries. Delicious red juicydrip taste. Then suddenly grotesquely beautiful. Suddenly out of place. How can these be *here*? And as these strawberries begin to taste unbecoming of this place and this cold, I end up feeling out of place as well. Eating these strawberries betrays something of those dippers and that ice and my living here.

II

> In the seventh month the Fire-star declines,
> In the ninth month winter garments are handed out.
> Spring days bring us the sun's warmth,
> And the orioles sing.
>
> (p. 9)

I recall growing up in southern Ontario, in what was then a small village crouched between Hamilton and Toronto, just at the west end of Lake Ontario—full of black-orange orioles, singing, and their droopnests branchended on silver maples or Royal Oaks, named like the red-and-white dairy trucks that delivered milk and cheese and butter and eggs.

Undeniable ecological memory, stored too deep, it seems, to switch. Earthy flesh memory born(e) in the body of the child I was raised. We carry memories of where we were born, and the triggers of such memories are themselves bodily:

> In the seventh month the shrikes cry
>
> (p. 10)

And in such a cry is borne part of my self crying back for the remembering of a seventh month, when strawberries arrived up out of our waiting and whiling (Ross, 2003, 2004; see Chapter 21).

So "bioregions" are not simply places with objectively nameable characteristics. They infest our blood and bones, and become odd, unexpected templates of how we carry ourselves, what we remember of the Earth, and how light and delicate are our footsteps in all the places we walk.

Burlington was, in the 1950s, a market garden area—small 40- to 60-acre farms bursting full and an area with many canning factories and wooden fruit-basket factories (up in Freeman, a once-named crossroad near the rail lines that has since disappeared). Back when such things mattered, Burlington was right at the hinge between the north–south rail route up from the fruit-growing areas of Lincoln County (Vineland, Jordan Harbour, east to Niagara-on-the-Lake) and the east–west rail routes to Toronto, Kingston, and on to Montreal, or west to London and Sarnia or down to Windsor and Detroit. Swimming, 1957, Lake Ontario, off the redbrick Legion Hall parking lot south of Water Street, just after the Aylmer Factory had burped out the leftover bilge of tomato canning, and how this hot-scented red-scummed flotation that made the water flapthick muffled and fly surface buzzy melded into the Polio Scares and the summers of no swimming at all.

I remember, growing up in Burlington—then a small village of 4,000, long since overgrown into the anyplace bedroom of nearby city condensations—having to *wait* for strawberries.

> In the fourth month, the small grass sprouts
> In the fifth month the cicadas sing.
> In the eighth month we harvest the field,
> In the tenth month the leaves begin to fall
>
> (p. 10)

Their appearance once meant something deeper and more difficult than their obvious bright pleasure-presence to the tongue: about place, about seasonality, about expectation, about era, about arrival, about remembering, about reliance, about resignation and hope and little-kid pleasures, about time and its cyclicalities. Strawberries once belonged *somewhere*. They thus arrived, not as objects but as bright and brief heralds. As heralds, they were always young, always new and fresh, always delicate and timely, always soon to take leave, leaving grief again at their passing.

III

> In the sixth month we eat wild plums and grapes,
> In the seventh month we cook sunflower and lentils.
> In the eighth month we strip leaves of their dates,
> In the tenth month we bring home the harvested rice,
> We make it into spring wine
> For the nourishment of the old.
> In the seventh month, we eat melons.
>
> (p. 11)

Pulling strawberries into continuous presence, into continuous, indiscriminate availability is, in its own way, a sort of objectivism. These Alberta winter strawberries are only in the most odd of senses here in my hands, even though, clearly, *here they are*. Something about eating them is potentially dangerously distracting. They are no longer exactly Earth produce even though, of course, they are just that. But they are commodities lifted off the Earth and floating above it, taking me with them. As they begin to float up into detached, oil-soaked commodification, I, too, begin to float, detached, unEarthly.

Such odd, objective strawberries, ripped out of the Earthy contexts of their arrival—no Earth to smell, no resignation to waiting fulfilled, no sunny warmth—can, however, also be alerting. This subtle disruption of a sense of seasonality (one that my own son was just barely raised up into) that transports and oils and technologies have brought us: odd pleasures, since, in the grip of cabin fevers, these strawberries have also saved my life. And yet, my pleasure . . .

I love them even though they are covered with oil this time of year. My love of them now, indiscriminately, is part of the "trouble in the Middle East." My pleasure is a reason for the war, just like the rainbow-stain gasoline that drove me out west to the edge of the Elbow River to see those dippers in the first place.

IV

I cannot stop remembering a tomato tossed out against the backyard fence in late Ontario fall and yielding, of itself, without me, beyond desire and necessity, a great green clump of bushes four feet across, with that unmistakable near-acrid smell of fat and furry vines. This dipper-place is a harsh place, which will yield potatoes and peas and not much else.

Another walk, moose cow, great Alert Being, chest deep in snow near the river. An odd coalescing point, a great gathering in what must be a large habitat. This moose body as a place of great intensity and great need. Seeing her munching on those small firtree tips seems near-ludicrous and courageous and near-impossible all at once. How large must the territory of tree tips be for there to be such a being? And me, in winter, here, sucking strawberries.

I am living in a place that a hunter should live or someone with animals to slaughter and offer and eat:

> In the tenth month we clean the threshing ground
> With a pair of goblets we hold a village feast.
> Let's slaughter sheep and lamb.
>
> (p. 11)

Out in the greenhouse, sheltered in part from the place, tomatoes. Great Alert Beings, here and yet not here.

An ecological grieving for that deeply imprinted place where I was raised and a joy over the potatoes burping up out of tilled soils, and the young gray jay just now flirting with the feeder.

Ecological grieving for the waiting that is no longer necessary.

V

> In the fifth month the locust stirs its legs,
> In the sixth month the grasshopper vibrates its wings.
> In the seventh month, out in the fields;
> In the eighth month, about the doors.
> In the tenth month the crickets
> Get under our beds.
>
> (p. 10)

Winter has cracked, or at least blinked. I, too, am a Great Alert Being, surprised to find that some of that alertness, as well as some grieving, is carried here, to Alberta, from the place I grew up.

It took me years to even begin to actually experience this place and its beauties. Too much of my thinking, too much of my experience is placeless. And yet here, summer, finally, heartbreaking blue against the yellow green of pines.

Hale-Bopp's nightly bristle, Mars between Leo's legs, Orion set already set, the great hunter that I am not.

And "*Liu-huo* ('cascading fire')" (p. 8), Antares, Great Red Giant in Scorpius, soon to rise.

Time to tend the tomatoes. Because, in the seventh month, the cascading fire of the Scorpion descends and winter begins its miraculous return.

17

"All Beings Are Your Ancestors"
A Bear Sutra on Ecology, Buddhism, and Pedagogy

DAVID W. JARDINE

> Transforming according to circumstances, meet all beings as your ancestors.
>
> (Hongzhi Zhengjue [1091–1157])

I

Just spotted a year-old black bear crossing Highway 66 at McLean Creek, heading north.

From a distance, struggling at first to resolve its color and lowness and lopey canter into dog or cat likenesses as it stretched up to the side of the road and across and suddenly slowed into distinctive roundhumpness—bear!

Stopped and watched him amble up the shalysteep creekedge. Wet. Greenglistening. Breath arriving plumey in the damp and cold after days of heat waves . . . been 33 degrees C. and more for four days running in the foothills of the Rockies west of Calgary. Here, roaming in the edge between prairie and forest, between flatlands and hills and mountains—here, when summers break, they tend to break deeply.

Cold rain. Cold.

It is so thrilling to not be accustomed to this sort of experience, to have it still be so *pleasurable*. Bear. His presence almost unbelievable, making this whole place waver and tremble, making my assumptions and presumptions and thoughts and tales of experiences in this place suddenly wonderfully irrelevant and so much easier to write because of such irrelevance.

Bear's making this whole place show its fragility and momentariness and serendipities.

Bear's making my own fragility and momentariness show.

That is what is most shocking. This unforeseeable happenstance of bear's arrival and my own happiness are oddly linked. This "hap" (Weinsheimer, 1985, pp. 7–8) hovering at the heart of the world.

My own life as serendipitous, despite my earnest plans. Giddy sensation, this.

Like little bellybreath tingles on downarcing childgiggle swingsets.

Felt in the *tanden* (Sekida, 1976, pp. 18–19, 66–67) in Walking Meditation (Nhat Hanh, 1995).

Breath's gutty basement. Nearby, the lowest Chakra tingles with an upspine burst to whitesparkle brilliance just overhead and out in front of the forehead.

In moments like this, something flutters *open*. Shifting fields of relations bloom. Wind stirs nothing. Not just my alertness and sudden attention, but the odd sensation of knowing that these trees, this creek, this bear, are all *already* alert to me in ways proper to each and despite my attention. Something flutters *open*, beyond this centered self.

With the presence of this ambly bear, the whole of things arrives, fluttered open.

II

All beings are your ancestors. The feary sight of him, teaching me, reminding me of forgotten shared ancestries, forgotten shared relations to Earth and Air and Fire and Water. That strange little lesson having to be learned again: that he has been here all along, cleaving this shared ancestry, cleaving this shared Earth of ours, making and forming my life beyond my "wanting and doing" (Gadamer, 1989, p. xxviii), beyond my wakefulness and beyond my remembering.

It is not so much that this bear is an "other" (Shepard, 1996), but that it is a *relative*, that is most deeply transformative and alarming to my ecological somnambulance and forgetfulness. It is not just that I might come awake and start to remember these deep, Earthy relations.

It is also that, even if I don't, they all still bear witness to my life.

Relations. Who would have thought? Coming across *one of us* that I had forgotten.

Coming, therefore, across myself *as also one of us*. Such a funny thing to be surprised about again. In the face of this Great Alert Being, I, again, become one of us!

Great Alert Being, this bear. Great Teacher. His and my meaty bodies both of the same "flesh of the [Earth]" (Abram, 1996, pp. 66–67), rapt in silent conversations (p. 49).

Where, my god, have I been? And what have I been saying, betraying of myself and my distraction?

III

This bear ambles in the middle of all its Earthly relations to wind and sky and rain and berries and roadsides and the eons of beings that helped hone that creek edge to just those small pebbly falls under the weight of his paws: "Even the very tiniest thing, to the extent that it 'is,' displays in its act of being the whole web of circuminsessional interpenetration that links all things together" (Nishitani, 1982, p. 150).

The whole Earth conspires to make just these simple events just exactly like this: "Within each dust mote is vast abundance" (Hongzhi, 1991, p. 14). "This is the odd butterfly effect" (Glieck, 1987, p. 17) fluttering in the stomach.

This, too, is the profound co-implication of all beings that is part of ecological mindfulness—that each being is implicated in the whole of things and, if we are able to experience it from the belly, from each being a deep relatedness to all beings can be unfolded, can be understood, can be felt, can be adored, can be praised in prayerful grace, a giving thanks (Snyder, 1990, pp. 175–185). Lovely intermingling of thinking and thanksgiving (Heidegger, 1968).

So the thrill of seeing this bear is, in part, the exhilarating rush felt in seeing it explode outwards, emptying itself into all its relations, and then retracting to just that black bear, now an exquisite still-spot ambling at the center of all things. And more! "*The center is everywhere.* Each and every thing becomes the center of all things and, in that sense, becomes an absolute center. This is the absolute uniqueness of things, their reality" (Nishitani, 1982, p. 146).

Like breath exhaled outwards and then drawn in deep drafts. This inwardness and outwardness of emptiness (Sanskrit: *sunyata*; Japanese: *ku*)—each thing *is* its relatedness to all things, reflecting, each in each, in Indra's netted jewels and yet each thing is always just itself, irreplaceable. Smells of the forests of mid-August and the sweetness of late-summer wild flowers. Winey bloomy blush. Intoxicating.

All Beings are your Ancestors.

IV

Hey, bear!

If we are to meet all beings as our ancestors, we must also meet all those very same beings as our descendants. This odd, fluid, difficult, shifting edge point between the ancestors and the descendants is where our humanity lives.

This is "the empty field" (Hongzhi, 1991) that opens and embraces.

It is also the lifespot of teaching and learning and transmission and transformation.

There are many Great Teachers.

All praise to bear and his subtle gift.

Bragg Creek, Alberta, August 8–10, 1997

18

"Some Say the Present Age Is Not the Time for Meditation"

Thoughts on Things Left Unsaid in Contemporary Invocations of "Traditional Learning"

RAHAT NAQVI AND DAVID W. JARDINE

I

> One cannot achieve realization merely by listening
> To the perfect teachings of Buddha.
> As a weak person may die of thirst
> While being carried away by a great river,
> So the Dharma is ineffective unless meditated upon.

The main title of this chapter and the passage above are cited from a translation of Dakpo Tashi Namgyal's (1511–1587) *Mahamudra: The Moonlight—Quintessence of Mind and Meditation* (2006, pp. 5, 9). This text happened to be next on the summer pile of reading as we began talking about the topic of this paper: how the term "traditional" is being bandied about once again in Calgary, Alberta, schools as a clarion call for often heated, often contradictory, desires regarding children and their education.

We are concerned that something profound is being lost and forgotten in how the terms "traditional learning" and (therefore) "traditional schools" are being used. Something about tradition, and what learning means in a living tradition, has been effaced. We are living, it seems, with a weird exaggeration of the worst that tradition might mean.

We cannot speak on behalf of universals in this matter, but can only invoke cases, instances, and threads of thought that suggest an always emergent "family resemblance" (Wittgenstein, 1968, p. 36). The words above from 15th century Tibet, translated through into English, strike something that seems familiar, familial—in many elementary school classrooms in and around Calgary, merely listening and repeating by rote, merely memorizing and regurgitating, merely remaining silent and having no questions of one's own, have come to be what is understood by "traditional" learning. Learning as a form of meditation and self-formation has been erased or, worse yet,

185

subjectivized as something beyond the reach of efficient and effective schooling.

What seems to be invoked in the use of the term "traditional" is, we suggest, a suppressed by-product of the early 20th century efficiency movement of Frederick Winslow Taylor (1911), wherein the logic of the assembly line (Taylor worked with Henry Ford [Wrege & Greenwood, 1991]) and army regimentation (Taylor studied the Prussian army as a model of efficiency [Wrege & Greenwood, 1991]) was used to re-cast the nature of public schooling and make it more manageable and efficient. Workers ("teachers") were handed simple instructions for repeated tasks, set to specific time limits and "quality" control measures. They each worked on an isolatable and definable piece of the overall task ("curriculum content" was thus subdivided and developmentally sequenced), such that there would be no confusion or thought required, and also such that, if there was a problem with the end results, the specific site of the problem could be found and fixed. If a child has trouble, for example, with certain grammatical forms, the specific grade in which this was "taught" can be located and assessed for its effectiveness in the production of knowledge of this grammatical form. And, of course, in the end, if there is no problem with the "line" and its "workers," the issue is then located in the child him- or herself and serviced by the proliferation of special needs interventions.

The term "traditional" in North American educational circles thus comes loaded with connotation. It is surrounded by clusters of negatively charged images:

- rote memorization done in orderly rows;
- silent, seated children all facing one way;
- authoritarian teachers;
- strict disciplinary and managerial orderliness;
- images of children as wild and willful and needing these wills to be broken (see Miller, 1989);
- questions as simply problems to be fixed so that silence can once again reign;
- mathematized forms of assessment—akin to statistically formulated experimental method—not only holding sway, but forming and shaping the very nature of pedagogy itself;
- curriculum content subjected to the logic of fragmentation and breakdown into its smallest, most easily manageable bits and pieces ("the basics," so to speak);
- the managed doling out of knowledge by the teacher and the passive reception of such fragmented bits by students, who then must dole them out themselves on examinations that are themselves designed under the auspices of fragmentation and management.

One of the most pernicious threads of this line of thinking is not simply that it has re-cast the nature of public schooling in light of industrial production images of manageability and efficiency. Far worse is that the very idea, the very possibility, of public accountability, the very idea of giving a warrantable account of the value and worth of an educational setting, has become linked with the manageability and efficiency of that account. Good schooling is about management, about manageable results. "Objective test scores" are themselves by-products of the dovetailing of the efficiency movement and a great early 20th century faith that schooling can become the controllable, predictable, and manageable (Habermas, 1972) object of the statistically based methods of empirical science, and that classrooms can be run with all the uncontaminated results of a well-run experiment.

If this bespeaks something of the present age, then meditation, inquiry, and scholarly reflection and debate certainly do seem childish, laughably arcane, unproductive. In such a light, reflecting, thinking, and worrying over how one's knowledge comes to shape one's life and character are not considered proper matters for school. Long and complex conversations in a Grade Ten social stud-ies class about British minister Jack Straw's comments about Muslim women wearing *hijabs* and one student's (a Muslim girl, wearing a *hijab*) comment that it is often seen as "hiding something"—such matters come to appear to be at best private or personal matters and, at worst, time-wasting, resource-wasting, unaccountable, subjective, emotionally laden, biased, unaccountable, liberal arts "frills" only pursuable by those with too much time on their hands. Such meditation becomes a term of elitism and intellectualism. School bespeaks no such scholarly leisure, even though its etymology (L. *schola*) suggests that, "traditionally," this is exactly what it was for in some bygone age—not the present—when there was time for such meditation.

Another one of those Grade Ten social studies students talks to me (D.J.) about how she understands that her *hijab* is seen by many as a form of oppres-sion. She explained how, in her tradition, if you wear a *hijab* simply because someone tells you to, you might as well not wear it at all. She also voiced a profound idea about herself and her classmates. Some of her female classmates believe that they are free to dress any way they want, and if a boy ogles them it is the boy's fault. She, on the other hand, suggested that how she is looked at affects who she is, and that it is her responsibility, at least in part, to protect how she is seen, because letting herself be seen a certain way is who she *is*.

Some say, however, that the present age is not a time for such meditations. In the present age, linking this student's comment up with work on Christian ideas of protecting the gaze (see Illich, 2001) seem at once trivial and extravagant.

II

The key issue is . . . the removal of the shadow thrown by economic structures onto the cultural domain. For this purpose we need to learn

188 • Naqvi and Jardine

> how to speak in a disciplined way . . . choosing words that do not surrep-
> titiously drag in assumptions of scarcity.
>
> (Illich, 1992, p. 45)

We would like to suggest that these Taylorized images of tradition and traditional learning are, in fact, profoundly impoverished. They are the by-
products of education imagined in light of what Ivan Illich (1992, p. 118)
named "regimes of scarcity," wherein economic or managerial discourse has
come to hold sway. In such a discourse, management and production become
central to our imagining of education itself. Again, this is, we suggest, a
suppressed by-product of Taylor's early 20th century industrial efficiency
movement inculcated into the educational imagination. Consider the words of
Ellwood P. Cubberley, dean of the school of education at Stanford, from his
book *Public School Administration*, originally published in 1916 (cited here
from Callahan, 1964, p. 97):

> Our schools are, in a sense, factories in which the raw products (children)
> are to be shaped and fashioned into products to meet the various
> demands of life. The specifications for manufacturing come from the
> demands of twentieth-century civilization, and it is the business of the
> school to build its pupils according to the specifications laid down. This
> demands good tools, specialized machinery, continuous measurement
> of production to see if it is according to specifications, [and] the
> elimination of waste in manufacture.

These images, experienced in contemporary circles as "traditional" in some
imaginary, Romanticized, ancient sense, are so deeply inculcated, so deeply
experienced to be simply "the real world" that, in fact, any questioning of such
eventually devolves into a seeming call for a return to *inefficiency* and for a
somehow wild and woolly overthrow of standards and accountability
altogether.

Perhaps in light of this intractability, many late 20th century critiques of
such industrial models of "traditional" education seem to have simply
abandoned the term "traditional" altogether and have therefore, we suggest,
unwittingly equated this term with its impoverished form. This is similar to a
phenomenon encountered in recent attempts to revive the phrase "back to the
basics" where the very idea of "basics" is identified with its impoverished form.
In such abandonment, what sometimes occurs is that the critique of "traditional" schools and schooling becomes fashioned as little more than the
inverse of the impoverished form: child-centeredness, an emphasis on
untethered individuality and the uniqueness of each child, soft, blurry, emotionally laden forms of "assessment" and "self-assessment" geared first and
foremost to the preservation of self-esteem, and the cowardly belief—a sort of
"vacuous licentiousness" (Smith, 1999, p. 139)—that any work a child does is

"good" because any judgment otherwise is a return to the authoritarianism of traditional learning that the critique has abandoned. (This line of thought refracts in wonderful ways with those Grade Ten social studies considerations of the *hijab*.)

We suggest that the inverse of impoverishment is still impoverished, and still tethered, unwittingly, to that which it rejects—a weak and debased understanding of "tradition."

There is a further step here that we must note with caution and concern. This is how the rumored logic goes around Calgary, Alberta. In the midst of all the calls for accountability and parent and student "choice," those "many" who say the present age is not the time for meditation are understood to be voicing a cultural preference. Wanting an education for one's children that is explora-tory, thoughtful, reflective, questioning, worldly, and authentic to the living disciplines of the world is a *cultural choice* in a multicultural city. The demand for schools and schooling that are "traditional" is thus understood as a cultural demand, as witnessed by the (so it is rumored) common desire for such schools from "new immigrants" to the country and to our city.

And here are the two final twists. First (so goes the hushed line of thought), Muslim families in particular often seek out such "traditional" schools and schooling because their cultural life is rooted in the commonplace cultural practice of the rote memorization of the Qu'uran. Second, critically reflecting upon or resisting this impoverished version of traditional schools and school-ing that is afoot in the city is a form of cultural prejudice. The University of Calgary's inquiry-based teacher-education program has been thus publicly and privately criticized as preparing new teachers for a type of schooling that is *culturally biased*, and that its promoting of inquiry and reflection and medita-tion as part of teacher-education is inculcating a cultural bias into new teachers entering the field.

In an ironic twist, just as education is beginning to effectively loosen the grip of all the old mind-numbing practices of 19th century pedagogy, where willful, wild children (see Miller, 1989) were stripped of their primitiveness in ways precisely analogous to the colonial civilizing of the Empire's "children" (see Jardine, 2005, 2006; Nandy, 1987; Smith, 1999, 2006), many immigrants to Canada are (so it is rumored) demanding precisely this sort of imperial pedagogy as an expression of their "cultural difference" and, even more bewildering, as a sign of a return to "traditional education."

The mind, of course, reels. In the name of diversity and difference and toler-ance, a form of schooling based on convergence, sameness, and an intolerance of any disruption of that self-same singularity is promoted. And the re-casting of Islam as especially "traditional" in this impoverished sense is, especially in these post-9/11 times, as understandable as it is unconscionable. We don't see much of the images of Islam as full of meditation and thought and care and love. There is no hint of how Islam protected knowledge and wisdom during the Dark Ages of Christian Europe. We see only Taliban-like children, where no child is left behind in the regime of blind, unthinking obedience.

III

In the Koran, the first thing God said to Muhammad was "Read."

(Baker, 2003)

As an immigrant parent with one young child in school and another soon to be, these matters leave me (R.N.) with a deep sense of insecurity. I come with a very strong sense of roots and ancestry—a strong sense of "tradition." My maiden name is Zaidi; derived from "Zaid" it literally means "aspiring for greatness." The Zaids held a privileged status in history; considered as direct descendants of the Prophet Muhammad's family they were known in history as warriors. The ways in which, in these post-9/11 times, my own roots and ancestry are culturally embattled and being used in weak and demeaning ways in heated public debates about schools have made me understand the need to be such a warrior. I am not going to let the dominant culture erase these notions of ancestry and tradition that are deeply embedded in me.

But what is this dominant culture? Our family lives in a "white," mainly Christian, suburban neighborhood, and my daughter attends the local school. Who am I in the midst of all of this? Who is my child? Is she a Zaidi or a Naqvi? Which does she need to be? What does it mean to be a Naqvi in Calgary, Alberta, today, in these times of war, at this time of Christmas greetings and green trees hauled into the house and lit up? What does it mean to aspire for greatness in what Judith Butler has called "precarious times" (2004; see also Naqvi & Prasow, 2007)? How can I hold on to some of what I can only express as "my traditions" and how might those traditions properly be understood? Have I—has my daughter—been turned into a blind and obedient memorizer of the Quranic verses? Is this what the *traditions* of Islam demand? Is this the nature of knowledge, of learnedness, of devotion, demanded of me and my child?

These matters can never be answered in general. In all traditions, Islam included, some people spend their lives as unthinking, obedient, memorizers.

One doesn't come to properly resist this unthoughtfulness by simply dumping tradition itself. My daughter has, until recently, attended the mosque where she spends her time with a script (in our case Arabic) and a book, the Quranic verses. She puts on her veil (*hijab*) and spends time learning this script and this scripture. Part of the work is learning this language and memorizing some of these verses. But these acts of memorization are not decontextual or without surrounding sense. Arabic was the language in which God spoke to the prophet.

But in her classes, until recently, *what it is that is memorable about those verses* is the real issue. Her teacher, in one session, spent time circulating a real apple and a plastic replica around the class, and the young children spent time thinking and talking and listening to conversations about what it means for something to be real and not fake, not plastic. What was discussed, as well, was the miraculous way in which humans have this ability to be conscious of and to experience the truth of things, to experience their reality and their gift, and to see through fakeness and phoniness.

As part of another day's work (and, yet, connected deeply with these apples), my daughter colored in a black-line-master drawing of a young girl, just awoken, sitting on the edge of her bed, morning sunshine streaming in the window. At the bottom of the sheet is a morning *do'a*, a morning prayer. The Arabic script is transliterated as *Allhamdullillahilladzii ahyaana ba'da maa amaata naa wa ilaihinnusyuur* and translated thus: *All Praises to Allah who has given us life (consciousness) after taking it away. And to Him we shall return.*

First of all, it is so interesting to note that these black-line-master school activities are oddly "transcultural" in ways that bear some future thought. Second, yes, part of Maria's work was to recite and practice and memorize the phrase at the bottom of this sheet, both in Arabic and in English translation. We all fully understand how repeated chanting and practice and memorization are themselves ancient practices. However, even if the *do'a*'s words are memorized, *what is being said, what it means about one's life, one's culture, one's family, one's future,* cannot be learned by rote but only by reflection and thought and conversation and application to oneself and one's circumstances. Memorization is inadequate to what tradition requires of us in such a statement about awakening, about consciousness and experience and praise. Thus, even to the extent that something like "rote memorization" is a part of what is occurring, it is not for its own sake or for the sake of simply being able to repeat it by rote on some measured and managed examination. Far from it. Simple rote memorization of such matters without application and thought and meditation, without time and occurrence and re-occurrence and venture and obligation and witnessing, without a family and friends, without others to converse and dispute and agree with about such matters and how we might live in a knowledge of them, is not only meaningless, mechanical, and imposed. It is *ridiculous*.

The "measure" of these words is one's life and how it is lived.

IV

For Petrarch, as for Bernard and Quintilian . . . when one unwittingly or from laziness quotes *verbaliter* because one's memory-design has been overwhelmed by the *turba* [like the turbulence of being carried away by a great river in the Buddhist image above] of all the pieces . . . that is a failure of memory. It makes oneself appear ridiculous and shameful, like a clown in ill-fitting clothes, whose garments are not "familiar" to him. It is a failure of invention because it is a failure of memory, that educated *memoria* of [one] who knows.

(Carruthers, 2005, p. 220; see Chapter 3)

Mathew Zachariah, a colleague of ours at the University of Calgary, once said that fundamentalists of different religions have more in common with each other than they do with many of those in their own religion. Darkness, closure, fear, paranoia, xenophobia, blind obedience, literalism, anger, a "monstrous state of siege" (Smith, 1999, p. 140) between self and others, us and them, young and old, the new and the established—these all have kin across traditions. These are "tradition," we suggest, at its worst, at its stupidest and most dull and dangerous. These are what becomes of tradition when it is cultivated with one's back against the wall, under threats of invasion or colonization or inquisition. In such ways in the world, we share a terrible common ancestry. And we need to understand, clearly and unequivocally, that, under threat, a reversion to the pretense of safety and security that such closures seem to offer makes a terrible sort of sense (see Jardine, Friesen, & Clifford, 2006, pp. 57–60). In these post-9/11 times, we have all, to varying degrees, retrenched back into manageable and monitorable border-security limits (it is not as if Frederick Winslow Taylor's management/surveillance/paranoia makes no sense at all. It is not as if basics-as-breakdown is simply meaningless. Far from it).

But tradition teaches us something else. All traditions are not constituted simply by what they display about themselves with their backs up against the wall. Islam, as much as any other tradition, also implores being mindful of the world and seeing the gift of knowledge and experience as the gift of care for what is known. Mindfulness, humility, hesitation, thought—these, too, are deep traditions held in kinship and kind.

When we provoke our children to remember things, to memorize, to make memorable, we suggest that impoverished versions of "traditional learning" have even misunderstood this phenomenon. The work of learning is, as St. Bede suggested, a meditative, memorial, memory-forming activity, "a process of meditative composition or collocative reminiscence—'gathering,' *colligere*" (Carruthers, 2003, p. 33). What is gathered in memory must not be simply stored up in some anonymous, automatically and efficiently retrievable inventory, but must be inventively worried over, worked, revisited, re-read, applied to one's life, mumbled, "murmured" (Carruthers, 2005, p. 164). If I do not thus meditatively compose myself and what I have come to know and understand, my memory will not be *my own*. "*Memoria* is most usefully thought of as a compositional art. The arts of memory are among the arts of thinking, especially involved with fostering the qualities we now revere as 'imagination' and 'creativity' " (Carruthers, 2003, p. 9). What I know will no longer be deeply ingrained and implicated in who I am. I might be able to repeat the words *Allhamdullillahilladzii ahyaana ba'da maa amaata naa wa ilaihinnusyuur* and such repetition can be manageably assessed in an efficient way, but such repetition by itself seems clownish, foolish, remiss of the real work of education. Even the insistence that the words be memorized even if you don't understand them

(Maria was eventually able to speak out loud the words of the Quran without necessarily understanding what many of the words meant) is done in the name of preserving and protecting the language in which God spoke.

Unless memory becomes a meditative, compositional act, one simply drowns in the turbulence that "traditional schools" seem to promote. We suggest that the core work of traditional education lies in the work of remembering what these words ask of me and composing my life in light of such knowledge—becoming someone because of what I know, and not simply being a repository for a memorized mass. Such meditative matters are at the heart of traditional education, and the difficulties we face in learning to live with such matters is part of their beauty and strength.

19

"The Profession Needs New Blood"

DAVID W. JARDINE

No sooner have you grabbed hold of it than myth opens out into a fan of
a thousand segments. Here the variant is the origin. In each of these
diverging stories all the others are reflected, all brush by us like folds of
the same cloth. If, out of some perversity of tradition, only one version of
some mythical event has come down to us, it is like a body without a
shadow, and we must do our best to trace out that invisible shadow.

> (Roberto Calasso, *The Marriage of Cadmus and Harmony*, 1993)

The blood is the life.

> (Deuteronomy 12:23)

Intimate Relations: On Education and Interpretation and the Image of "New Blood"

"I enjoy having student-teachers in the school. It keeps things lively, keeps us
on our toes. And anyway, it's our responsibility. The profession needs new
blood."

These words of an elementary school principal are, on the face of it, rather
commonplace and familiar. We all know what he means in some colloquial
sense in that we can all recognize these lived features of the community of
teaching and the wonders and difficulties of student-teaching they bespeak.
This commonplace, lived familiarity is a fascinating phenomenon because it
suggests that, prior to any deliberate and methodical "educational inquiry," we
find ourselves somehow already in relation to this principal, already sharing in
a complex, ambiguous, often unvoiced understanding of the constitution of
the community of teaching. This realm of ambiguous, lived familiarity and the
evocations of sense and significance enfolded within it defines the field of study
for interpretive inquiry.

If playfully allowed to "expand to their full breadth of illuminative meaning," (Norris-Clarke 1976, p. 188) this principal's words echo down into a rich
"implicate order" (Bohm 1983) of metaphors, mythologies and traditions.
They contain images of education's relation to and responsibility for the
young, as well as images of the mysterious "liminal period" (Turner 1969;
1987) indicated by the hyphenation "student-teacher." The movement through

such "threshold times" (Mahdi et al. 1987, p. ix) is full of "ambiguity and paradox, a confusion of all customary categories" (Turner 1987, p. 7) and as such, the tales told of such times lend themselves to a discourse that is itself "incurably figurative and polysemous" (Clifford, J. 1986, p. 5). In this sense, such tales lend themselves to interpretive work—they call for a reading which does not take them literally but rather figuratively, full of haunting figures and forms that stalk our profession and give it its life and its vigour.

These phenomena of liminality and transition and thresholds and passage are nothing new. The entrance of the young into the community, our responsibility for them, and the initiatory movement from student to teacher—all these bear a "family resemblance" (Wittgenstein 1968, p. 32) or "kinship" (p. 34) to long-standing tales told in many cultures and in many communities. Most pointedly, the graphic notion of "needing new blood" suggests archaic images of fleshy vitality, regeneration, transfusion, fertility/fecundity, reproduction, blood sacrifice, menstruation, child bearing, renewal, healing/wounding, transformation and the whole cascade of bloody events surrounding the Christian worship of the consuming of flesh and blood and its intimate coupling with crucifixion and resurrection.

"Needing new blood" also suggests a deeply ecological and ethical imperative—that the Earth (ecos)/the community (ethos) somehow *needs* the young/ the initiate for its own sustenance, continuance and renewal.

These commonplace words of an elementary school principal are, in this sense, not so commonplace. "In this short passage, we have an embarrassment of symbolic riches" (Turner 1987, p. 18)—multiple meanings, "interweaving and criss-crossing" (Wittgenstein 1968, p. 32) (*textus* originally means "to weave," like textiles). These words are thus clearly not simply an autobiographical tidbit and to treat them as such would serve a dual abandonment. We would abandon this principal to the isolation of "personal knowledge" (where we "become stuck in the case without a vision of its soul" [Hillman 1983, p.23]) and we would equally abandon the inter-weaves of tradition and language and the mythologies that house our profession to remaining uninvigorated by this suggestive rebirth of an age-old tale.

It is vital to note here that such a dual abandonment leaves both sides at work in their worst aspects. The young/new case/individual is left unable to find itself a voice in the midst of the established/long-standing, and thus appears pathetic (the etymological opposite of *ethos* is *pathos*—the one with no home). This is the potentially pathetic character of "teacher narratives" when these are left as simple self-announcements of teachers who have been abandoned to the isolation of the classroom. Clearly, we must overcome the hegemonies that have silenced and isolated such teachers. However, when these "narratives" are left unread out into the world, teachers are re-abandoned and re-isolated to the pathos of "my own story" which can only be "shared" with others in equally pathetic situations. In this way, the re-invigoration that the young/the new case could have provided the world is forgone in favour of merely puerile self-annunciation.

And, conversely, once the new case refuses to read itself out into the world, the old/established closes in on itself and is no longer visible as the senatorial, accumulated wisdoms of age and experience, able to provide comfort to the young (i.e., common fortitude, strength). Bereft of "new blood," the senatorial becomes merely senile.

Contrary to this dual abandonment, an interpretive understanding suggests that the words of this principal are not only expressions of this principal's personal experiences, feelings, beliefs, images and the like (although they are certainly all of these in some sense). These words are *the new, unanticipated* (and most likely *unintended*) *re-voicing of a world*, a world full of multiple tales that are folds of the same cloth (the same weave). This principal is, however unwittingly, folded into a world—implicated in it—a world full of blood relations. Such implication does not mean that his words are identical to that world (so we can simply explore that world and tell this principal what he means). But neither are they simply different. His words bear a "family resemblance" to tales we have heard before but now, having heard this principal's tale, we will never hear those old tales quite the same way again. Differently put, this principal has "kin" even though he may not know it or experience it. This is why, interpretively speaking, simple reflection on experiences is not necessarily enough. The inverse of this is also true. Citing authoritative and established texts on "blood mythology" is *also* not enough, interpretively speaking, since this fecund new case rips open those texts (itself a bloody-minded metaphor) and makes them *readable* again by re-enlivening them, re-living them. It is the old and the young, the established and the new *together* that make interpretation possible.

This is the hermeneutic dance of part (new, young) and whole (established, old), where the new tale (just like "new blood") is not simply additive to the whole but restorative and thereby transformative of it and where, because of the generous arrival of new case, "the whole" is never a *given* that could be simply described. Thus, interpretively understood, what "new blood" *means* cannot be stated once and for all as if it were an object: what it means is always in a state of "interpretive suspense" (Jardine 1992) always "yet to be decided" (Gadamer 1989, p. 361). For example, having heard a principal of a school full of young children speak of "needing new blood," Christ's role as a teacher and his summoning of the "little children" (Matthew 18:3) (which we may have heretofore considered ourselves to have "understood") begins to "waver and tremble" (Caputo 1987, p. 7) with new, unanticipated interpretive potency and power. Christ's summoning of the "new blood" and his saying that we must become like these children if the gates of heaven are to be open to us—this merges with images of Hermes as himself a young boy (the young as the portend of a hermeneutic-interpretive life—Hermes was also "a phallic god and a god of fertility" [Crapazano 1986, p. 52]), but also as a guardian and opener of the portals, the gates (which itself bespeaks images of open, bleeding wounds as mythological signs of vulnerability and sensitivity and openness to the world (precisely the vulnerability and sensitivity and openness that we see in those student-teachers that provide the school with "new blood").

From this admittedly overextended interpretive spinning, we see that this principal (of a Catholic school, I might add) is "in" a living world full of its own histories and ways and we, too, are "in" this world along with him, and our knowing of its ways is attested to by the original familiarity of the tale he has told, and the spins of significance and sense enfolded within that familiarity/ family resemblance:

> Language itself contains sedimented layers of emotionally resonant metaphors, knowledge, and associations, which when paid attention to can be experienced as discoveries and revelations. . . . [The interpretive task] is to inquire into what is hidden in language, what is deferred by signs, what is pointed to, what is repressed, implicit, or mediated. What thus seem initially to be individualistic autobiographical searchings turn out to be revelations of traditions, re-collections of disseminated identities.
>
> (Fischer 1986, p. 198)

As we have been witnessing, "stories [like this principal's tale] never live alone: they are branches of a family" (Calasso 1993, p. 9), and a telling story bespeaks a family (a "familiarity," if you will) to which we already somehow belong. This is why interpretation is often equated with a form of recollection—a sort of family gathering (a gathering of blood lines), where "gathering" takes on anew that archaic sense of a way of deeply *knowing*.

It is becoming obvious that this particular phenomenon of new blood has a more intimate relation to interpretation than being just another possible topic of investigation.

Generativity, renewal and the need for "new blood" can be read as evocative descriptions *of the nature of interpretation itself* in its concern for the delicate interplays between tradition/community and the "fecundity of the individual case" (Gadamer 1989, p. 38; Jardine 2006a). Interpretation is caught, in a fashion similar to education itself, in the ongoing, living tension (one might say, "the blood relations") between the old and the young, between the established and the new. As with education itself, the interpretive task is not to *cure* this tension, but to care for it, nurture it and protect it—to *read* it for its most generous possibilities. Because it does not aim to cure but rather to care for and attend to the living ambiguities and tensions that inform our lives, interpretation has been described as "restoring life to its original difficulty" (Caputo 1987, p. 1).

In this way, interpretation is not simply a "method" that can have the tales of student-teacher initiation and their parallels to philosophical and mytho-logical literature simply as its *topic*. Interpretation is also "akin" to that of which it speaks—interpretive activity itself bears a "family resemblance" to the notion of "needing new blood." Thus, the tale cited above from a school principal is as telling of interpretive inquiry as interpretive inquiry might be telling of it. This is vital to understanding the conduct of interpretive work (and it re-capitulates Wittgenstein's images of "family resemblance"): "The practice of understanding is the expression of the affinity of the one who understands to the one whom he understands and to that which he understands" (Gadamer 1983 p. 48).

Interpretation seeks out its affinity to its "topic." One does not have "inter-pretation" in hand as a method and *then* go out looking for a topic—scouring transcripts, for example, and "doing" an interpretation of them. Rather, some-thing *becomes* a topic only when its interpretive potency strikes or addresses the one doing the interpretation. The words of a school principal cited in this paper form a small fragment of countless conversations. I did not *select* it as an "interesting" topic and then "do" an interpretation of it. Interpretation does not begin with *me*. It only begins when something *happens to me* in my reading of a text, when something *strikes* me, tears me open, "wounds" me and leaves me vulnerable and open to the world, like the sensitivities of open flesh. Through such sensitivities, a world begins to open around these words, and the interpretive task is to use sniff out this "new blood," "to put a finger on the wound" (Grossman 1988, p. v; see Jardine 1992a) and from/through this "opening," to re-enchant and re-awaken that world. As such, these words themselves became echoes of the process of interpretation itself. Not only did they become interpretive "portals" into a whole world of mythologies and symbols—"needing new blood" is itself *about* interpretive portals. Interpret-ation thus "finds itself" in its topic. Differently put, only in and through the topography of the world can interpretation "come to" and realize its place and limits.

There is a further convolution in this "kinship" between "new blood," interpretive inquiry and student-teacher education. Education has long suffered under the auspices of our Enlightenment legacy which suggests that separation, isolation and the severance of ambiguous kinships, family resem-blances and relationships are the route to secure a solid foundation of under-standing. We have, in the name of such security, sub-divided the ambiguous, texts/weaves of the tales of student-teacher education into a babble of indi-vidual skills and techniques and objective checklists of separate competencies and the like, all of which has torn apart the ambiguous, living fabric of the community of education in the name of clarity and manageability. Educators, like much of North American culture, have suffered the alienation and loss of meaning that results from having our lives dissected into the bits and pieces requisite of experimental design. One could consider, for example, how the principal's words cited above would not count if we were pursuing an "object-ive" account of student-teaching: his words are too fluid, too evocative, too "poetic" and slippery and wet, too subject to multiple, generative responses.

Under the auspices of our Enlightenment legacy, many educational studies would "marginalize and instrumentalize [his words] into a rhetorical figure called metaphor" (Gadamer 1989, p. 432) which, because of its ambiguous and evocative character, is not considered to be "true." Since student-teaching, under such a legacy, is considered to be an univocal, unambiguous and object-ive state of affairs, multivocal and ambiguous language such as "needing new blood" cannot possibly correspond to this state of affairs without blurring and "subjectivizing" what is (following the Enlightenment presumption) "in reality" clear and distinct and objective.

One of the aims of interpretive work is to recover the narrative/metaphoric interrelations and kinship systems that give human life meaning and to work against the legacy of severance and its consequences. Interpretive work thus wishes to read this principal's tale for its *truth*, but truth in such a case no longer means unambiguous correspondence to an objective state of affairs. Rather, the interpretive truth of this tale lies in whether it can be read in a way that might help us more openly and generously understand the lives we are already living, that is, whether it can be read in a way that provides us with the re-invigoration of new blood.

Differently put, the truth of an interpretation lies not simply in the fact that a tale has been told (although this, of itself, is often difficult enough, being able to finally tell *at all*) but in how and whether this tale can be made *telling*.

A sure sign of the interpretive truth of such a tale is whether it provokes those who hear it to speak, i.e., whether it provokes generative, creative partici-pation. In presenting such work to teachers, student-teachers and colleagues I have found, over and over again, that hearing such tales provokes others to themselves tell a tale that bears a family resemblance to the ones I have offered—"have you read Alice Walker's *The Temple of my Familiar?*," "what about D.H. Lawrence? He's full of blood," "as soon as you started talking about blood, I remembered my student-teacher talking about feeling drained," "this talk frightens me. It reminds me of lambs to the slaughter. We don't do that. We *don't*." Interpretive telling thus opens up a haunted space full of tell-tale famil-iarities that bind Earthly lives together, kinship systems, blood relations whose "truth" is not a given state of affairs but is always yet-to-be-decided by *this* reader's or *that* reader's giving of new blood to what is written. Interpretation thus requires active, creative, risk-laden participation, not distanced, objective, methodological documentation, nor a pathetic, pathological withdrawal into "my story." *Both* of these are refusals to read the deep kinships that bind our lives together. Both of these are forms of institutionalized illiteracy which orbit each other and which assume the severance of blood relations that interpretation is wont to heal.

This puts a peculiar demand on those who *read* an interpretive study. An interpretive study does not centre around the presentation of *facts* (the past participle of *facere*—"to make"), as if the phenomenon of "new blood" were simply a given object whose characteristics could be documented and simply handed over to a reader or as if it were "my story" which I could simply tell. Rather, "needing new blood" is a nest of ambiguous signs that need to be *read* and *re-read* to be understood. Interpretation thus centres around a movement from what initially appears to be merely literal/factual (the *fact* that this is what this principal said—these literal words—or the *fact* that similar words appear frequently over the transcripts of several principals) down into the "make up" or "forming" or "fashioning" of these facts, down, that is, into the generous possibilities of meaning that they embody. Interpretation is thus a movement from the past participle towards the (re-)generative case: it "opens" what has been made (what presents itself as "facts") out into its "makings." This not only allows "the making" to become visible to the reader and thus allows the sedimented layers of meaning encrusted in "the facts" to be subject anew to transformation, healing and change. Interpretation also necessitates that the reader him or herself must somehow *participate in the making*. To read an interpretive study is to bring forward the ways in which what is being addressed is part of my living "make up." I must attempt to "make" something out of what I read *and* I must read my life into the words. I must both make these words mine *and* I must explore how these words *make a claim on me* and reflect back to me "kinships" of which I might not have been aware. This principal has "kin" *whether he likes it or not, whether he knows it or not*. So it is not enough, in attempting to understand this principal's words, to simply explore what *he* thinks "new blood" means, as if he *owns* the kinship system of which "new blood" is a part. "Stories never live alone," and to make them live this way in the name of voice and individuality and empowerment is to do ecological, spiritual and ethical violence.

In this sense, interpretation is a form of *fiction* (the generative case of "to form" or "to fashion" which nuzzles up close to *facere*) that moves to re-imagine and re-enchant the world that has fallen prey to the degenerate closures of factuality and literalism. Such closures have no room left for the young—the new blood is not summoned and welcomed but shut out. However, to use Wittgenstein's metaphors, "family resemblances" and "kinships" cannot go on without the new ones entering into the flesh of the family ("the familiar") and making it new: the "family resemblances" evoked in this chapter cannot go on without the reader's entrance into the haunted spaces between the lines. Without such entrance, interpretive work looks like little more than clever textual trickery.

Moving against this mathematical dismemberment of the Enlightenment legacy (*and* against the ways that teacher narrative leaves this dismemberment in place but simply rejects the mathematics) towards re-membering makes interpretive work a profoundly *ecological* enterprise. It cares not simply for the fecundity of the individual case (without which the world would not be renewed, without which the story will not be re-membered), but cares also for the openness and generosity of the world (without which the new case could not enter and could therefore not provide re-membering and re-generation to the world). It attempts, therefore, *to make the individual case readable* by opening it out into the world, and it attempts *to make the world readable* anew by introducing into that world this new case.

Interpretation works against the dual consequences of this dissection of blood relations—against *both* our relentless focus on objective documentation (where we cannot read our lives out into the world with its brutal, closed, objective, literal surfaces) and against its dark twin, the potential isolation inherent in "everybody telling their own story" when such stories are left *unread* in any strong sense except as "mine." To play with Wittgenstein's metaphors again, interpretation works against *both* the brutal patriarchal father who silences all his kin in favour of a singular voice. And it works, too, against the abandoned, isolated, self-affirming child who can bear no comfort from the world. Interpretation is focussed, rather, *both* on the entrance of the young/ the initiate into the world *and* upon the restoration and renewal of the world that can ensue from such entrance. As with the figure of Hermes, interpretation stands at this portal, constituted by "a consciousness that must leave the door ajar," (Hillman 1979a, p. 154) ready for the arrival of the "new blood" (the next teacher's / principal's / child's / student-teacher's tale) that will not be left to its own devices, but will help transform the world and make it new.

An Admission of our Need

> We keep hearing from principals that some of the best people are the new, young, fresh blood in the system.
> (Jon Ed, Human Resources Superintendent, Calgary Board of Education. *Calgary Herald*, March 23, 1993, page B1)

> We see in [images of new blood and bleeding] inflation and enthusiasm. The vitality of the [young] spreads and stains like the red tincture of the alchemist's *lapis*. His bleeding is *multiplicatio*, the infectious giving out of essence for the sake of transforming the world.
> (Hillman 1979, p. 111)

The passage of the initiate into the community of education and the "original difficulties" that ensue is a phenomenon that defines that community at many levels. Education is constituted, first and foremost, by the arrival of the young (the arrival of new blood), year after year, and this cycle of arrival and its consequent images of inflation and enthusiasm (one could think of the bounties of the new growth of spring, for example, which are themselves iterated in Easter ceremonies of life resurrected and, at a more mundane level, the "bunnies and chicks and eggs" of this celebration—a wonderful pagan underbelly of the Christian legacy) reiterates many other cycles in our lives as well as Earthly cycles of season and planting and growth and harvest. The images of the arrival of "new blood" thus suggests an image of pedagogy itself. This arrival is full of possibility and full of hope for a re-invigoration of the course (*currere*) of our human inheritance. Differently put, with the image of "new blood," it will not do to imagine that our course (our curriculum) is simply fixed and given. Our course—what will come of us and our preciously held ideas and ideals and learning objectives and the like—is always available to us only in a state of interpretive suspense, yet to be decided in relation to the arrival of this child, and this. Education thus sits at an irresolvable point. It must prepare our course for the arrival of the young (so it must understand that course openly and generously), and it must prepare the young to enter our course (so it must understand the young as "new blood" for our course). It must cradle *both* the child and the world in nursing *caritas*.

Education is also concerned after the arrival of "the young" in the sense of the arrival of new teachers into the profession.

The initiation of new teachers into the community of education is full of "pedagogic intent" (Turner 1987, p. 15). It is a time wherein prospective teachers become "vividly and rapidly aware of what may be called the 'factors' of their culture." (p. 14) However, the lessons learned by student-teachers in their initiatory travails crack open beyond mere *epistemology*—beyond "teacher knowledge." The initiation of "new blood" into the community of education is not simply a matter of what the initiate explicitly or implicitly *knows*. The smooth transmission of "cultural knowledge about teaching" (White, 1989) is not the sole, centre point of initiatory phenomena. Rather:

> The term initiation in the most general sense denotes a body of rites and oral teachings whose purpose is to produce a radical modification . . . of the person to be initiated. Initiation is equivalent to an ontological mutation of the existential condition. The novice emerges from his ordeal a totally different being: [s]he has become *another*.
>
> (Eliade 1975, p. 112)

Underlying the potentially bloodless passing on of knowledge is a deeper, more bloody mystery wound up in the entrance of student-teachers into the community of education. It has to do with *ontological* transformations in who the student-teacher *is*, not simply *epistemological* transformations in what they *know*. Through the rites of passage and initiation, student-teachers not only can claim to know things they did not know before. They *are* something they were not before: they *are* "new blood" for the community of teaching. They *are* (becoming) teachers.

This deeper and more bloody mystery hints at a terrible fact we hardly ever raise in our teacher preparation programs: *the fact of natality*—that pedagogy is premised on the inevitable, continual arrival of the young (Arendt 1969)—and its dark twin, *the fact of the mortality of the world*:

> We are always educating for a world that is or is becoming out of joint, for this is the basic human situation, in which the world is created by mortal hands to serve mortals for a limited time as home. Because the world is made by mortals, it wears out; and because it continuously changes its inhabitants, it runs the risk of becoming as mortal as they. To preserve the world against the mortality of its creators and inhabitants it must be constantly set right anew. . . . Our hope always hangs on the new which every generation brings.
>
> (Arendt 1969, p. 192)

Or, linked more directly with anthropological and mythological tales:

> Through its own duration, the World degenerates and wears out; this is why it must be symbolically re-created every year. [But note how, with the arrival of new children in my Grade One class, it is not simply *symbolically* re-created every year].
>
> (Eliade 1968, p. 76)

> It is a living world—inhabited and used by creatures of flesh and blood, subject to the law of becoming, of old age and death. Hence it requires a periodic renewing.
>
> (p. 45)

So, just as the initiate brings renewal, he or she also brings a vision of the *need* for renewal and therefore a vision of the mortality, fragility and dependency of the community of which we are all a part. Our "course," our "community," is not a given which can be simply documented and detailed. It is not a given because the entrance of the young, fresh blood makes that community different than it would have been without them. Moreover, that the arrival of "new blood" is *also* not a given that can simply be taken for granted. There is something miraculous about this fact of natality. The arrival of the renewal of the young simply *happens*.

Through the image of "new blood," what we often assume to be relations of (inter)dependency are strangely reversed. We are so accustomed to identifying "the young" or "the new ones" with being (our) *dependents*. Now we can begin to see *our own dependency*. We can begin to see how our hope hangs upon the young and their ability to open up what has become closed, to re-new what has become no longer workable—to find the portals, the openings, the life in what we do.

Because of the inherent mortality of the community of education, the strength and stability of that community cannot be established through its calcification and closure. It will simply "wear out" if it remains closed. Stability and strength can be achieved only through an open and generous relation to the young. More strongly put, it can be achieved only through an admission of our need.

This admission is strangely absent from the literature on teacher education. We speak so often about how the student-teacher needs and depends upon the cooperating school, the cooperating teacher, the administration of their practicum school, the University, the curriculum guides, the lists of teaching techniques or classroom management techniques, or the educational theories and so on. Rarely do we admit how the community of education needs "new blood." Simply put, without new initiates entering in the community of education—without the continual arrival of new children, new teachers, new knowledge, new worldly circumstances—that community itself would cease to be. The community of education is not only a haven for our dependents. That community itself *depends*.

The profession *needs* new blood.

"New Blood" and the Healing Return to the Origins

> Our blood will water the dry, tired surface of the Earth
> We will bleed. We will bleed. We will
> bleed until we bathe her in our blood and she turns
> slippery like a new baby birthing.
>
> (Bass 1989, p. 53)

The creation of the world was no single, irrevocable act. If the world and its seasons are to continue, the original drama has to be re-enacted every year.

(Tannahill 1975, p. 20)

"The profession *needs* new blood." This evokes a dark memory of the mortality of the world and an equally dark memory of our own dependency. It foreshadows a memory of the original making of the world (a memory of its *interpretability*) and of our own dependency on the fact of natality as figuring in that origination (as interpretation recalls its own dependency on the fecundity of the individual case). New blood thus provides an image of the *return to [our] origins*.

The initiate represents that which is first, that which is "initial." The initiation of student-teachers into the community of education thus keeps us oriented to what is first, what is originary in what we do.

This notion of originariness can be understood in two interrelated senses:

1). Education requires an orientation to what is chronologically first. Education entails a relation to the young, the vulnerable, the new. Going back to what is first for the community is going back to what is at its heart: the fact of natality, the fact that children are born into the world and that the community can go on only through its concerted attention to this arrival and to the conditions under which such arrival can be generously sustained. With such a return, hope is renewed that things might be different this time, that things can start again from the beginning, that things can be set right, that things can be put back on course. One can think, for example, of how September can often figure in the imagination of a teacher: a fresh start, a new beginning, starting again.

Here we have a wonderful cross-over effect: the entrance of the initiate into the community of education bears an affinity to the entrance of the child into the world. Both are the new ones and both figure in the "new blood" entrails of "starting again." Hence the powerful images of a student-teacher's description of entering her first practicum school:

> When I went to my practicum school the first day, I felt about this high, like a little kid again, going to school for the first time, beginning all over again, right from the beginning. And my cooperating teacher was, like, *my* teacher and I was a little kid in Grade One.

2). A return to the origin can also be understood as a return to what is foremost, what is foundational, what is "originary" and "initial" in the sense of what is long-standing, what persists, what pertains. To the extent that initiates return us to the origin in *this* sense, initiation ceremonies are often described as the re-laying of the foundations of the world (Eliade 1975, p. 175). Or, in the words of a cooperating teacher:

> Having student-teachers in my class makes me go back to what I thought I knew and question it again: "Why do I do that in my math lessons?" They make me ask the questions I have forgotten to ask. They make me *say* what I know. They help me clear away the crap.

Thus, the arrival of "new blood" is an event which potentially "washes away the sins of the world." That is to say, the arrival of the young requires that we sort out what is necessary to our world, what is most true and sustainable and generous about it. It is a cyclical, repeated gesture that is restorative and healing (Eliade 1968, p.79). It invokes the cleaning away of the unnecessary accretions of time and a re-invoking and re-membering (i.e., not only bringing back to memory, but gaining new members the initiate, as the new one, re-members the community by becoming a new member of it) what has been forgotten. This is what the innocent question of the new student-teacher can evoke: "keep[ing] us on our toes" and requiring that what has become mute habit be uttered. "They make me *say* what I know." Not only must I re-think what is vital to this community through the initiate's questioning. I must *profess* what is vital to the very symbol of vitality that stands before me.

The Shadow-Side of the Need for New Blood

What are we to make of the red symbolism which, in its archetypical form in the initiation rites, is represented by the intersection of two "rivers of blood"? This duality, this ambivalence, this simultaneous possession of two contrary values or qualities is quite characteristic of redness in the Ndembu view. As they say, "redness acts for both good and ill."

(from Victor Turner, *The Forest of Symbols*, cited in Tannahill 1975, p. 77)

[With the entrance of the initiate] there is a "return to the origin" in the literal sense, that is, a relapse of the Cosmos to the amorphous, chaotic state, followed by a new cosmogony.

(Eliade 1968, p. 52)

A relapse into such originary chaos can be considered as healing and restorative. But this relapse, for all its fecundity and regenerative, also portends something dark and dangerous, akin to the day between the crucifixion and the resurrection (itself a perfect example of "interpretive suspense"). This is the "fallow chaos" (Van Gennup 1960) of the liminal, initiatory period (like the "–" in "student-teacher").

The old needs not only the renewal that the young bring: "[the] redness [of new blood] acts for both good and ill." The old needs *protection* from the young and, strangely enough, *the young need protection from themselves.*

New blood portrays more than simple renewal. It also suggests wildness, chaos, things being out of control, torn apart, growth that is out of control, cancerousness, over-stimulation. The "opportunity" that the young provide also opens a portal to a potentially dangerous "chaos of possibilities" (Hillman 1979a, p. 123). In short, there is a shadow side to the re-generativity that new blood portends.

We have suggested above that the strength and stability of the community of education can be achieved only through an open and generous relation to the young. But this cannot mean a limitless free-for-all, as if *anything* will do in the constitution of the community of education. Here is the rub: we must open that community to the new ones while, at the same time, preventing simple licentiousness, simply spilling blood without any orientation to what we are spilling it *for.*

So the shadow awakes and it has a dual aspect. The notion of "new blood" signals a danger to the community. But it also signals a danger to the initiate as well:

1). "I just got the kids settled down and now this new face arrives"—the arrival of new blood is also the arrival of the disruption of what has been settled, the violation of boundaries that have been set, the re-opening of issues that had been closed. There is a delicate matter involved here. Not wanting the new face to arrive can signal calcification and closure as much as it can signal a healthy desire for stability, order, continuity, memory, community, and the like. The continuous, uncurbed, unprepared arrival of new blood is not necessarily sustainable. With such an arrival, new blood is no longer re-generative of the community: it simply becomes what Arendt (1969) names an "onslaught." Sustaining the arrival of new blood requires time and attention and care. It requires preparing the soil, so to speak. It requires sometimes *refusing* the arrival of new blood on behalf of sustaining the fertility of the soil and not overworking, overstimulating or over-questioning what has been established and settled.

The notion of "new blood" thus signals a potential danger to the community: the danger of a relentless, unbridled onslaught of change.

2). James Hillman (1979, p. 113) describes the young as "afflicted by openness." The danger here is that, "through his[/her] own wounds, [the initiate] may feed others, but may himself [/herself] be drained thereby" (p. 112). Here lies the possibility that the initiate may "burn themselves out" by giving too much, too quickly, taking on the task of "re-inventing the wheel" at every turn, feeling responsible for every happenstance. The vulnerability and openness and sensitivity that new blood provides can suggest that the initiate is *too* vulnerable, *too* sensitive, *too* open: in the desire to love all the children all the time, and provide perfect, stimulating, life-changing lessons coupled with perfect classroom management etc., the initiate can easily twirl out of control, endangering not only the community but themselves.

Lurking here too is the possibility that the old may take advantage of the young and "bleed them dry." Student-teachers are sometimes given the tasks that no one else wants or are over-burdened with too much planning, too much teaching too early.

This is perhaps why "myths show divine-child figures each with special nursing attendants" (Hillman 1979, p. 113) who have a dual function: they not only protect the child from giving too much; they protect the world from being overrun by the growth the child portends. Coupled together, this is an image of our role as those involved in initiating student-teachers into the community of education: opening both the world and the initiate to the convolutions involved in the fact that "the profession needs new blood," and protecting the world and the initiate from the dangers found in such convolutions.

There is, as we have come to expect, a parallel in the work of interpretive inquiry. Once things start to "happen"—as with this topic of new blood—it is very difficult to get such happenstances to stop. In producing this chapter, how can I refuse the cascade of new instances that continually arrive: Yeats' notion of blood memory? the coincidence of our cultural severances of blood relations through empowerment of the individual and the fact of AIDS and the potential deadliness of blood relations? the rush of children in the halls between classrooms as blood pulsing between the "vital organs" (the science classroom, the library, each of which represent "organons" of knowledge and each which need the new blood's arrival)?

Stop.

As with the arrival of "new blood" itself, there is no set of rules regarding when enough is enough. All of this has to be worked out in the particular, living case, and it has to be worked out in a way that is full of "interpretive suspense." As with education, so too for interpretive inquiry: there is no set of rules that save us from the agonies of deciding anew, in *this* case, the delicate balance between our responsibility for the world and our responsibility for the young. As with education, so too for interpretive inquiry: one learns that an open and generous (but not licentious and chaotic) relation to "new blood" is an irresolvable, "original difficulty" that we can only learn to live with well.

Concluding Remarks: New Blood and the Interpretability of the World

The arrival of "new blood" bespeaks the possibility of "keeping the world open."

(Eliade 1968, p. 139)

The arrival of the fecund new case bespeaks the possibility of keeping the world *interpretable*: full of portals, openings, through which the initiate may enter.

"The profession needs new blood": the profession of teaching must not take itself or its tasks literally. The curriculum must needs be *interpretable*— enterable.

"New blood" bespeaks the interpretability of the world: not only the possibility but the *necessity* of renewal.

Interpretation, as a relation between the old/established and the young/new case, is an intimately pedagogic activity. (Thus, as literalism is the enemy of interpretation, literalism is the enemy of pedagogy.)

Education, as a relation between the old/established and the young/new case, is an intimately interpretive activity.

"Stories never live alone: they are branches of a family."

End.

Scenes from Calypso's Cave
On Globalization and the Pedagogical Prospects of the Gift

DAVID W. JARDINE, PATRICIA CLIFFORD,
AND SHARON FRIESEN

Beginning

We will try to understand why our society, which, more than any other, insists that each individual is unique, systematically tends to dismiss those primary social ties that enable people to affirm and shape their uniqueness and promotes those abstract and secondary ties that, at least in theory, make people interchangeable and anonymous, only to later create an ersatz personalization through identification with work or the state.

(Godbout, with Caille 1998, pp. 19–20)

The economy of the gift is a knitting of such primary social ties, an exemplary form of which is our relation to our children (Godbout with Caille 1998, p. 27), because it involves one of the most intimate ways a living community of relations "renews itself in renewing the pact with every 'generation' " (p. 30). The character of the gift is in its movement (Hyde 1983, p. 16), in its being handed along (Gadamer 1989, p. 284) and, in such movement, in the forfeit of its measure and the forfeit of the expectancies of return.

It is giving up.

It is always and necessarily unnecessary. It is excessive (Schrift 1997, p. 7). It is an abundance (Hyde 1983, p. 22) that does not diminish but increases in the giving away.

It is a form of love because, "as in love, our satisfaction sets us at ease because we know that somehow its use at once assures its plenty" (Hyde 1983, p. 22).

Introduction

Borders have been crossed and re-crossed since the dawn of human civilization. If globalization is something new, it must involve more than a series of proliferating cross border exchanges. As people have thought about the contemporary period, it is not so much that borders are crossed or even opened up. Rather it is that they are *transcended*. Global phenomena are those that extend across widely dispersed locations simultaneously and can move between places anywhere on the earth simultaneously. Hence, we often speak of globalization as a matter of *compressing space and time*. So territorial distance and borders have limited significance; the globe becomes a single place in its own right.

(McMaster Website)

Our conversations about globalization and the pedagogical prospects of the gift began with the recognition of the ambiguous and alluring power released in our classroom conversations and work through the use of the Internet. Our beginning questions turned out to be deceptively simple: "Why do people put up all these great papers and links and sites for nothing?" "Why are all these people just giving away their stuff?" The three of us had been struck by the generosity of scholars, researchers and amateurs in sharing freely the fruits of their labour on what appeared to be every imaginable topic.

Such free and generous arrivals were not without risk. What is transcended first and foremost with the onrush of Internet possibilities is the taken-for-grantedness of the warrant of what we receive in such gifts. As Hillman (1979, p. 123) has suggested, "opportunities are not plain, clean gifts. They trail dark and chaotic attachments." They are thus inherently ambiguous and tricky: "reciprocity as rivalry, generosity as interested, the free return as obligatory" (Schrift 1997, p. 9) always remains a series of open possibilities, since the economy of the gift "refuses to attend to egoistic and interested calculations of exchange while at the same time remaining aware of that very logic of exchange" (p. 14).

Therefore, phrase "given away for nothing" has stayed with us, because it still rings of a proximity to commodified forms of exchange that have been, somehow, for some mysterious, dark and chaotic reason, transcended, even though it is not yet quite plain and clean what has arrived through such transcendence. Therefore, also, we have begun to read the movement from commodified relations towards the economy of the gift as a way of understanding the transcendence of boundaries characteristic of the phenomenon of globalization.

These beginning questions helped us to listen differently to the roiling conversations in the classroom as one child or another would grab the whiteboard marker to insist on showing another, better way of thinking about a problem; as one or the other of them would follow University researchers around the classroom, arguing the fine points of distinction between human and natural structures. Again, similar questions arose: "Why did they bother, these children, to argue pink-cheeked in favour of their preferred solutions?" "Why did they care to be clear or controversial or interesting?" "What were they giving us in these exchanges?"

Why don't they just *stop?*

And what of that experience of standing stockstill in the middle of sixty Grade Seven students and feeling the propulsive movement of one utterance on top of the other, with waves of dissent from this corner or that issued to each pronouncement, clearly giving the feeling of a sort of "surfing" more bodily, grounded, work-like and generous than the panicked rush from one thing to another that underwrites many post-modern love-laments about such issues? It may be that:

> the subject of postmodernity is best understood as the ideal-type channel-hopping MTV viewer who flips through different images at such speed that he/she is unable to chain the signifiers together into a meaningful narrative, he/she merely enjoys the multiphrenic intensities and sensations of the surface of the images.
>
> (Usher & Edwards 1994, p. 11)

Even though such "flipping" was occurring here and there in the middle of this classroom movement, those who "flipped out" were more often than not overwhelmed when their flip answers were taken seriously, were taken up, were sometimes read as more generous gifts than the giver could have imagined alone. How they were taken, then, moved them into the movement that underwrites a gift economy. "Gift" is thus not an objective property of something. Rather, "the way we treat a thing can sometimes change its nature" (Hyde 1983, p. xiii) from gift to commodity to gift and return.

"If we are so bold to affirm [the image of the gift], it can only mean that we are incapable of penetrating the veil. For the modern sophisticate . . . innocence is no longer possible unless leavened with irony" (Godbout with Caille 1998, p. 3). We affirm this image of the gift as essential to pedagogy and especially essential to understanding the place of new technologies and the moving, gifted "chaos of possibilities" (Hillman 1979, p. 123) they can release into the work of pedagogy. These children—sometimes unwittingly, sometimes even unwillingly—were giving us something for nothing, something that sidestepped the venerated irony, cynicism, withholding, anger and urban(e) hyperliteracy (Smith 1999) that some post-modern accounts of this phenomenon might sometimes require. And, in engaging them in these conversations, it seems that we were doing the same, all of us now caught up in the play, caught up in the *Spiel* (Gadamer 1989, pp. 101–34), caught up in the "circular movement" (Hyde 1983, pp. 11–16) of something playing itself out all around us, something moving in wider and richer arcs than the commonplace boundaries and borders of seemly schooling often allow.

The Language of Pedagogical Commodification and the Intransigence of its Boundaries

Could we escape the limits of the . . . ideal of autonomy—the *nomos* of the *autos*—as a law of the self, which might make it possible to exceed the limits of ourselves and enter into the between of self and other without losing ourselves in the process? To free ourselves from the oppositional logic of "self vs. all others" might allow for our self-construction as something other than isolated and atomistic subjectivities. Freed from the constraints of an atomistic and autonomous individualism, might possibilities be opened for establishing nonproprietary relations . . . in which a fully intersubjective self could be at home in the between of self and other? And might such . . . relations facilitate the formulation of an alternative logic of the gift, one liberated from the presuppositions of more classic exchangist logics that imprison gift giving within the constraints of the economic assumptions of commodity trading?

(Schrift 1997, p. 20)

(*The true locus of hermeneutics is this in-between.*

[Gadamer 1989, p. 295])

Much traditional educational research and classroom practice can be under- stood as operating within the borders and boundaries of the language of commodity-trading, and therefore within the language of a sort of atomistic individuality that cannot envisage any in-between other than distanced, monitored forms of anonymous, zero-sum exchange.

Such commodification of pedagogical relationships is part of the deep mal- aise we as educators experience in our daily work and in our scholarly efforts to understand the logic we are living out. Images of commodification, their prem- ises and their consequences infest the classroom with the most intransigent of boundaries. In this imagining, the "to and fro motion" (Gadamer 1989, p. 104) of the gift disappears and with it, we suggest, the very possibility of pedagogy.

Without the free and unself-conscious (Hyde 1983, p. 152) movement of the gift, education loses its abundance. It loses its love, not only of children, but also its love of the ways that the worlds we are entrusted with (mathematics, language, and so on) are themselves great and ambiguous gifts, great move- ments into which we might step. Things become leaden. Things stop and take on the measured click of the machine, where "time is always running out" (Berry 1987, p. 44) and where knowledge becomes scarce and there is never enough for everyone. Without the movement of the gift, we live, in our class- rooms, unable to be moved or to feel the movement of the living disciplines of the world.

There are many faces to this pedagogical commodification, both in edu- cational theory and educational practices: it begins, first, with an image of "the individual" as separate and autonomous, and, therefore, an image of inter- relatedness as a matter of optional, discretionary, wilful, withholdable exchanges with other equally autonomous individuals. Thus education becomes full of a language of cross-border exchanges between teacher and

student, between student and text, between consuming knowledge and reproducing it on tests, between the accumulating and hoarding of knowledge and
the exchange of such knowledge for marks. Commodification marks the break-
up of the living disciplines of the world into carefully packagable, dispensable,
consumable and manageable curriculum resources and such a break-up lends
itself perfectly to talk of the marketability of skills and widespread images of
accountability and monitoring. Knowledge begins to appear to be scarce,
something hoarded by teachers and dispensed in developmentally graded
increments. And this reproduces images of second and third worlds, of under-
developedness and of the desire of development as underwritten by the opening of new markets: a horrifying image of educating our children in order to
open up them to being new markets for our own profit. Of course we do this
"for their own good" (Miller 1989) because they, too, *if they make the grade, if
they measure up,* will become autonomous producers and consumers along
with us, able, like us, to survive and profit.

Since the premise of these moves is what could be called a "metaphysics of
self-containment" (and therefore subsequently containable exchanges between
"individuals"), such exchanges must commodify the "worth" of those
exchanges such that no self-contained individual loses out in the rounds of
exchange. The space "in between" individuals thus becomes "the market"
where exchanges occur.

Moreover, those exchanges that become most "valued" are those that *allow*
such commodification. It is therefore interesting to note how images of "the
basics" in education are themselves produced out of this logic. It turns out that
"the basics" are those elements which can be most easily packaged and
delivered in discreet, sequenced, monitorable exchanges; they are also those
elements which can be most easily tested and assessed by having children give
back to us what we have given them. They are also those elements which can
and must be learned and understood "individually." There is no need for one
child to converse with another about a "basic math fact" question on a test. In
fact, this would be "cheating."

Another buried consequence of this logic is evident in how so much of the
discourse of beginning teachers begins by revolving around issues of "management." If classrooms are ideally/ideologically constituted by the logic of
containable exchanges, and teachers are those entrusted to monitor and facilitate such exchanges in ways fair to each "individual child," then *how to manage
this* becomes paramount. Teachers become "good facilitators" of seemly
exchanges. Add to this another odd logic we are living out and a great deal of
classroom turbulence is laid out.

From our inheritance of late 19th century pedagogies (Miller 1989), children are understood to be the uncivilized, the wild, those who will wilfully
attempt to despoil civil, commodifiable and containable relations (see, on this
point, Ivan Illich's [1980] profound tracing of the movement from the infidel

to the wild man to the native to the "underdeveloped"; see also Smith 2008). Thus, classroom management becomes even more central to our ability to imagine the contours of educational theory and practice. Worse yet, the much heralded arrival of constructivism becomes visible as a way to co-opt the wilderness/wildness of children by offering them a part in the dampening down of their own audacities (see Chapter 6), a part in their own "civilization," a part in their own self-containment: they now produce knowledges that are already and ahead of time co-opted in the rounds of exchange that constitute schooling and school success and future employment prospects. The invitation that constructivism thus offers children is one that keeps in place their diminishment but now lures them into doing it to themselves. Perfect: children, as reflective-constructive participants in their own education, become self-monitoring, self-assessing, self-managing, self-containing.

And we end up, in a weird and horrifying ecological backspin, calling wilderness forests "natural resources" and calling our children "our *greatest* natural resource."

In such an imaginal space, the idea of "globalization" gets collapsed into a happy gloss for the colonizing imposition of marketspeak in all aspects of our lives. The language of the market, the language of commodity, has become the only warranted form of publically speaking. And, as educators, we have all experienced how knowledge has become a commodity, students and parents have become "stakeholders" and customers, and teachers have become "accountable" in ways that no longer have any hint other than "are we getting our money's worth?"

All else seems merely naive, unable to understand "the realities" of things. And, although it might seem naive to suggest otherwise, this is not the sort of transcendence of boundaries that globalization can portend.

The Language of the Gift and the Transcendence of Boundaries: Globalization as Working in the Economy of the Gift

A brief entry in a mid-nineteenth-century collection of English fairy tales tells of a Devonshire man to whom the fairies had given an inexhaustible barrel of ale. Year after year the liquor ran freely. Then one day the man, curious to know the cause of this extraordinary power, removed the cork from the bung hold and looked into the cask; it was full of cobwebs. When the spigot next was turned, the ale ceased to flow.

The moral is this: the gift is lost in self-consciousness. To count, measure, reckon value, or seek the cause of a thing, is to step outside the circle, to cease being "all of a piece" with the flow of gifts and become, instead, one part of the whole reflecting upon another part. We participate in the esemplastic power of a gift by way of a particular kind of unconsciousness.

(Hyde 1983, pp. 151–2)

Just as the relation between the speaker and what is spoken points to a dynamic process (a "to and fro motion" [Gadamer 1989, p. 104]) that does not have a firm basis in either member of the relations, so the relation between the understanding and what is understood has a priority over its relational terms. Understanding [thus] involves a moment of "loss of self." (Gadamer 1977, pp. 50–1)

In some of our earlier work (Jardine 1998b), we have already explored some of the philosophical underpinnings of the image of the gift and its pedagogical character. We suggested that the idea of data or a datum is defined as that which is freely given and therefore, following Heidegger (1968) in one of his wonderfully wild etymologies, *thinking* (*Denken*) about the living realities of classroom events might best be described as a form of *thanks* (*Danken*) of the gift of the given. This line of thought provided us with a wonderful way of thinking through Gadamer's (1989) idea of taking up what is freely given in a classroom conversation. He suggests that, rather than combating what has been offered up in argumentative ways in order to weaken it in favour of something else, one might rather attempt to strengthen it (p. 367) by taking it up by taking seriously its claim (pp. 126–7) on us, taking seriously its claim to be, in some sense, true of something. It should, that is, be taken up as a gift and read back perhaps more generously than the giver intended or knew or desired.

This is especially evident in one of the most telling passages in Gadamer's *Truth and Method* (1989, p. 294) where he states that "it is only when the attempt to accept what is said as true fails that we try to 'understand' the text [what is written or said] as another's opinion." Understanding what a child offers in a classroom conversation as "their opinion" might be intended well, but it is also understandable as a refusing of the gift that is offered by handing it back to them as belonging to them. It is refusing to let it lay claim to us, to address us, to obligate us by its arrival to enter into the movement of thinking it sets forth. It is, however much unwittingly, a re-invoking of the whole metaphysics of commodification where experience is something an individual *has* (think of all the rhetoric of "ownership" in educational discourse) and conversation is something where individuals simply enter into relations of exchange. Forcing the gift back into "another's opinion," although it is meant as a way of honouring each child, in fact reinforces a zero-sum game in which every utterance rests inert beside any and all others, each having lost its power of address, i.e., its power to draw us into some larger, richer, more mysterious movements of ancestry and obligation than the narrows of owned-and-exchanged subjectivities. In fact, we begin to glimpse that "the focus on subjectivity [and its reliance on images of autonomous individuality] is a distorting mirror" (Gadamer 1989, p. 276).

All of this came home to us when we began to think of our recent experiences in studying a version of Homer's *Odyssey* with a group of fifty Grade Two children. We had chosen the *Odyssey* deliberately, as a tale we knew to be full of wondrous images, wondrous questions, wondrous topographies. We had taken several other groups of children into this place before. We knew, as Gadamer (1989, p. 21) has noted, that "youth [in fact, anyone 'new' to something] demand images for its imagination and for the forming of its memory. [We must, therefore] supplement the *critica* of Cartesianism [i.e., methodological issues of *how* to teach children to read] with the old *topica* [imaginal topographies that involve issues of what is worthy of the imagination and involvement of teachers and children alike, where is a rich, recursive, rigorous, interrelated (Doll, 1993) place in which we might meet? See Chapter 3]."

We did invite these children to read in a particular way that we also expected of ourselves. We enticed them to "give their hearts away," to find in the tale the images, characters, words, (the "good bits" as we and the children called them) that really spoke to each one of them and that were the opening or portal or door into what this tale might help us understand about ourselves and the great, mysterious arcs that tether us to this alluring place. Pairs of children carefully mapped out elaborate illustrations to different moments in the story that had for them a special hesitation. These pictures were sweated over for weeks, and the classroom became simply filled up with the images the children carefully, thoughtfully, diligently laboured over. These pictures, with the appropriate re-telling by each child, were posted on the school's Internet site. Part of the labour of understanding this tale, then, involved all of us giving away what each of us found in favour of wider, more generous, more worldly rounds of movement in which each of us were intimately involved. We each found ourselves involved in the movement of "primary social ties that enable[d each of us] to affirm and shape [our] uniqueness" (Godbout with Caille 1998, pp. 19–20) This was no longer part of the curriculum that had to be "covered" and, in such "covering" "promotes those abstract and secondary ties that, at least in theory, make people interchangeable and anonymous" (Godbout with Caille 1998, pp. 19–20) and subject to "ersatz personification" (p. 20) through an anonymous identification with Grade Level Expectations.

Hyde (1983) mentions that a peculiar characteristic of the gift and its movement is that it always, so to speak, has to go around a corner, out of sight. The movement set in motion by the gift always just might re-turn, like the unanticipated converses of a good conversation, drawing us out of ourselves into a movement greater than we could have experienced alone. The gift is always experienced as arriving from elsewhere, somewhere unexpected, undeserved, unearned. It is impossible to know in advance how it will be taken up, just as Homer himself could not have imagined that these children, here, in these times, would give their hearts away like this.

Three years after the Grade Two children completed their work, the following (excerpted) letter arrived at the School Division Office and was eventually directed to us and, through us, to the children and parents involved:

I am a Professor of Nuclear Engineering, Purdue University, and write to you from Athens, Greece where I am spending the current semester.

I have translated the first rhapsody of Homer's Odyssey into modern Greek and am in the process of publishing it in Greece. This translation differs from others in the sense that I use all the words of Homer that are still in use today even though the modern Greek reader might have difficulty in recognizing some of them as they have changed over time and only the root of the word remains. These words (more than forty percent of the original dates to ca. 800 BC), are printed in the old and modern Greek in red.

For some time I have been in search of an appropriate cover for my translation. It was my good luck to find via the Internet the beautiful drawings of the Grade Two class of Banded Peak School as they retell the Odyssey in words and pictures.

I am considering using one of the following two:

Calypso's Cave by A. and A.

Odysseus Escapes by M. and M.

Will you please grant me the appropriate permission to do so? Looking forward to your reply.

Sincerely, (signed) Paul S. Lykoudis, Professor Emeritus

Purdue University, West Lafayette IN.

Teachers, children and parents alike experienced the vertigo rush in this wonderful, unexpected arrival. Because the children had accepted the gift-movement of Homer's work, their pictures that were themselves given away set in motion a cascade of transcendences: between school-work and the work of the world; between children's work and the work of adults; between the work of careful illustration and the ebullience of the playful pleasures of real work; between teachers and learners, between the cultural boundaries of Canada and an American scholar now working in contemporary Greece; between "Ancient Greece" as a mandated curriculum demand and "Ancient Greece" as a living place inhabited by children's and teachers' imaginations; and, from Lykoudis's letter, between ancient and contemporary Greek words and the fact that his translation is premised precisely on long-forgotten rootednesses of contemporary terms and their origins. So his reading of the *Odyssey* in this way is itself in part a releasing of the gift-movement of contemporary usage back into its living inheritance.

The image of the gift helped us glimpse something we had taken for granted in this work and the rounds it seemed to take. We found that we had been deliberately taking up those things entrusted to us as teachers of young children as living gifts, living inheritances, rather than as commodifiable, inert, exchangeable objects. We had been acting on the belief that, for example, the tales and images of Ancient Greece are not simply deadened curriculum mandates that have to be somehow "covered." Rather, they "possess [their] own original worldliness and, thus, the centre of its [their] own Being so long as [they are] not placed in the object-world of producing and marketing. Our orientation to [such things, unlike our orientation to the object-world] is always something like our orientation to an inheritance." (Gadamer 1994, pp. 191–2). We chose it, therefore, not because it is some sort of "great book" but because it is *already on the move* in our culture, in the imaginations of children, in our images of journeys, in tales told and monsters imagined, in ideas of travel and home and family and fates and return. We had been reading a version of Homer's *Odyssey* with a group of Grade Two children with an eye to its movement in our lives as a gift, as an arrival, not, then, with an eye to what we might get from it, but with an eye to how we might give ourselves to it and, in such giving of our attention and love, keeping in motion its character as a gift.

Commodification stops the movement. It stops things from being "moving" and makes it possible to understand "being moved" as little more than being emotional, subjective, idiosyncratic and personal and therefore dismissible in light of more cynical, more "realistic" insights. This relationship between the movement and the stopping has always been a topic for us with the children and student-teachers we engage. What is becoming clear is that questions of how to motivate children have disappeared in favour of questions of how to find what is moving, how to find the movement, the living generosity, of the subjects we teach. We are finding that *this movement is what defines for us the idea of what is "basic" to any discipline with which we have been entrusted.*

The *Odyssey* is thus not some "thing" whose characteristics can be hoarded in the back of some seminal text and withheld and then dispensed for marks. Unless we enter wholeheartedly into the movement of thinking that it offers us, it remains anonymous and dead and takes on all the deadliness of school-as-consumption-and-production.

The conversations that interest us are not part of this zero-sum game of monitored dispensation. The conversations that interest us and that take our breath away are purely and clearly *excessive*. We are suggesting that what is "basic" to any of the work we do in education is *precisely in such excessiveness.* What is basic is the abundance, the gift in what we teach.

Endbit

Back, at this tail end, to our fascination with the gift-character of the Internet. We cannot avoid the fact that, in the midst of all this joyous transcendence and excessiveness, other, more silent borders are heightened in such a way that *their* transcendence becomes even less likely than before. As Ivan Illich (1970, p. 2) reminds us, "every technological response to a deeply human need creates a new level of poverty." Every gift can also sometimes subtly, sometimes grossly and intentionally diminish those outside the circles of its movement. We know that we have come upon "something else" (Godbout with Caille 1998, p. 3) here and we understand the terrible dangers of treating such matters naively, as if the political and economic forces at work in the new globalization were all somehow either non-existent or beneficent.

Without a careful critique of commodification, globalization turns out to be nothing more that the new colonialism. But without imagining "something else" than such commodification, such a critique is ripe and ready for the sort of cynicism, paranoia and exhaustion that, as teachers, we cannot readily afford.

On the While of Things

DAVID W. JARDINE

It's like making a path through the forest. At first it's rough going, with a lot of obstructions, but returning to it again and again, we clear the way. After a while the ground becomes firm and smooth from being walked on repeatedly. Then we have a good path for walking in the forest.

(Chah, 2005, p. 83)

I

What is it that makes classroom experiences worthwhile? This formulation hides too much of the deep etymological inheritances of such a question: what makes a classroom experience worth, not simply zero-sum school-grade exchange and the quick-time pace of acceleration, but, rather, *while*? What makes some experiences worthy of rest and repose, worthy of returning and being careful, worthy of tarrying and remembering, of taking time, of whiling away our lives in their presence?

These questions are framed, for me, as a way to think through some of the classroom work I have witnessed over several decades of attention to a specific phenomenon: how, in vigorous and intellectually challenging and pleasurable classrooms, time and memory gather together, both things and thinking accrue and return, and there is a sense of plenitude wherein the panics of schooling are cooled in favor of good, worthwhile work. Even as far back as 1991, when I first started hanging around Patricia Clifford and Sharon Friesen's classrooms, there was a different sense of time—not slowing, exactly, but *lingering*. It was a temporality I recognized from my own life and my loves of music and books and the wilds of cutting wood for the winter, something I recognized, too, from haphazard bouts of walking meditation and lolling over the smell of poplar trees early in an Alberta spring blue sky.

The fragmentation and scattershot acceleration that have come to define much of North American life and even more of our children's school-lives seems more and more like a bizarre hoax.

On darker days, it seems that it is purposefully wrought in order to induce the terrifying belief that acceleration and an increased (and increasingly mindless) consumption of pretty fragments will save us.

It seems, on darker days, that our children are being prepared to become unthinking consumers of *purposefully* less and less satisfying junk (for, of course, "satisfaction" might mean the breaking of the consumptive spell).

It seems, on darker days, that we, as teachers, have swallowed wholesale our role in ensuring this preparation. It seems like Sharon and Pat were right, years ago, when they said that we can't do to children what we haven't already done to ourselves, and that their infantilization and dumbing down are premised on our own. This is the great pedagogical trauma of anti-intellectualism that is passed off in many schools of education as "No Child Left Behind," "accountability," and "the real world."

We should be ashamed of ourselves, even if our complicity is a result of simple neglect. We have been *had*.

II

But there is little sense attempting to break this spell until we see that the understandings of the topics at hand that are available to us so often in schools have already been intellectually broken. We are no longer especially entrusted with living traditions but simply bits whose management is our task. Many of the tasks asked of teachers and students in schools are not worth *while* in this very particular sense: they are not worth lingering over, meditating upon, remembering, and returning to. They don't gather us together and demand gathering of us (an archaic way of saying "knowing"), but rather they isolate and pathologize and accelerate attention into scattershot pursuit. And this pursuit is not of the marks and vestiges (L. *vestigia*, "tracks"—root of the word "investigation" [see Chapter 3]) of the living topic under consideration and its living, scholarly place in the life of knowledge, but is, rather, the pursuit of the marks of schooling itself. In short, the purpose of, say, learning about a topic like "sovereignty" in social studies (a Grade Ten mandate in Alberta, Canada) is not to articulate one's life and make it more knowledgeable and perhaps livable (sovereignty, after all, is part of the *topos* that teachers and students and citizens inhabit day to day, in multifarious ways). Rather, the purpose of studying such a topic is to pass the upcoming examination. "Sovereignty," which still reigns as one leaves the examination room, is often dropped from memory at the moment that the examination is over, and the reason for this is that it is never taught as something memorable, something that forms and shapes our lives. Once dropped at the examination room door, this living *topos* remains at work in students' (and teachers') lives, but it remains a silent ghost that haunts and sways but never reaches living speech. In many schools, we never actually become *educated* in such matters, just well informed enough to "pass," and with such passing so too passes, too often, any memory of such matters.

With many examples of classroom work, no matter which aspect of which living discipline is under consideration, in schools, so often, the real topic is, as Ivan Illich told us over 30 years ago (1970), "school" and how to survive it.

In some schools, students who want to think about it and while over it get mocked, thus reproducing in students the very sort of "anti-intellectualism" that Raymond Callahan (1964, p. 8) noted as commonplace in contemporary schooling's efficiency ancestry.

This helps us get a glimpse of why it is that many of the tasks asked of students are *purposefully designed* precisely to rebuke whiling away over. In light of provincial test scores, sovereignty, for example, *is* the definition that can be rattled off. It *is* (a). & (c). or "none of the above." In light of industrial images of time-lines and efficiency and task-management, whiling over such matters seems archaic, useless, or, even worse, merely unproductive, hazy, liberal, snobbish, intellectualistic, "not-the-real-world" laziness. Many school tasks don't *need* a while because "needing a while" is understandable only as gumming up the works. Since most school curriculum is delivered in such a fragmented way as to not need a while, "needing a while" is understandable only as a "special need" (a need of what used to be called, ironically, "slow" children). Here, a while is understood only as a slowed-down version of that which "normal" students can do quickly and efficiently. The while needed to properly take up a topic like sovereignty in one's life is thus pathologized into the slow-wittedness of the one considering such a topic.

III

Given Frederick Winslow Taylor's insinuation of the efficiency-movement industrial assembly line into the consciousness of schooling (Taylor, 1911; Wrege & Greenwood, 1991; see Chapter 18 and our Preface), students and teachers are, more often than not, living in the midst of industrial temporality and its measures. It is in light of these measures that most schooled tasks have been stripped of that character which would take a while. A "continuity of [our] attention and devotion" (Berry, 1986, p. 32) to some classroom work is very often not simply *unnecessary* but *impossible* because the school-matters at hand have been stripped of the very memorability and relatedness and demand that might require and sustain and reward such attention and devotion. From the point of view of efficiency and management, intellectual whiling in the leisures (L. *schola*) of school simply seems dense and unproductive.

Worth *while* instead of simply worth cramming-as-time-runs-out-for-upcoming-examinations speaks, therefore, to a sense, not just of the tempo of human affairs, but of the temporality that some things have and the time that some things ask of us. "While" and what might be worthy of it is about time. One can't while over disconnected fragments. They don't ask this of us and will reject any such efforts at whiling.

There is thus a hidden ontology here, that *to be* worthy of while means not being a disconnected, fragmented, distanced, manageable object, but to be lived with, "*lebensweltlich* (close to the living world)" (Ross, 2004). Living disciplines full of topics we are living in the midst of and to which we belong in contested and multifarious ways need a while. Manageable objects do not.

Whiling over a topic—working at it, composing it, composing ourselves over it, remembering and cultivating one's memory of it—defines the work of hermeneutics.

Interpretation *whiles*.

And such whiling, I suggest, defines pedagogy at its best.

IV

The way we treat a thing can sometimes change its nature.

(Hyde, 1983, p. xiii)

Worthwhileness is not simply some sort of objective property or set of properties pertaining to certain topics and not to others. We can't just get a list of "great classroom ideas" and splay them out for students, or hand over to student-teachers some sure-fire "activities" that just need to be "done." This just leads, more often than not, to the complaint that "it didn't work with my kids."

Worthwhileness has to do with a way of treating things, a way of composing our understanding of something, seeking its kinships (Wittgenstein, 1968, p. 36) and versimilitudes (Gadamer, 1989, p. 21), and, in the same breath, composing ourselves, finding our composure in the face of what we have encountered.

The old and tired terminology of "objectivity" and "subjectivity" is inadequate to this phenomenon. Equally inadequate are the squeals of "accountability" and "what about assessment?" as if talk of something being worthwhile means the end of such matters. One of the great hoodwinks is that, if we try to disrupt the machine of efficient assembly, then all matters becomes subjectivized and issues of students doing good work can no longer be judged (since "to do good work" has itself already been rendered into the efficient production of high marks on examinations). Such alternatives already bespeak the severing of the often hidden or occluded or forgotten, sometimes contested, sometimes revelatory, kinships and "family resemblances (*Familienahnlichkeiten*)" (Wittgenstein, 1968, p. 32) upon which whiling relies. Stripped of all their relations, fragments don't draw us in. Fragments leave us as worldless, obligationless, willful agent-subjectivities whose only recourse is methodology. In its worst case, we become the authors of any relations we "find" in the world: "Accordingly, the spontaneity of understanding becomes the formative principle of receptive matter, and in one stroke we have the old mythology of an intellect which glues and rigs together the world's matter with its own forms" (Heidegger, 1985, p. 70).

Constructivism, initially meant to disrupt the assembly-line consciousness of contemporary schooling, simply aggravates it and replaces it with a sort of ego-imperialism which makes consumptiveness more violent and willful. In its worst aspect, the state becomes the sole constructor and we become its silenced products. As a senior advisor to the Bush administration suggested, here is the terrible truth that whiling is up against and that is killing teachers and students and the living disciplines which have been entrusted to them in schools:

> We are an empire now, and when we act, we create our own reality. And while you're studying that reality—judiciously as you will—we'll act again, creating other new realities, which you can study, too, and that's how things will sort out.
>
> (cited in MacMillan, 2006, p. A19)

Studiousness becomes a form of inaction and an object of mockery. Thinking about the acts of this rendering empire becomes unpatriotic (see Jardine, 2005, 2007; Smith, 2006, 2008).

Once constructivism is underwritten by an ontology that portends a world of disconnected fragments, once we fall for the fragmentation that leads us to believe that "we make all the patterns" (Berry, 1987, p. xv), the only outcome can be that "constructivism means war" (Jardine, 2007), geopolitically, in terms of personal politics, and, of course, against the green of things (see Bowers, 2006; Orr, 2004).

And in all this, time seems to accelerate and slip away. Nothing accrues and nothing is remembered. Nothing lasts.

V

Whiling, on the contrary, pulls at us, because it seeks kinships, bloodlines. Whiling is the work of someone looking not to be the gluer and rigger of a constructed world, but to be implicated in and witnessed by what they while over, looking to "recognize themselves in the mess of the world" (Hillman, 1983, p. 49) ("we do not understand what recognition is in its profoundest nature if we only regard it as knowing something again that we already know. The joy of recognition is rather the joy of knowing *more* than is already familiar. In recognition, what we know emerges, as if illuminated. It is known *as* something" [Gadamer, 1989, p. 114]).

More simply, yet more mysteriously put, when we experience something worthwhile, we experience something over and above our wanting and doing (this is Frederick Winslow Taylor's worst nightmare, as well as something beyond the comprehension of contemporary American foreign policy—that we might be *thought about* differently than we think about ourselves, that others might understand us differently than we are able to understand ourselves). We experience something being *asked of us*. "Understanding begins when something addresses us" (Gadamer, 1989, p. 299), or, as the old man put it in his 94th year, fragmented bits and pieces (like those requisite of assembly-schooling) are not in any living sense "the basics" (see Chapter 1): "something awakens our interest—that is really what comes first!" (Gadamer, 2001, p. 50).

In asking after worthwhileness, we are asked to find our measure in such things that awaken us and our interest. We are asked to learn *from* things, not just *about* them, and, in such learning, to become something more than we had been before such encounters. A worthwhile matter "would not deserve the interest we take in it if it did not have something to say to teach us that we could not know by ourselves" (Gadamer, 1989, p. xxxv).

VI

Part of my initial interest in these matters stems from this being the 12th year that I have taught a course that involves reading Hans-Georg Gadamer's *Truth and Method* (1989) cover to cover. This experience of re-reading—this experience of whiling away over this work with others for so many years—doesn't exactly fit the image of up-to-date research agendas. But it always ends up the same. Something always unanticipatedly *happens*, and a heretofore timid thread of Gadamer's work spins around and finds a face and faces me with something of its own to say. Consider that one of the threads of Gadamer's text is precisely the whiling time of "works," and how this hit full force in combination with how many years I've been precisely lingering over this work of Gadamer's.

In this happenstance, I was aided by happening upon Sheila M. Ross's brilliant article "Gadamer's Late Thinking on *Verweilen*" (2004). This text helped me see vestiges in *Truth and Method* that I had not experienced before, and yet, reading Ross's article was a peculiar act of recognition, of knowing something more in knowing the same thing.

This experiential sense of vestige links up with earlier work (see Chapter 3) on the composition of memory and how such composition involves the effort, not to "amass verified knowledge" (Gadamer, 1989, p. xxi) but rather to *keep something in mind*. And the act of keeping something in mind is the act of shaping my life (*Bildung*) as one who carries himself this way, with this in mind. In such memorial whiling-work, I become someone lodged in the multifarious memory of the world. I come upon myself making myself up, getting a hold of myself, composing my self in the middle of this worldly life.

There is something about such matters that provides clues to understanding an intimate form of classroom practice that sidesteps the panics of industrial time-consciousness and provides for whiling. And this interweaves with the opportunity I have had over the past year of working, in some small ways, with a group of wonderful teachers and students at a local high school. This has given me a site of meditation, a site of attention to consider again the issue of worthwhile work in the face of the particular ways in which it arises in the work of students and teachers and the curriculum topics entrusted to them in schools (some of this is also discussed, in a different context, in Chapter 18).

I was recently a very small part of some conversations in a Grade Ten social studies class about British minister Jack Straw's comments (from October 5, 2006 [see news.bbc.co.uk]) regarding Muslim women wearing the *hijab*. Minister Straw was suggesting that Muslim women unveil in his presence, and that their refusing to do so is nothing more than a way of cutting themselves off from British culture. One student's (a Muslim girl, wearing a *hijab*) comment was that it is often seen as "hiding something" and that, perhaps, helps start to explain the hushed conversations and stares on the bus on the way to school. I've wryly laughed since over the terrifying coincidence of George Bush's security fetishes and images of Texan wild-west outlaws with their faces obscured—bandannas, banditos ready to violate any and every border of civility, plundering, robbing us of house and home. The glare of the unobstructed, irresistible, you-have-no-say-in-it security-gaze, and the demand to uncover, to strip down, is occurring precisely in a time of great secrecy and cover-up, a time of the deliberate and systematic "enfraudening" of the public sphere (Smith, 2006). Frederick Winslow Taylor's security and surveillance-based line-ups that underwrite much contemporary schooling have made us ripe for accepting and even embracing the contemporary zeal for entrenching of security-paranoia. We've been *schooled* into experiencing a world that asks nothing of us beyond what we ask of it. And we've equally been schooled into believing that relentless surveillance shouldn't bother you if you've got nothing to hide. Differently put, if you hold something in reserve, you are guilty, because the very act of doing something "off the grid" of Taylor's stopwatch checklist—something not glued and rigged under the management of the line—is itself subversive.

As I meditate upon Smith's words about the deliberate veil of enfraudening that has fallen over the public sphere, that Grade Ten conversation starts to turn, to converse, to shape and form itself and seek verisimilitude ("the spontaneous and inventive seeking out of similarities" [Gadamer, 1989, p. 432]). I start to "think it over," or "ruminate" or "worry" this bone of contention. Memory, in such a case, doesn't simply "store" these events nor does it store separately these ideational, recurrent, image-filled speculations that these events engender (including a terrible hesitation over the fact that Islam turns its back on the image in vital and telling ways that have as yet had little truck in schools except through the ridiculous recent dance of Islamic iconoclasm and Danish cartoonists. The anti-intellectualism of public discourse about such matters is heartbreaking for anyone interested in *education* and *thoughtfulness*. This alone is one reason why Chapter 4 above is the most meager of beginnings of thinking and wholly inadequate to the task of thinking that recent events have laid out for us all).

Memory "works" each event *in relation* to the other, working to "place" them properly and safely. This might sound a bit contrived, but consider: that link between Taylor's efficiency-movement schooling of our attention and contemporary security fetishes needs to be calmed down a bit, worked over a bit, not just blurted out. It needs to find its proper measure, its proper proportionality to the matters at hand that are emerging in memory and its ways. We cannot know in advance or once and for all if it will turn out to be a grotesque exaggeration or a timid understatement. Again, the phenomenon of memory, here, is continually in suspense, because what is being formed is susceptible to a future that is still arriving. Who would have thought, for example, that we would have come to see the eruption of the old iconoclastic/iconophilic Second Council of Nicea arguments in violent responses to newspaper cartoons? Or that something of North America's spell-bound love of unveiled access to increasingly flickering images might be worth *thinking about* in light of voices from outside of that spell?

The inventive seeking out of similarities is necessarily premised upon a slow and gathering memorial inventory, a "niche" where things are not simply stored but restored, measured, shaped, and formed in relation to and in the witness of each other. This leads to an emergent experience of the memorability of a place (a "topic") rather than to the simple memorization of fragments to which I bear no memorial obligation and which ask nothing of me in return. In this cultivated, worked and whiled-over space that develops "in between" (Gadamer, 1989, p. 109), each initially seemingly "separate" tale becomes more than it might have been without the other. Oddly enough, in such memorial working, the "time" of each event changes as well. Each enters into the same *while* as I while away over them, caring for them, placing and replacing in the *invenio* memory-dance that is both inventive and inventorial (Carruthers, 2003, p. 11). My "making something" of these events (my formative activity) is, at the same time, also "made" by the formative encounter with the fleshy "otherness" of the experiences undergone and remembered:

> Thinking is not a disembodied "skill"; there is no thought without matters to think with. People can only think with the contents of their memories, their experiences. And human memories are stored as images in patterns of places (or "locations" or "topics").
>
> (Carruthers, 2003, p. 89)

About a week after this class, one of those Grade Ten social studies students talked to me about how she understands that her *hijab* is seen by many as a form of oppression. She explained how, in her tradition, if you wear a *hijab* simply because someone tells you to, you might as well not wear it at all, but she understood how some Canadians, some of her classmates, have trouble understanding how anyone would *choose* such a thing (of course, we might say, unmediated unveiledness seems so "ordinary" in North American consciousness, and veiledness seems so, well, *exotic*—even though I can recall my next door neighbor, Eva [the wife of Harry from Chapter 15], covering her head when she entered the Catholic Church while Harry removed his hat, and how the Royal Canadian Legion would, for a while, not admit Sikhs because turbans were consider to be "hats" and therefore disrespectful of fallen comrades. All this and *yarmulkes*, too, hardly ever came to memory or speech in arguments over Muslim women's veils. Too much thinking is required, too much cultivated memory and snobbish intellectual venture. Instead, news programs ask for our opinions, and 70 percent of x think y, and [the greatest lie of all] "We want to hear from you. We want to know what *you* think").

This girl admitted, as well, and without hesitation, that, of course, some in her tradition simply do what they are told. We commiserated a bit over how this is a deep kinship that many traditions share that we, here, share face to face, of mindlessly simply doing what you are told and remaining silent and silenced (see Chapter 18).

There is something, here, about the decision *to be regarded* a certain way and what that says about who you are in a profoundly worldly sense, here, in relation to, in standing with, others. There is also, echoing here, an issue of having to simply submit to another's demands for their right to have my self as the object of their unveiled regard, as with Minister Straw. It seems that Minister Straw did not while over those women who might visit his ministry office. It seems that he did not ask himself what they might have to say about him and his unveiling presumptions. At least that is what the media has left us with— fragments of a fragmented story that flitters by our attention and leaves us flittering and, once again, bereft of the possibility of whiling except through great effort. Faint echoes of that old Grade Ten social studies topic of (for Canadians especially, British) sovereignty and (American-style) self-sovereignty and the nature, occasion, and limits of submission. But the topic speeds by and becomes no topic at all, just a flicker.

Echoes, then, of a decision to be seen to belong in this multifarious world *this* way, veiled from something of its gaze and telling us something of the origins and nature and limits and enculturedness and ethnicity of the unremitting glare of that gaze and its pretenses.

That student also voiced a profound idea about herself and her classmates. Some of her female classmates believe that they are free to dress any way they want and, if a boy ogles them, it is the boy's fault. She, on the other hand, suggested that how she is looked at, the gaze she attracts, affects who she is, and that it is her responsibility, at least in part, to protect how she is seen, because letting herself be seen a certain way is who she *is*. You become who you are in the witness of the world with which you surround yourself. If you surround yourself with ogling gazes, you become someone.

This, among, of course, clusters of other threads, is a reason for the troublesome demand to remove the *hijab*. This is also a troublesome reminder of the hollowing effect of being a young female who is *nothing but gazed at*—Paris, Lindsay, Britney, Nicole, and the Olsens come to mind, and the fact that this list will seem positively ancient and out of date in a year is, of course, *precisely the point*. We bounce, here, between anorexia and obesity, between too much and too little, between darkness and hiddenness and security threats, and paparazzi's unveiled glare.

Again, "understanding begins when something addresses us" (Gadamer, 1989, p. 299). But what occurs in such moment of address is that something starts to slow around these classroom events and the memorial ruminations they spawn, and memory starts to double in on itself and coalesce and become compositional. I want to *remember* this, but this remembering is not simply an issue of brute storage, but of exaggerating (Gadamer, 1989, p. 115), forgetting (pp. 15–16), seeking out resemblances or versimilitudes or family resemblances as places to place such a memory safely, a place it can take root, be restored and recalled. To remember it, then, is to place it such that it can remain not simply as a slot into which to unthinkingly pigeon-hole what arrives next, but as something ready to be re-membered. Only as something ready to be re-membered does it remain in *living* memory. Only as such does it refuse to become a concept ready to wreak conceptual violence by con-structing what newly arrives (see Chapter 15 on the idea of "conceptual violence").

Something, in remembering, starts to form, to shape (this is what that whole "transformation into structure" section is about in *Truth and Method*, when the "to and fro" [1989, pp. 114ff.] of play starts to become "a play," that is, a "work" that somehow begins to "stand there" with a life of its own [this is the *Da* of Heidegger's (1962) *Dasein*]). But something else starts to happen in such memory work.

I gather things in memory, but then, as Clarissa Pinkola-Estes (1992, pp. 27–28) describes so wonderfully (and as has been raised in a different con-text in Chapter 8 regarding the phenomenon of animism and its consorts), I also sing over these bones and something happens:

> The sole work of *La Loba* is the collecting of bones. She is known to collect and preserve especially that which is in danger of being lost to the world. . . . Her specialty is said to be wolves.
>
> She creeps and crawls and sifts through the *montanas* . . . and *arroyos* . . . looking for wolf bones, and when she has assembled an entire skeleton, when the last bone is in place and the beautiful white sculpture of the creature is laid out before her, she sits by the fire and thinks about what song she will sing.
>
> And when she is sure, she stands over the *critura*, raises her arms and sings out. That is when the rib bones and leg bones of the wolf begin to flesh out and the creature becomes furred. *La Loba* sings some more, and more of the creature comes into being; its tail curls upward, shaggy and strong.
>
> And *La Loba* sings more and the wolf creature begins to breathe.
>
> And *La Loba* sings so deeply that the floor of the desert shakes, and as

she sings, the wolf opens its eyes, leaps up, and runs away down the canyon.

Right in the midst of dwelling on these old bones and worrying them in memory, something leaps up with a life of its own (which is precisely what the phenomenological presumption of hermeneutics pursues in its compositional work, an experience of the *Lebensweltlichkeit*—the "life-worldliness"—of something). Here, however, is one great difference between phenomenology and hermeneutics. For phenomenology, this life-worldliness is a given that is presented to consciousness in phenomenological reflection and that is ripe for nothing but *description* of it in its givenness. For hermeneutics, it is not a given. It is experienced as "a task for consciousness and an achievement that is demanded of it" (Gadamer, 1989, p. 127). In *Lebensweltlichkeit*, something is asked of us beyond what issues from our experience (*Erlebenisse*). An experience (*Erfahrung*—a venture, a travel, full of faces and voices and efforts and grief of those who've travelled before us, our ancestors [*Vorfahrung*]) is in store.

Properly worried over, properly cared for and remembered, these things keep "coming up," erupting and interrupting of their own accord, asking for attention, needing something from me, it seems. This is a reason why Gadamer (1989, p. 366) suggests that understanding is "more a passion than an action. A question *presses itself upon us*," thus undermining the subjective-activity centeredness of constructivism and its consorts (see Jardine, 2006d, pp. 123–136), as well as the pretense to givenness in experience of Husserlian phenomenology. Moreover, insofar as what is composed and formed and shaped and remembered is hermeneutically understood only insofar as it remains susceptible to the future (see Chapter 19 on the idea of "new blood" and its arrival; see also Jardine & Batycky, 2006), this also undermines the tendency of phenomenology towards an "eidetic reduction" (see Husserl, 1970a) which, through "eidetic variation," renders instances into essences, resulting in an ever *decreasing* susceptibility to what the next case may have to say (once we know what something essentially is, the next instance is, in essence, "already understood" before its arrival). Husserl (1970a) states of his phenomenology that "the great task can and must be undertaken of investigating the . . . fact . . . as belonging to its essence, and it is determinable only *through* its essence" (p. 177). "The life-world does have, in all its relative features, a *general structure*. We can attend to it in its generality and, with sufficient care, fix it once and for all in a way equally accessible to all" (p. 178).

This is not how whiling works in hermeneutics. It was, of course, the great and sometimes terrible work of Martin Heidegger that began the great hermeneutic "turn" away from such confident subjectivizing and essentializing towards the work of whiling over works (see Chapter 15 for some comments on Heidegger's efforts regarding works of art). In a very literal and deeply bodily, deeply experiential sense, these events worry *me* and draw me in as much as *I* worry over *them* and attempt to draw memory and knowledge from encountering them:

> I am not anthropomorphizing. It's more like a thing is a phenomeno-logical [in a very non-Husserlian sense, clearly] presentation, with a depth, a complexity, a purpose, in a world of relations, with a memory, a history. And if we look at it this way we might begin to hear it. It's an aesthetic appreciation of how things present themselves [see Gadamer, 1989, for how he uses the work of art as a way in to discussing hermen-eutic experience (*Erfahrung*)] and that therefore they are in some way formed, ensouled, and are speaking to the imagination. This way of look-ing is a combination of the Neoplatonic *anima mundi* and pop art: that even a beer can or a freight car or a street sign has an image and speaks of itself beyond being a dead throwaway object.
>
> (Hillman, 1982, pp. 132–133)

Thus, the image of being culpable for the gaze I attract and a realization that is deeply ecological in character, that, in seeing, I am also *visible*. In remembering such events, what begins is a shift in temporality and an ontological shift. What begins is a whiling over them, a whiling that seeks out the worth of that while (the keep-seeking of kinships and family resemblances that shape the invento-rial, root of *invenio*), while, at the same time, making the thing worth while through whiling (the inventive root of *invenio*).

What starts to occur is an experience of things that breaks the surveillance-gaze and mastery-pretensions of subjectivity (and its rude con-sort, "objectivity," and the consequent possibilities of Frederick Winslow Tay-lor's "scientific management"). Whiling "breaks open the being of the object" (Gadamer, 1989, p. 382) and we begin to experience how things are not sim-ply arm's length objects in which we have no stake and we are not worldless subjects living inside our own experiences. Such a belief in the being of things and the nature of our selves is simply an outcome of how they have been treated.

Rather, in whiling, things start to *regard us* and tell us about ourselves in ways we could not have experienced without such whiling. And we become selves that recognize themselves in the recognition of the world:

> All things show faces, the world not only a coded signature to be read for meaning, but a physiognomy to be faced. As expressive forms, things speak; they show the shape they are in. They announce themselves, bear witness to their presence: "Look, here we are." They regard us beyond how we may regard them, our perspectives, what we intend with them, and how we dispose of them.
>
> (Hillman, 1982, p. 77)

But they will only regard us, speak to us, if we treat them properly. "Look, here we are" is not a phenomenological or ecological given. It is a task to be taken up, a dedication whose consequences must be suffered.

VII

Several weeks after that cluster of conversations and musings, I returned to a lovely website that houses "unpublished" work by Ivan Illich. I'd been reading Illich's work on fragmentation, commodification, and regimes of scarcity as a way of thinking through what might be meant by "curriculum in abundance" (Jardine, Friesen, & Clifford, 2006). All this was a follow-up to considering how classrooms might function as gift economies (see Jardine, Clifford, & Friesen, 2003, pp. 211–222) rather than market economies where regimes of scarcity reign.

In such market economies, "time is always running out" (Berry, 1983, p. 76). The time involved here, in the efficiency movement's fragmenting of the living disciplines entrusted to teachers and students in schools, is not while-time simply sped up. Rather, this time is "empty"—"measuring time [as distinct from whiling time] requires a separation of the temporal units which measure from that which is measured; to separate time from its contents is to 'empty' it" (Ross, 2004, discussing Gadamer [1970]). In light of such an empty measured time, things are no longer understood to have a time of their own. Rather, things are rendered measurable by such empty, formal, clockwork temporality and thus things lose their while—things no longer *are* all of their relations and kinships and family resemblances, not any of the beckonings that might haunt us and call for our thinking (see Heidegger, 1968). We can no longer say of something that "only in the multifariousness of voices [does it] exist" (Gadamer, 1989, p. 284). Empty time fragments things, cuts their bloodlines, and reduces their multifariousness to singularity—the singular voice of empty, leveling, measurable surveillance.

Once time becomes detached from that which it measures, quite literally nothing holds time at bay, nothing can cause it to linger or tarry. Worse yet, once time becomes thus clocked independently of that which it measures, this temporality of industrial fragmentation *demands the fragmentation of that which it measures* and measures the truth of things by the ability to control, predict, and manipulate such fragments. This is why, following James Hillman's admonition (cited on p. 234), we might suggest that such empty time is a form of anthropomorphism, but it is a special form. It isn't the living, Earthly body (*morphos*) of humanity or the Earth-bodies of things that are the measure. It is the morphology of an abstract idea into which we have shaped ourselves: clock-watchers whose lives have become machined. *Anthropos* has rendered itself into surveillable DNA sequences, or into the image of computer storage and retrieval, or scannable identity cards and the like. As many teachers have said, in one way or another, we and our students and the disciplines entrusted to us all become rendered to fit the institutional machine of schooling.

Once it is compositionally and topically unheld, fragmented time can only try to become fulsome through *accelerating* (this again is a lived experience in schools caught in empty time and its effluence). Cut off from the while of things, there is nothing to hold memory and attention and experience in place, nothing to call it to collect itself or attend or return. Time speeds up. Whiling appears as a luxurious waste of time that many teachers have told me they would pursue with their students if it were not for how many fragmented things needed covering and the fact that time's running out.

To repeat, there is something worse yet. We start to believe that we live in a world where *nothing requires a while*. We experience a world in which nothing is asked of us beyond what we ask of it:

> The Gadamerian dystopia is not unlike others. In his version, to be glib, little requires human application, so little cultivates it. Long alienated from abiding in inquiry as a form of life and a way of being, a restless humanity defers to models, systems, operations, procedures, the ready-made strategic plan.
>
> (Ross, 2004)

The time things need from us is forgone in favor of the time we have to "cover" them in class, and in such measured time, as every teacher has experienced in the institution of schooling, there is never enough time to take a while over something and make it worthwhile. Thus rendered under the demand of another, measured time becomes akin to the Straw-gaze that Muslim women were asked to submit to.

It *renders* (see Chapter 14 and also Jardine 2005, 2006d).

The sovereignty of the fragmented, measured-time curriculum disassembly is, of course, on behalf of the ease of management and surveillance. In measured time, ideally, nothing *happens*. Things just occur according to the rules that measured time has measured out for things, or they deviate from such a measure and need realignment. In such a light, whiling now appears as a potential threat to the security and orderliness and manageability and surpriselessness that measured time demands of that which it renders.

In whiling you can happen upon something unanticipated.

Insurgency is possible. Something can "come up" of its own accord, "over and above our wanting and doing" (Gadamer, 1989, p. xxviii). Whiling is *epiphantic*, and, thus, because it cannot lay out in advance what will happen, it appears veiled and suspicious.

After all, the voices say, what are those teachers and students up to who while over the *hijab* even though the curriculum guides don't say that it needs to be covered? (A pitiful pun, I know.)

VIII

On this Illich-related website (see www.davidtinapple.com/illich) there are two papers I spotted that I hadn't quite seen before. My susceptibility to seeing them was a vestige of memory and its composition. Their titles have now become full of address: "Guarding the Eye in the Age of Show" (2001) and "The Scoptic Past and the Ethics of the Gaze" (2001a). In these papers Illich speaks of what he names, in another context (2005, p. 108), the "*custodia oculorum*, the guarding of the eye" that was once a commonplace idea in European thought (and clearly, from that Grade Ten conversation, an idea borne somewhere near the heart of Islam):

> Until quite recently, the guard of the eyes was not looked upon as a fad, nor written off as internalized repression. Our taste was trained to judge all forms of gazing on the other.
>
> (Illich, 2001, p. 5)

> In 726, the emperor Leo III had the icon of Christ torn from the tympanum of his palace's bronze gate, to be replaced by a naked cross. In this event, three distinct currents find a common expression: the Old Testament awe rejecting any visualization of the Word of God that touches the flesh, the heart of the believer; the later Muslim exaltation of the sound of the Koran with whose majesty and beauty no picturing of the Almighty could possibly compete; and, of course, the Greek Ikonoskepsis, the philosophical hesitancy in giving the weight of truth to representations.
>
> (Illich, 2001a, p. 7)

Like any of the good fields entrusted to teachers and students in school, (curriculum) topics emerge and show their fullness and richness and abundance if they are worked carefully and in ways proper to them and their (sometimes contested, sometimes contradictory, sometimes worthy of repudiating or valuing or re-evaluating in light of new circumstances) familial limits. After all, who would have imagined on September 10 that the vitality and difficulty and particular ancestries and worries about Canadian social studies curriculum topics like "multiculturalism" or "sovereignty" would have turned out quite like this?

They need our while anew (which is why believing that we know "in essence" what sovereignty is always constitutes an error that time will, of necessity, outrun. Good teachers know that understanding "sovereignty" in its *Lebensweltlichkeit* means that we must listen to how it is being read back to us by our students and the world in which it lives and breathes and becomes).

If we are surrounded, not by the living world but by surveilled and manageable fragments rendered by measured time, this has an effect. As with the zero-sum scarcity regimes of market economies, "it nullifies precedent, it snaps the threads of memory and scatters local knowledge. By privileging individual choice over the common good, it makes relationships revocable and pro-visional" (Gray, 1998, pp. 35–36). We become something under the gaze of such revocability. If we surround ourselves with fragments, we become fragmented, isolated, entrenched, tribalized, paranoid, and any sense of relatedness or worldliness is simply a site of a possible security breach (again, images of Taylor's assembly-line stopwatch and whistle). If we surround our-selves with things that are trivial and cheap, our lives become trivial and cheap. If learning becomes just "for show" on an exam and no longer about the formation of our lives, our lives become susceptible to the trivializing and infantilizing flicker of the business of show (this hides the great critiques in hermeneutics of the metaphysics of *presence*). In being formed by such flickering, I become:

> the ideal-type channel-hopping MTV viewer who flips through different images at such speed that she/he is unable to chain the signifiers together into a meaningful narrative, he/she merely enjoys the multiphrenic intensities and sensations of the surface of the images.
>
> (Usher & Edwards, 1994, p. 11)

This was written in 1994. The enjoyment of such multiphrenic intensities and sensations of the surface of things is now, post-9/11, underwritten by a para-noia about what is hidden behind the imaginal veil. And it links back, too, to those older musings about regimes of scarcity and market economies:

> People whose governing habit is the relinquishment of power, com-petence and responsibility, and whose characteristic suffering is the anx-iety of futility, make excellent spenders. They are the ideal consumers. By inducing in them little panics of boredom, powerlessness, sexual failure, mortality, paranoia, they can be made to buy virtually anything that is "attractively packaged."
>
> (Berry, 1986, p. 24)

Illich (2001, p. 3) asks us " 'What can I do to survive in the midst of show?' not 'how do I improve show business?' " But now, in these post-modern times, the image-flicker is no longer veiling anything at all. The real world is either scientific management or it is shifty referentialities all the way down, and whil-ing is for intellectual snobs (as one science teacher said at the high school where I'd been working this past year, when she heard about our class, "Sounds nerdy!").

IX

Tarrying, involving the "temporal structure of being moved" and occasioning "durationless" time ... suggests a most practical and accessible solution [to this issue of how to survive in the midst of show],

demonstrating how practice is a solution. "The *Weile* [the 'while' in *Verweilen*, tarrying] has this very special temporal structure."
(Ross, 2004, citing, at the end of this passage, Gadamer, 2001)

Obviously such streams of consequence and gathering get out of hand very easily when whiling is trying to be portrayed in narrative form, because each of these incidentals and their "interweaving and crisscrossing" (Wittgenstein, 1968, p. 36) is only especially sensible if such matters are compositionally *experienced* and *undergone*, not simply rattled off in some "brainstorm" wherein none of the possibilities tossed around are taken especially seriously. That is what is meant by suggesting that the scattershot fragmentation of attention has a practical solution.

Whiling must be *practiced* in order to be understood (see the lamentations in Chapter 3 regarding how to help readers experience how students' work has been accomplished). This is why hermeneutics cannot be adequately described procedurally and why the proper first response to the question of "How do you do hermeneutics?" is "What is your topic?" Without the worldly resistance of a topic and the topical work of memory, composition, and composure around *this* or *that* topic—without the "fecundity of the individual case" (Gadamer, 1989, p. 33)—hermeneutics doesn't "work" because it has nothing to work in concert with, no "other" to heed, no vestiges, no need to compose myself, nothing over which to while.

Equally obvious is that what starts to occur in the task of whiling is that we begin to experience the matters we are whiling over as something that "outplays" us. We begin to experience the fact that the thing under consideration is *itself* and not us. With measured time, the thing measured comes more and more into our purview, under our gaze, in our control and subjected to our demands. With spending time over things that are worth while, something else occurs, something worth repeating from the first edition of this text:

> When any of us think of those things in the world that we dearly love— the music of Duke Ellington, the contours of a powerful novel and how it envelopes us if we give ourselves over to it, the exquisite architectures of mathematical geometries, the old histories and stories of this place, the rows of garden plants that need our attention and devotion and care, varieties of birds and their songs, the perfect sound of an engine that works well, the pull of ice under a pair of skates, and on and on—we understand something in our relation to these things about how excessiveness might be basic to such love. We do not seek these things out and explore them again and again simply for the profit that we might gain in exchanging what we have found for something *else*. What we have found, in exploring and coming to understanding, to learn to live well with these things is not an arms-length commodity but has become part of who we are, and how we carry ourselves in the world. We love them and we love

what becomes of us in our dedication to them. And, paradoxically, the
more we understand of them, the better—richer, more intriguing, more
complex, more ambiguous and full and multiple of questions—*they*
become, and the more we realize that gobbling them up into a knowing
that we can commodify, possess and exchange is not only undesirable. It
is impossible. We realize, in such knowing, that the living character of the
things we love will, of necessity, outstrip our own necessarily finite and
limited experience, memory, and exploration.

(Jardine, Clifford, & Friesen, 2003, p. 208)

X

So long as [these curriculum topics are] not placed in the object-world of
producing and marketing [the object-world, of course, of measured
time, not of while], [they are able to] draw us entirely outside of ourselves and impose [their] own presence on us. [They] no longer [have]
the character of an object that stands over against us; we are no longer
able to approach this like an object of knowledge, grasping, measuring
and controlling. Rather than meeting us in our world, it is much more a
world into which we ourselves are drawn.

(Gadamer, 1994, pp. 191–192)

This final section is, in part, a memo to myself as a teacher. I have witnessed,
over and over again, the profound thoughtfulness that teachers and students
can display in their whiling over the world, if their time and the topics they
while over are treated properly and they are allowed to become untethered
from the time-measured panics of schooling. Such untethering is difficult, life-
long work and, given the pervasiveness of the spells of measured time, engaging
in such work is not necessarily viewed as honorable by one's colleagues. This,
again, is Gadamer's version of dystopia: in the day-to-day work of most
schools, "little requires human application, so little cultivates it" and those who
pursue such whiling can seem pretentious, perhaps even mad.

I have witnessed, too, over the 20 years I've worked in schools in the Calgary
area, how intellectually vigorous and sound is the work so many teachers and
students have done once they are able to get their bearings in the often-wild
whiles of things. The intellectual and spiritual pleasure to be experienced, and
the honorability of the suffering such whiling requires, is beautiful and true.

Finally, there is another connection that links up some of the phenomenological rootedness of hermeneutics with what I believe is a profoundly ecological idea. Here is a difficult hint in a commentary by Hans-Georg Gadamer
on the work of one of his great teachers, Martin Heidegger:

The existing thing does not simply offer us a recognizable and familiar
surface contour; it also has an inner depth of self-sufficiency that
Heidegger calls "standing-in-itself." The complete unhiddenness of all

beings, their total objectification (by means of a representation that con-
ceives things in their perfect state [fully given, fully present, fully presented, finished]) would negate this standing-in-itself of beings and lead
to a total leveling of them. A complete objectification of this kind would
no longer represent beings that stand in their own being. Rather, it would
represent nothing more than our opportunity for using beings, and what
would be manifest would be the will that seizes upon and dominates
things. [In whiling over something rather than rendering it in measured
time] we experience an absolute opposition to this will-to-control, not in
the sense of a rigid resistance to the presumption of our will, which is
bent on utilizing things, but in the sense of the superior and intrusive
power of a being reposing in itself.

> (Gadamer, 1977, pp. 226–227)

Worthwhile things are thus experienced as standing-in-themselves, "over
and above our wanting and doing" (Gadamer, 1989, p. xxviii). As anyone rapt
of the Earth's ways will understand, it takes quite a while to experience the
while of the Earth and its ways.

As hinted at above, having become more experienced about some thing
through whiling our time away over it has a strange result: *what is experienced*
"increases in being" (Gadamer, 1989, p. 40) while our knowledge of such things
becomes more and more incommensurate with the thing itself. Things become
experienced as having their own measure. We begin to experience them as
there. Understanding such things is no longer a matter of mastery and control
which forces things to face this way and unveil. Things reposing in themselves
do not just face this way.

But we must work to cultivate an experience of such repose. It takes time
and practice to learn how to treat things well. It takes a while to let things
repose ("letting things be" is how Heidegger [1962] defined phenomenology).
Even here, in the meager beginnings of ventures in this chapter into the gaze,
into sovereignty and the strange positioning of Islam in the iconophilic midst
of a contemporary Canadian high school, we can start to recognize ourselves in
this mess of the world. We can start to experience ourselves, not as having such
matters belonging to us, but as *belonging to and implicated in such matters.* This
is what is meant by something being worthwhile:

> Our knowledge of the world instructs us first of all that the world is
> greater than our knowledge of it. To those who rejoice in abundance and
> intricacy, this is a source of joy. To those who hope for knowledge equal
> to (capable of controlling) the world, it is a source of unremitting defeat
> and bewilderment.
>
> (Berry, 1983, p. 56)

This constitutes an *ontological* assurance about the abundant while of things
and about the worthwhileness of treating things with such soft and loving

assurance. This love of the while of things is an assurance around which pedagogy, hermeneutics, and ecology turn. It is also that around which a more livable sense of "the basics" might accrue in educational theory and practice— learning to experience "curriculum in abundance" as a source of joy and the time of whiling, the time involved in "thinking the world together," in all its intellectual and spiritual delight.

References

Aardema, V. (1981). *Bringing the rain to Kapiti Plain.* New York: Dial.

Abram, D. (1996). *The spell of the sensuous: Language in a more-than-human world.* New York: Pantheon Books.

Aitken, R. (1982). *Taking the path of Zen.* San Francisco: North Point Press.

Arendt, H. (1969). *Between past and future.* New York: Penguin Books.

Baker, A. M. (2003). From the *New York Times*, July 27, 2003. Cited in Jeanette Winter (2005). *The librarian of Basra: A true story from Iraq.* New York: Harcourt.

Bass, E. (1989). Tampons. In J. Plant (Ed.), *Healing the wounds: The promise of ecofeminism* (pp. 33–36). Toronto: Between the Lines Press.

Bastock, M. (2005, July). *Suffering the image: Literacy and pedagogic imagination.* Unpublished doctoral dissertation, Faculty of Education, University of Calgary.

Berk, L. (1985). Back to basics movement. In *The international encyclopedia of education: Research and studies* (Vol. 1, pp. 223–225). Oxford: Pergamon Press.

Berman, M. (1983). *The reenchantment of the world.* Ithaca, NY: Cornell University Press.

Berry, W. (1983). *Standing by words.* San Francisco: North Point Press.

Berry, W. (1986). *The unsettling of America: Essays in culture and agriculture.* San Francisco: Sierra Club Books.

Berry, W. (1987). *Home economics.* San Francisco: North Point Press.

Berry, W. (1989, March). The profit in work's pleasure. *Harper's Magazine,* 19–24.

Berry, W. (1990). *What are people for?* New York: North Point Press.

Birkerts, S. (1994). *The Gutenberg elegies: The fate of reading in an electronic age.* New York: Fawcett Columbine.

Bly, R. (n.d.). *When a hair turns to gold.* St. Paul, MN: Ally Press.

Bogdan, D. (1992). *Re-educating the imagination: Toward a poetics, politics and pedagogy of literary engagement.* Portsmouth, ME: Heinemann Educational Books.

Bohm, D. (1983). *Wholeness and implicate order.* New York: Ark Books.

Bowers, C. A. (2006). *The false promises of constructivist theories of learning: A global and ecological critique.* New York: Peter Lang.

Boyle, D. (2003, June). The man who made us all work like this . . . *BBC History Magazine.* Retrieved August 5, 2006 from http://www.david-boyle.co.uk/history/frederickwinslowtaylor.html

Bright, W. (1993). *A Coyote reader.* Berkeley: University of California Press.

Bruner, J. (1990). *Acts of meaning.* Cambridge, MA: Harvard University Press.

Buck, G. (2000). Technology integration in the mediaeval period: Factors relevant to the present. *Journal of Curriculum Theorizing, 16*(4).

Bull, M. (n.d.). *Malcolm Bull's Calderdale companion.* Retrieved June 2005 from http://members.aol.com/calderdale/h992_b.html

Butler, J. (2004). *Precarious life: The power of mourning and violence.* London: Verso.

Calasso, R. (1993). *The marriage of Cadmus and Harmony.* New York: Alfred Knopf.

Calkins, L. (1986). *The art of teaching writing.* Portsmouth, ME: Heinemann.

Callahan, R. (1964). *Education and the cult of efficiency.* Chicago: University of Chicago Press.

Caputo, J. (1987). *Radical hermeneutics.* Bloomington: Indiana State University Press.

Caputo, J. (1993). *Against ethics: Contributions to a poetics of obligation with constant reference to deconstruction.* Bloomington: Indiana State University Press.

Carroll, L. (1966). *Alice's adventures in wonderland, and Through the looking glass.* New York: Macmillan.

Carruthers, M. (2003). *The craft of thought: Meditation, rhetoric, and the making of images, 400–1200.* Cambridge, UK: Cambridge University Press.

Carruthers, M. (2005). *The book of memory: A study of memory in medieval culture.* Cambridge, UK: Cambridge University Press.

Carruthers, M., & Ziolkowski, J. (2002). *The medieval craft of memory: An anthology of texts and pictures.* Philadelphia: University of Pennsylvania Press.

Cayley, D. (1992). Introduction. In I. Illich & D. Cayley (1992), *Ivan Illich in conversation.* Toronto: House of Anansi Press.

Cecil's Mail Bag, Straight Dope Science Advisory Board. Retrieved October 30, 2005 from http://www.straightdope.com/mailbag/mnewmath.html

Chah, A. (2005). *Everything arises, everything falls away.* Boston, MA: Shambhala Press.

Cleary, T., & Cleary, J. C. (1992). Introduction. In *The Blue Cliff record* (pp. xvii–xxx). Boston, MA: Shambhala Press.

Clifford, J. (1986). Introduction: Partial truths. In J. Clifford & G. Marcus (Eds.), *Writing culture: The poetics and politics of ethnography* (pp. 1–26). Berkeley: University of California Press.

Clifford, P., & Friesen, S. (1994, October). *Choosing to be healers.* Paper presented at the JCT Conference on Curriculum Theory and Classroom Practice, Banff, Alberta.

Clifford, P., Friesen, S., & Jardine, D. (1995). Whole language, edgy literacy and the work of the world. *Applying Research to the Classroom, 13*(2), 4–5.

Coles, R. (1989). *The call of stories: Teaching and the moral imagination.* Boston, MA: Houghton Mifflin.

Corbett, J. (2003). *New Advent: The Catholic encyclopaedia.* (Original work published 1907) Retrieved May 2005 from http://www.newadvent.org/cathen/02547a.htm

Crapazano, V. (1986). Hermes' dilemma: The masking of subversion in ethnographic description. In J. Clifford & G. Marcus (Eds.), *Writing culture: The poetics and politics of ethnography* (pp. 51–76). Berkeley: University of California Press.

Craven, M. (1973). *I heard the owl call my name.* New York: Dell Publishing.

Dan, J. (1986). Midrash and the dawn of Kabbalah. In G. Hartman & S. Budick (Eds.), *Midrash and literature* (pp. 122–132). New Haven, CT: Yale University Press.

DeMott, B. (1964). The math wars. In R. W. Heath (Ed.), *New curricula* (pp. 54–67). New York: Harper & Row.

Doll, W. (1993). Curriculum possibilities in a "post"-future. *Journal of Curriculum and Supervision, 8*(1), 277–292.

Dressman, M. (1993). Lionizing lone wolves: The cultural romantics of literacy workshops. *Curriculum Inquiry, 23*(3), 239–263.

Egan, K. (1986). *Teaching as story telling: An alternative approach to teaching and curriculum in elementary schools.* London, Ontario: Althouse Press.

Egan, K. (1992). The roles of schools: The place of education. *Teacher's College Record, 93*(4), 641–645.

Eliade, M. (1968). *Myth and reality.* New York: Harper & Row.

Eliade, M. (1975). *The quest.* New York: Harper & Row.

Estes, C. P. (1992). *Women who run with the wolves: Myths and stories of the wild woman archetype.* New York: Ballantine Books.

Everest, B. (1996). [Untitled]. Calgary, Alberta.

Evetts-Secker, J. (1994, June). *In being able to imagine.* Paper presented at the Early Childhood Education Conference, Calgary, Alberta.

Fischer, M. (1986). Ethnicity and the post-modern arts of memory. In J. Clifford & G. Marcus (Eds.), *Writing culture: The poetics and politics of ethnography* (pp. 196–233). Berkeley: University of California Press.

Foucault, M. (2005). *The hermeneutics of the subject.* New York: Palgrave Macmillan.

Freedman, J. (1993). *Failing grades.* Red Deer, Alberta: Society for Advancing Educational Research.

Gadamer, H.-G. (1970, Winter). Concerning empty and ful-filled time. *Southern Journal of Philosophy, 8,* 341–353.

Gadamer, H.-G. (1977). *Philosophical hermeneutics* (D. E. Linge, Trans.). Berkeley: University of California Press.

Gadamer, H.-G. (1983). *Reason in the age of science* (F. G. Lawrence, Trans.). Boston, MA: MIT Press.

Gadamer, H.-G. (1989). *Truth and method* (J. Weinsheimer, Trans.). New York: Crossroads.

Gadamer, H.-G. (1994). *Heidegger's ways* (J. W. Stanley, Trans.). Boston, MA: MIT Press.

Gadamer, H.-G. (1995). Foreword. In Jean Grondin, *Introduction to philosophical hermeneutics* (pp. ix–xii). New Haven, CT: Yale University Press.

Gadamer, H.-G. (2001). *Gadamer in conversation: Reflections and commentary* (R. Palmer, Ed. and Trans.). New Haven, CT: Yale University Press.

Gatto, J. (2006). The national press attack on academic schooling. Retrieved July 2007 from http://www.rit.edu/~cma8660/mirror/www.johntaylorgatto.com/chapters/9d.htm

Glieck, J. (1987). *Chaos: The making of a new science.* New York: Penguin Books.

Godbout, J., with Caille, A. (1998). *The world of the gift.* Montreal and Kingston: McGill and Queen's University Press.

Goodman, K., Bird, L., and Goodman, Y. (1991). *The whole language catalogue.* New York: Glencoe/McGraw-Hill.

Gray, J. (1998). *False dawn: Delusions of global capitalism.* New York: New Press.

Green, V. (Ed.). (1991). *Rhythm of our days: An anthology of women's poetry.* Cambridge, UK: Cambridge University Press.

Greene, M. (1978). *Landscapes of learning.* New York: Teachers' College Press.

Greene, M. (1988). *The dialectic of freedom.* New York: Teachers' College Press.

Greene, M. (1993). Diversity and inclusion: Toward a curriculum for human beings. *Teachers College Record, 95*(2), 211–221.

Gregory, B. (1990). *Inventing reality: Physics as language.* New York: John Wiley.

Grimm Brothers (1972). *The complete book of Grimm fairy tales.* New York: Pantheon.

Grondin, J. (1995). *Introduction to philosophical hermeneutics.* New Haven, CT: Yale University Press.

Grossman, D. (1988). *The yellow wind* (H. Watzman, Trans.). New York: Bantam Doubleday.

Grumet, M. (1993). The curriculum: What are the basics and are we teaching them? In J. Kinchloe & S. Steinberg (Eds.), *Thirteen questions: Reframing education's conversation* (pp. 5–22). New York: Peter Lang.

Habermas, J. (1972). *Knowledge and human interests.* Boston, MA: Beacon Books.

Hanh, Nhat. (1986). *The miracle of mindfulness.* Berkeley, CA: Parallax Press.

Hanh, Nhat. (1995). *The long road turns to joy: A guide to walking meditation.* Berkeley, CA: Parallax Press.

Heidegger, M. (1962). *Being and time.* New York: Harper & Row.

Heidegger, M. (1968). *What is called thinking?* New York: Harper & Row.

Heidegger, M. (1971). *Origin of the work of art.* New York: Harper & Row.

Heidegger, M. (1985). *The history of the concept of time.* Bloomington: Indiana University Press.

Hiebert, J. (2005, May 5). From best research to what works: Improving the teaching and learning of mathematics. Albert Shanker Institute. Retrieved November 1, 2005 from http://www.shankerinstitute.org/Downloads/Forum%20Transcript.5.5.05.doc

Hillman, J. (1979). Notes on opportunism. In J. Hillman (Ed.), *Puer papers* (pp. 152–158). Dallas, TX: Spring Publications.

Hillman, J. (1979a). Senex and puer: An aspect of the historical and psychological present. In J. Hillman (Ed.), *Puer papers* (pp. 3–53). Dallas, TX: Spring Publications.

Hillman, J. (1982). Anima mundi: The return of soul to the world. *Spring: An Annual of Archetypical Psychology and Jungian Studies,* 174–188.

Hillman, J. (1983). *Healing fiction.* Barrytown, NY: Station Hill Press.

Hillman, J. (1991). *Inter Views.* Dallas, TX: Spring Publications.

Holt, M. (1996). A cautionary tale: School reform in England. *Journal of Curriculum and Supervision, 12*(1), 4–6.

Hongzhi, Z. (1991). *Cultivating the empty field: The silent illumination of Zen Master Hongzhi* (T. D. Leighton & Y. Wu, Trans.). San Francisco: North Point Press.

Hood, M. (1996). Getting lost in a book. Unpublished manuscript.

Humboldt, Wilhelm von (2000). Theory of Bildung (Gillian Horton-Krüger, Trans.). In Ian Westbury, Stefan Hopmann, & Kurt Riquarts (Eds.), *Teaching as a reflective practice: The German Didaktik tradition* (pp. 57–61). Mahwah, NJ: Lawrence Erlbaum. (Original work published 1793–1794)

Husserl, E. (1970). *Cartesian meditations.* The Hague: Martinus Nijhoff.

Husserl, E. (1970a). *The crisis of European science and transcendental phenomenology.* Evanston, IL: Northwestern University Press.

Husserl, E. (1972). *Logical investigations.* London: Routledge & Kegan Paul.

Hyde, L. (1983). *The gift: Imagination and the erotic life of property.* New York: Vintage Books.

Illich, I. (1970). *Deschooling society.* New York: Harper & Row.

Illich, I. (1980). Vernacular values. Retrieved August 3, 2007 from http://www.preservenet.com/theory/Illich/Vernacular.html#empire

Illich, I. (1992). *In the mirror of the past: Lectures and addresses.* New York: Marion Boyars.

Illich, I. (1993). *In the vineyard of the text: A commentary on Hugh's Didascalicon.* Chicago: University of Chicago Press.

Illich, I. (2000). Disabling professions. In I. Illich, I. Zola, J. McKnight, U. Caplan, & H. Shaiken, *Disabling professions* (pp. 11–40). New York: Marion Boyars.

Illich, I. (2001). Guarding the eye in the age of show. Retrieved July 2007 from http://www.davidtinapple.com/illich/

Illich, I. (2001a). The Scoptic past and the ethics of the gaze. Retrieved November 2006 from http://www.davidtinapple.com/illich/

Illich, I. (2005). *The rivers north of the future.* Toronto: House of Anansi Press.

Illich, I., & Cayley, D. (1992). *Ivan Illich in conversation.* Toronto: House of Anansi Press.

Illich, I., & Sanders, B. (1988). *ABC: The alphabetization of the popular mind.* Berkeley, CA: North Point Press.

Inhelder, B. (1969). Some aspects of Piaget's genetic approach to cognition. In H. Furth (Ed.), *Piaget and knowledge: Theoretical foundations* (pp. 9–23). New Jersey: Prentice-Hall.

Jardine, D. (1992). *Speaking with a boneless tongue.* Bragg Creek, Alberta: Makyo Press.

Jardine, D. (1992a). The pedagogic wound and the pathologies of doubt. In B. Levering, M. Van Manen, & S. Miedema (Eds.), *Reflections on pedagogy and method* (Vol. II, pp. 97–112). Montfoort, Netherlands: Uriah Heep.

Jardine, D. (1998). *"To dwell with a boundless heart": On curriculum theory, hermeneutics and the ecological imagination.* New York: Peter Lang.

Jardine, D. (1998a). Student-teaching, interpretation and the monstrous child. In D. Jardine, *"To dwell with a boundless heart": On curriculum theory, hermeneutics and the ecological imagination* (pp. 123–134). New York: Peter Lang.

Jardine, D. (1998b). Awakening from Descartes' nightmare: On the love of ambiguity in phenomenological approaches to education. In D. Jardine, *"To dwell with a boundless heart": On curriculum theory, hermeneutics and the ecological imagination* (pp. 5–32). New York: Peter Lang.

Jardine, D. (2000). *"Under the tough old stars": Ecopedagogical essays.* Brandon, VT: Psychology Press/Holistic Education Press.

Jardine, D. (2000a). Reflections on hermeneutics, education and ambiguity: Hermeneutics as a restoring of life to its original difficulty. In D. Jardine, *"Under the tough old stars": Ecopedagogical essays* (pp. 115–132). Brandon, VT: Psychology Press/Holistic Education Press.

Jardine, D., Clifford, P., & Friesen, S. (Eds.). (2003). *Back to the basics of teaching and learning: "Thinking the world together."* Mahwah, NJ: Lawrence Erlbaum.

Jardine, D. (2004). "A single truth alone": Some cultural currents from up north. *International Journal of Education.* Retrieved from www.taylorandfrancis.metapress.com/index/J9UBYV6ADNWDQ2VP.pdf

Jardine, D. (2005). *Piaget and education: A primer.* New York: Peter Lang.

Jardine, D. (2006). On hermeneutics: "What happens to us over and above our wanting and doing." In K. Tobin & J. Kincheloe (Eds.), *Doing educational research: A handbook* (pp. 269–288). Amsterdam: Sense Publishers.

Jardine, D. (2006a). "The fecundity of the individual case": Considerations of the pedagogic heart of interpretive work. In D. Jardine, S. Friesen, & P. Clifford, *Curriculum in abundance* (pp. 151–168). Mahwah, NJ: Lawrence Erlbaum.

Jardine, D. (2006b). "Under the tough old stars": Pedagogical hyperactivity and the mood of environmental education. In D. Jardine, S. Friesen, & P. Clifford, *Curriculum in abundance* (pp. 179–184). Mahwah, NJ: Lawrence Erlbaum.

Jardine, D. (2006c). Welcoming the old man home: Meditations on Jean Piaget, interpretation and the "nostalgia for the original." In D. Jardine, S. Friesen, & P. Clifford, *Curriculum in abundance* (pp. 73–86). Mahwah, NJ: Lawrence Erlbaum.

Jardine, D. (2006d). Cutting nature's leading strings: A cautionary tale about constructivism. In D. Jardine, S. Friesen, & P. Clifford, *Curriculum in abundance* (pp. 123–136). Mahwah, NJ: Lawrence Erlbaum.

Jardine, D. (2006e). Youth need images for their imaginations and for the formation of their memories. *Journal of Curriculum Theorizing, 22*(4), 3–12.

Jardine, D. (2007, March 12). Constructivism means war. Unpublished talk, Center for Pedagogy and Culture, Faculty of Education, University of Alberta, Edmonton, Alberta.

Jardine, D., & Batycky, J. (2006). Filling this empty chair: On genius and repose. In D. Jardine, S. Friesen, & P. Clifford, *Curriculum in abundance* (pp. 213–226). Mahwah, NJ: Lawrence Erlbaum.

Jardine, D. W., & Field, J. C. (2006). "Disproportion, monstrousness and mystery": Ecological and ethical reflections on the initiation of student-teachers into the community of education. In D. Jardine, S. Friesen, & P. Clifford, *Curriculum in abundance* (pp. 107–119). Mahwah, NJ: Lawrence Erlbaum.

Jardine, D., & Misgeld, D. (1989). Hermeneutics as the undisciplined child. In M. Packer & R. Addison (Eds.), *Entering the circle: Hermeneutic investigations in psychology* (pp. 259–273). Albany: State University of New York Press.

Jardine, D., & Naqvi, R. (in press). Learning not to speak in tongues: Thoughts on the librarian of Basra. *Canadian Journal of Education.*

Jardine, D., & Novodvorski, B. (2006). Monsters in abundance. In D. Jardine, S. Friesen, & P. Clifford, *Curriculum in abundance* (pp. 103–106). Mahwah, NJ: Lawrence Erlbaum.

Jardine, D. W., Clifford, P., & Friesen, S. (1999). "Standing helpless before the child." A response to Naomi Norquay's "Social difference and the problem of the 'unique individual': An uneasy legacy of child-centered pedagogy." *Canadian Journal of Education, 24*(3), 321–326.

Jardine, D., Friesen, S., & Clifford, P. (2006). *Curriculum in abundance.* Mahwah, NJ: Lawrence Erlbaum.

Jardine, D., Grahame, T., LaGrange, A., & Kisling Saunders, H. (2006). Staying within the lines: Re-imagining what is "elementary" in the art of schooling. In D. Jardine, S. Friesen, & P. Clifford, *Curriculum in abundance* (pp. 233–244). Mahwah, NJ: Lawrence Erlbaum.

Johnson, B., Fawcett, L., & Jardine, D. (2006). Further thoughts on "Cutting nature's leading strings": A conversation. In D. Jardine, S. Friesen, & P. Clifford, *Curriculum in abundance* (pp. 139–148). Mahwah, NJ: Lawrence Erlbaum.

Kant, I. (1964). *Critique of pure reason.* London: Macmillan. (Original work published 1767)

Kay, A. C. (1995). Computers, networks and education. *Scientific American Special Issue: The Computer in the 21st Century,* 148–155.

Kilpatrick, J. (1997, October 4). *Five lessons from the new math era.* Paper commissioned for the symposium Reflecting on Sputnik: Linking the Past, Present, and Future of Educational Reform held at the National Academy of Sciences in Washington, DC. Retrieved October 19, 2005 from http://www.nas.edu/sputnik/kilpatin.htm

King, T. (1992). *A Coyote Columbus story.* Toronto: Groundwood Books.

Lattin, H. P. (1961). *Lattin: Letters of Gerbert.* New York: Columbia University Press.

Lazere, D. (1992). Back to basics: A force for oppression or liberation? *College English, 54*(1), 7–21.

Le Guin, U. (1987). *Buffalo gals and other animal presences.* Santa Barbara, CA: Capra Press.

Le Guin, U. (1989). Woman/wilderness. In Judith Plant (Ed.), *Healing the wounds.* Toronto: Between the Lines Press.

Lopez, B. (1990). *Crow and weasel.* Toronto: Random House.

Lugone, K. (1996, March). Internet message. *Kidsphere.*

Lui, W. C., & Lo, I. (Eds.). (1990). *Sunflower splendor: Three thousand years of Chinese poetry.* Bloomington: Indiana University Press.

Ly, Y. (1996). Family tree 1. Unpublished story.

MacMillan, M. (2006, February 4). What would Kissinger do? *Globe and Mail* (Toronto), A10.

Mahdi, L., Foster, S., & Little, M. (1987). *Betwixt and between: Patterns of masculine and feminine initiation.* LaSalle, IL: Open Court.

Manning, T. (2001). *The internet Biblia Pauperum.* Retrieved July 2005 from http://amasis.com/biblia/index.html

McMaster website (1998). www.humanities.mcmaster.ca/~global/themeschool/globaliz.html

Melnick, C. (1997). Review of Max Van Manen and Bas Levering's *Childhood secrets: Intimacy, privacy and the self reconsidered. Journal of Curriculum Studies, 29*(3), 370–373.

Meschonnic, H. (1988, Autumn). Rhyme and life. *Critical Inquiry, 15*(1), 90–107.

Miller, A. (1989). *For your own good: Hidden cruelty in child-rearing and the roots of violence.* Toronto: Collins.

Minh-Ha, T. (1994). Other than myself/my other self. In G. Robertson, M. Mash, L. Tickner, J. Bird, B. Curtis, & T. Putnam (Eds.). *Travellers' tales: Narratives of home and displacement* (pp. 9–26). London: Routledge.

Morris, M., & Weaver, J. (2002). *Difficult memories: Talk in a (post) Holocaust era.* New York: Peter Lang.

Namgyal, D. T. (2006). *Mahamudra: The moonlight—Quintessence of mind and meditation.* Boston, MA: Wisdom Publications.

Nandy, A. (1987). *Traditions, tyranny and utopia.* Delhi: Oxford University Press.

Naqvi, R., & Prasow, C. (2007). Precarious positionings. *Journal of the American Association for the Advancement of Curriculum Studies.* Retrieved from http://www.uwstout.edu/soe/jaaacs/

Nation at Risk, A: The Imperative for Educational Reform (1983, April). Retrieved from http://www.ed.gov/pubs/NatAtRisk/index.html

Neeson, J. M. (1996). *Commoners, common right, enclosure and social change in England, 1700–1820.* Cambridge, UK: University of Cambridge Press.

Nishitani, K. (1982). *Religion and nothingness.* Berkeley: University of California Press.

Norris-Clarke, W. (1976). Analogy and the meaningfulness of language about God. *The Thomist, 40,* 176–198.

Okri, B. (1991). *The famished road.* Toronto: McLelland & Stewart.

OnLine Etymological Dictionary [OED]. Retrieved April 17, 2006 from http://www.etymonline.com/

Orr, D. (2004). *The last refuge: Patriotism, politics, and the environment in an age of terror.* Washington, DC: Island Press.

Palmer, P. (1993). *To know as we are known: Education as a spiritual journey* (2nd ed.). San Francisco: Harper.

Peterson, R. T. (1980). *A field guide to the birds east of the Rockies* (4th ed.). Boston, MA: Houghton Mifflin.

Piaget, J. (1952). *Origins of intelligence in children.* New York: International Universities Press.

Piaget, J. (1965). *Insights and illusions of philosophy.* New York: Meridian Books.

Piaget, J. (1968). *Six psychological studies.* New York: Vintage Books.

Piaget, J. (1970). Piaget's theory. In P. Mussen (Ed.), *Carmichael's manual of child psychology* (Vol. 1, pp. 703–732). Toronto: Wiley & Sons.

Piaget, J. (1970a). *Structuralism.* New York: Harper & Row.

Piaget, J. (1971). *Genetic epistemology.* New York: W. W. Norton.

Piaget, J. (1971a). *Biology and knowledge.* Chicago: University of Chicago Press.

Piaget, J. (1971b). *The construction of reality in the child.* New York: Ballantine Books.

Piaget, J. (1972). *Judgement and reasoning in the child.* Totowa, NJ: Littlefield & Adams.

Piaget, J. (1974). *The child's conception of the world.* London: Paladin Books.

Piaget, J. (1977). The mission of the idea. In *The essential Piaget.* New York: Basic Books.

Piaget, J., & Inhelder, B. (1969). *The psychology of the child.* New York: Harper & Row.

Piaget, J., & Inhelder, B. (1976). Gaps in empiricism. In B. Inhelder & H. Chipman (Eds.). *Piaget and his school: A reader in developmental psychology* (pp. 25–35). New York: Springer-Verlag.

Pinar, W. (2006). Foreword: The lure that pulls flowerheads to the sun. In D. Jardine, S. Friesen, & P. Clifford, *Curriculum in abundance* (pp. ix–xxii). Mahwah, NJ: Lawrence Erlbaum.

PISA (2003). Program for International Student Assessment. Organisation for Economic Co-operation and Development. Retrieved from www.oecd.org

Plato (trans. 1956). *Phaedrus.* New York: Liberal Arts Press.

Postman, N. (1995). *The end of education: Redefining the value of school.* New York: Alfred A. Knopf.

Professional standards for teaching mathematics. (1991). Reston, VA: National Council of Teachers of Mathematics.

Ricoeur, P. (2004). *Memory, history, forgetting.* Chicago: University of Chicago Press.

Ross, S. M. (2003, August). *Event hermeneutics and narrative: Tarrying in the philosophy of Hans-Georg Gadamer.* Unpublished doctoral dissertation, Department of English, Simon Fraser University.

Ross, S. M. (2004). Gadamer's late thinking on *Verweilen. Minerva—An Internet Journal of Philosophy, 8.* Retrieved June 2007 from http://www.ul.ie/~philos/vol8/gadamer.html

Schmidt, W., McKnight, C., & Raizen, S. (1997). *A splintered vision: An investigation of U.S. science and mathematics education.* Norwell, MA: Kluwer Academic Press.

Schrift, A. (Ed.). (1997). *The logic of the gift: Toward an ethic of generosity.* New York: Routledge.

Sekida, K. (1976). *Zen training.* New York: Weatherhill.

Shepard, P. (1996). *The others: How animals made us human.* Washington, DC: Island Press.

Skuce, T. (2007). Unpublished doctoral dissertation research on secondary school and melancholy. Faculty of Education, University of Calgary.

Smith, D. (1999). *Pedagon: Interdisciplinary essays in the human sciences, pedagogy and culture.* New York: Peter Lang.

Smith, D. (2006). *Trying to teach in a season of great untruth: Globalization, empire and the crises of pedagogy.* Amsterdam: Sense Publishers.

Smith, D. (2008). From Leo Strauss to collapse theory: Considering the neoconservative attack on modernity and the work of education. *Critical Studies in Education, 49*(1), 33–48.

Snyder, G. (1969). *Earth house hold.* New York: New Directions Books.

Snyder, G. (1977). *The old ways.* San Francisco: City Lights Books.

Snyder, G. (1980). *The real work.* New York: New Directions Books.

Snyder, G. (1990). *The practice of the wild.* New York: North Point Press.

Snyder, G. (1995). *The practice of the wild.* San Francisco: North Point Press.

Stanic, G. M. A., & Kilpatrick, J. (1992). Mathematics curriculum reform in the United States: A historical perspective, *International Journal of Educational Research, 17,* 407–417.

Stigler, J., & Hiebert, J. (1999). *The teaching gap: Best ideas from the world's teachers for improving education in the classroom.* New York: Free Press.

Stock, B. (1983). *The implications of literacy: Written language and models of interpretation in the eleventh and twelfth centuries.* Princeton, NJ: Princeton University Press.

Sumara, D. (1995a). Counterfeiting. *Taboo: A Journal of Education and Culture, 1*(1), 94–122.

Sumara, D. (1995b, December 2). *Understanding response to reading as a focal practice.* Paper presented at the National Reading Conference, New Orleans.

Sumara, D. (1996). Using commonplace books in curriculum studies. *JCT: An Interdisciplinary Journal of Curriculum Studies, 12*(1), 44–50.

Tannahill, R. (1975). *Flesh and blood: A history of the cannibal complex.* London: Hamish Hamilton.

Taylor, F. W. (1911). *Scientific management, comprising shop management, the principles of scientific management and testimony before the special house committee.* New York: Harper & Row.

Tennyson, A. (1986). *The lady of Shalott.* Oxford: Oxford University Press.

Thomas, D. (1967). Reminiscences of childhood. In *Quite early one morning.* London: Adline Press.

Thompson, W. I. (1981). *The time falling bodies take to light: Mythology, sexuality and the origin of culture.* New York: St. Martin's Press.

TIMSS (1995). Trends in International Mathematics and Science Study 1995. Retrieved from http://timss.bc.edu/timss1995.html

TIMSS (1999). Trends in International Mathematics and Science Study 1999. Retrieved from http://timss.bc.edu/timss1999.html

TIMSS (2003). Trends in International Mathematics and Science Study 2003. Retrieved from http://timss.bc.edu/timss2003.html

Tingley, K., & Brownlee, K. (2005). *Alberta remembers: Recalling our rural roots.* Red Deer, Alberta: Red Deer Press.

Trungpa, C. (1988). *The myth of freedom and the way of meditation.* Boston, MA: Shambhala Press.

Turner, V. (1969). *The ritual process.* Chicago: Aldine.

Turner, V. (1987). Betwixt and between: The liminal period in rites of passage. In L. Mahdi, S. Foster, & M. Little, *Betwixt and between: Patterns of masculine and feminine initiation.* LaSalle, IL: Open Court.

Usher, R., & Edwards, R. (1994). *Postmodernism and education.* London: Routledge.

Van Gennup, A. (1960). *Rites of passage.* Chicago: University of Chicago Press.

Voneche, J., & Bovet, M. (1982). Training research and cognitive development: What do Piagetians want to accomplish? In Sohan Modgil & Celia Modgil (Eds.), *Jean Piaget: Consensus and controversy* (pp. 83–94). London: Holt, Rinehart and Winston.

Wallace, B. (1987). *The stubborn particulars of grace.* Toronto: McLelland & Stewart.

Weinsheimer, J. (1985). *Gadamer's hermeneutics.* New Haven, CT: Yale University Press.

Werner, M. (1994). *Managing monsters: Six myths of our time* (Transcriptions of the Reith Lectures, BBC Radio). London: Vintage Books.

White, J. (1989). Student teaching as a rite of passage. *Anthropology and Education Quarterly, 22*(1), 177–195.

Williams, W. C. (1991). Spring and all (1923). In *The collected poems of William Carlos Williams* (Vol. 1: 1909–1939). New York: New Directions Books.

Wittgenstein, L. (1968). *Philosophical investigations.* Cambridge: Blackwell.

Wrege, C. D., & Greenwood, R. (1991). *Frederick W. Taylor: The father of scientific management: myth and reality.* New York: Irwin Professional Publishing. (Currently out of print. The text of Chapter 9 is available on-line at www.johntaylorgatto.com/chapters/9d.htm)

Yates, F. (1974). *The art of memory.* Chicago: University of Chicago Press.

Index

DATE DUE

Demco, Inc. 38-293